In Him was life, and the life was the light of men. And the light shines in the darkness, and the darkness did not comprehend it.

John 1:4

And the LORD God said to the woman, "What is this you have done?" The woman said, "The serpent deceived me, and I ate."

Genesis 3:13

FIFTEEN MINUTES
INTO ETERNITY

The War Between the Human Spirit

and the Holy Spirit

Lynn Baber

Fifteen Minutes into Eternity is the continuation of

Rapture and Revelation

© Lynn Baber 2016

ISBN – 978-1-938836 – 19 – 0

"Where am I?"

Something is different. Your eyes are drawn to a clock-like digital display as you wake from the deepest sleep you've ever experienced. Brilliant numerals are backlit by an unidentifiable color.

24:15

> *"What does that mean? Is 24:15 the time? Where am I and what kind of time is 24:15? In military time midnight is 24:00. One minute past midnight is 00:01. What does 24:15 mean? Is it morning or evening, daytime or nighttime?"*

All you see is the display—24:15.

The natural world defines days in 24-hour periods. The duration of one cycle of light and dark wasn't established by politicians, religious doctrine, or human whim. Daytime and nighttime are values defined by simple observation and explained by both the rotation and orbit of the Earth. Since our time exists in 24-hour increments, is 24:15 beyond midnight but yet not morning?

Where will you be fifteen minutes into Eternity?

Your eternal neighborhood will be determined by who you are and what you believe—and whether what you believe has any relationship to what actually is.

> *"Choose today whom you will serve. As for me and my house, we will serve the LORD."—Joshua 24:15*

Author's Note

ω

It doesn't matter what you believe at your last breath unless what you believe is true. The lies of the world have no power in eternity. There is only one source of Truth. It not only matters *why* you believe *what* you believe, it matters if what you believe is *real*.

New Creations in Christ aren't 30-day wonders or one act plays. We are flesh and blood people on a journey of continuing discovery, transformation and purpose, daily becoming more like Jesus by the grace of God. The path is bumpy and the hazards great because we have all been deceived.

The world shifted from *God over man* to *Man over god* in 1859 when much of the world left the past behind in favor of progressive doctrines intended to deny God. While researching this book I learned that almost everything wrong in western cultures today was either introduced or altered course in 1859. It was the beginning of humanism, "settled science", modern medicine, progressive sociology, and a theology based on human nature rather than God's Holy Spirit.

The fuse that detonated the 1859 explosion was lit in the Garden of Eden and we are in free-fall. Little that is recognizable will remain when the dust settles. Where you find yourself in eternity depends on what you believe and what you do about it. You must declare your choice because there is no more time on the clock. The span between 23:59 and 24:15 cannot be measured by mortals. The passage from life to eternity is known only by God.

"It was the best of times; it was the worst of times."

Both Charles Dickens' A Tale of Two Cities and Charles Darwin's *On the Origin of Species* were published in 1859. Events of 1859 launched the American Civil War. Major news stories of 1859 include abortion, children on drugs, rapture, racism, troubles with Mexico and Cuba, and man-made climate change.

Such topics today are news stories with constituencies. Every special interest, from abortion activists to *#BlackonCampus*, thinks it should be King of the Hill and that all others should endorse them and live on leftovers. No unity remains in the United States of America except what pulls the lost into self-centered microcosms of human fear. Human nature seeks to exclude, banish, contain, or exterminate those who aren't *like we are*. Because "they" are different we can't predict what "they" will do. The natural human response is fear.

There is nothing everyone in the USA would agree on. There is nothing every "Christian" would agree on. Nothing unites, and the result is infighting. Jackals rip at the carcass of a once united people to wrest their *fair share* from other jackals. The USA is no more immune to human nature than were the Israelites. Human law changes based upon which "we" is in charge. The only law unchanged from the beginning is that established by God. Because human nature fears, rejects, and seeks to eliminate that which it does not understand or is not *like we are*, God has been banished from the land.

> *"Over the last 50 years our Supreme Court has made four explosive decisions that have so weakened the moral and spiritual structure and foundation of our country that our inevitable collapse is certain. Right now we're simply living between that time of the explosions that have weakened our basic foundation, and the coming implosion."—Pastor Robert Jeffress*

In the following chapters you'll discover the sources and history of many worldly falsehoods, including the most powerful –isms, economic theories, intellectual lies, scientific inaccuracies, and some of the stranger religions tried throughout history, and the one thing common to them all, Human Nature.

Consciously consider the historical substance and tidbits of trivia in *Fifteen Minutes into Eternity* from God's perspective rather than the world's. Resolve to make that choice every morning. That choice determines where you will be fifteen minutes into eternity.

TABLE OF CONTENTS

Introduction

ω

"And what will be the sign of Your coming, and of the end of the age?" And Jesus answered and said to them: "Take heed that no one deceives you. For many will come in My name, saying, 'I am the Christ.' Then many false prophets will rise up. And because lawlessness will abound, the love of many will grow cold. But he who endures to the end shall be saved." —Matthew 24: 3-5, 11-13

The world is divided into two camps. The issue that divides is control, who has it and who wants it. Control is a function of power, who has it and who wants it, because whoever has power has control. The division, however, is not one of nationality, race, gender, socio-economic status, or political affiliation. People are divided on almost every issue, whether cultural, scientific, historical, legal, or biological. The underlying cause of every disagreement, whether social or spiritual, is MY campmates versus YOUR campmates. The division is between the folks who walk in the Light and those who live in the darkness.

No matter who you are, how old you are, where you live, how you were raised, or what you believe - you have been deceived. Everyone is a victim of deceit. The greatest lie ever told is that everything is all about *you*. The trap was set in Genesis 3. What could be more important than what you think, feel, want, or believe?

Nothing. That's the problem.

The Lord Jesus Christ is the sole subject of the Bible. From creation to Abraham, Egypt to Bethlehem, and Calvary to the New Jerusalem, everything was, is, and will be about Jesus. Jesus of Nazareth is absolutely God or He is not. Jesus is a real flesh-and-blood human who was born into the world from outside of the world. He walked dusty roads, thirsted, wept, and loved His mother.

Jesus was born, died, was resurrected, ascended, and lives forever in glory. Jesus is alive and He is coming back. There is only one Jesus who can save you. Jesus is Immanuel, God with us, who has spoken to us about Himself. This Jesus is one with God the Father.

Who is this "jesus" we hear so much about today who loves all, judges none, and is a political liberal? At best, this jesus is a humanist fabrication and at worst a demon in shepherd's robes. This convenient jesus is led about like a lapdog, dressed in whatever costume will persuade or mislead the uninformed or the gullible. It is this jesus that artists malign and social progressives quote. There is only one Jesus. Any preaching or teaching about some jesus that contradicts the Bible is not Jesus, but only a puppet-jesus with no power to save.

Your eternity was purchased by the blood of the Jesus who is not conflicted about abortion, creation, human nature, biology, or truth. One camp will spend eternity with this Jesus; the other will not.

Deception

Where you find yourself fifteen minutes into eternity depends on what you believe and if what you believe is real or a delusion. The rest of this book describes where we came from and how we got to where we are today. You will find both secular and religious history, philosophy, science, and plain-speaking about topics most folks shy away from.

Pastors, politicians, authors, scholars and teachers will tell you that there is more than one way to eternal life; that there is more to the concept of *god* than what the Bible speaks; that truth is relative and that "my truth" may not be the same as "your truth." *What if my God and your God aren't the same?*

Truth is a constant. Anyone who thinks otherwise has been deceived. The choice between God and Not God should be a simple one. If the God of the Bible exists, how much power does He have? Some familiar words no longer mean the same thing to everyone.

They used to, but no longer. Words like, God, Jesus, Bible, Christian, and Grace.[1]

Humans are hardwired to quibble about what words mean and balance the importance of their feelings against God's Word. Vocabulary is an issue of power and control (i.e. the N-word). In western cultures today, political correctness defines what words mean and established who is or is not entitled to use them.

"You shall have no other gods before Me."—Exodus 20:3

God commands that every thought, belief, and action be defined and evaluated based on His Word. Any person, cause, excuse, ideal, feeling, allegiance, or philosophy that teaches God is something other than who He says He is errs, lies or blasphemes. Elevating any –ism or creed above God's Word is idolatry. God is God. Whether He is my God or yours, He is who He is. He is I AM.

The Jesus with the power to save is the Son of *this* God. Jesus was obedient unto death; even death on the Cross. He has not changed. His message has not changed. Debates over vocabulary, semantics, and the relative importance of human sensibilities in a sinful world change nothing. Eternity with Christ depends entirely on what He says, what He thinks, what He commands, and whether you choose His camp or the other camp.

Pastors can be deceivers. Teachers can be deceivers. Humans eagerly swallow deception when it offers power, safety, forgiveness, and a Get-Out-of-Jail-Free card. Human ears have a distinct tendency to itch. (2 Timothy 4:3) Believing the pretty lies self-serving men tell is to choose Not God. Some pastors and teachers don't realize they're peddling deception because they are themselves firmly trapped under the weight of delusion.

"But evil men and impostors will grow worse and worse, deceiving and being deceived"—2 Timothy 3:13

---

[1] A detailed discussion of these words are included in Rapture and Revelation (Lynn Baber).

Some Christians argue that:

- Abortion is good.
- Man evolved from a rock.
- God makes mistakes.
- Jesus saves whether He is loved or cursed.
- Every "good" person will go to heaven.

If you agree with any of these, you may get along pretty well with the world. The problem is, they are all lies. How did abortion become acceptable? How did Evolution and Climate Change become "settled science"? What led to President Obama's decision to bathe the White House in rainbow-colored lights the day the Supreme Court recognized same-sex marriage as a constitutional right?

Daily headlines bring additional examples of the power of delusion. In August 2014, Michael Brown, an18-year-old black man, was killed in self-defense by 28-year-old white police officer Darren Wilson in Ferguson, Missouri.

Eyewitness accounts and physical evidence prove the facts of the case. Yet the false narrative that Brown was killed with his hands in the air saying, "Don't shoot!", continues to be a powerful rallying cry. When activists are forced to admit that their mantra is a lie, we discover that the truth isn't important.

Someone is in control. Someone seeks power. Another lie is that protests about race, gender, education, the environment, abortion, immigration, and religion seek parity. Protests are about power and control; who has it and who wants it. Protest is a tactic used to delude the masses into serving the organizers. Protesters are a new mercenary class. Some are true believers in the lie while others serve organizers for either a fee or a feel good.

God hasn't changed. Human nature hasn't changed. Fighting to maintain control and power over others in the name of something good is nothing new. The Apostle John addressed this issue in the first century.

"I wrote to the church, but Diotrephes, who loves to have the preeminence among them, does not receive us. Therefore, if I come, I will call to mind his deeds which he does, prating against us with malicious words. And not content with that, he himself does not receive the brethren, and forbids those who wish to, putting them out of the church. Beloved, do not imitate what is evil, but what is good. He who does good is of God, but he who does evil has not seen God."—3 John 9-11

Diotrophes' sin was pride; a church leader refusing delivery of the Apostle John's letter and emissaries. Doctrine in his church was settled; no dissenting voices allowed. The only way Diotrophes maintained power and control was by isolating congregants so they were unaware of his deception or other voices.

What complicates the matter further is how each camp of Christians believes it is the one loyal to the Word of God and other camps live in error. How have you been deceived? Are you listening to authorities who see delusion as truth? Does it matter?

Did you know…

- that The Holy See (Vatican) officially records the death of the Apostle John during the time of Evaristus, the *fourth* pope? (w2.vatican.va)
- that Charles Darwin had one college degree – in Divinity?
- that secular humanism originated in the writings of a man suffering from unrequited love and mental illness?
- that in 1859 Democrats called the Republican Party a criminal conspiracy because it spoke against slavery.

Political and moral hot buttons of 1859 America are the same ones we face today. From abortion to racism, Islamic jihad to evolution, and man-made climate change to raging conflicts in Congress – the roots of delusion have only grown deeper in the past century and a half. The term settled science is used today for the same purpose Diotrephes barred the Apostle John from his congregants. It has nothing to do with anything being proven or even scientific. It has everything to do with maintaining power and control. The goal is keeping people encamped in pleasant delusion so they won't choose God.

When you finish this book, you will know things you never imagined and the role the year 1859 played on the road to the End Time.

> *"Not everyone who says to Me, 'Lord, Lord,' shall enter the kingdom of heaven, but he who does the will of My Father in heaven. Many will say to Me in that day, 'Lord, Lord, have we not prophesied in Your name, cast out demons in Your name, and done many wonders in Your name?' And then I will declare to them, 'I never knew you; depart from Me, you who practice lawlessness!'"—Matthew 7:21-23*

Walking in Darkness

ω

Then Jesus said to them, "A little while longer the light is with you. Walk while you have the light, lest darkness overtake you; he who walks in darkness does not know where he is going."—John 12:35

There has never been a more treacherous or difficult time to be a faithful follower of Jesus Christ than the present. More people were martyred for their faith in Christ in the past century than the totality of previous human history[2]. The difficulty of keeping your dusty sandals on the narrow path increases both daily and exponentially (Matthew 7:14). This trend will continue unabated until the end of the age. You live in the End Time. The narrow path is far more difficult to travel today than in past centuries because you have been deceived.

Deception is everywhere. Every person is deceived. Every Christian is deceived. We continue to believe lies, spread lies, and convince ourselves that something is true when it is not. Lies, repeated often enough, become truth. Deception is widespread and constant.

Time is Short

Where will you be fifteen minutes into eternity? The answer depends on what you believe and whether your belief has any relationship to reality. Whoever or whatever controls your present also determines your future.

Curiosity led me to read Tom Doyle's *Dreams and Visions*, a book documenting the increasing incidence of Jesus visions converting Middle East Muslims to Christ. Middle East Christians wake each morning knowing it may be their last; yet they smile, enjoy peace, produce sweet fruit, and are secure enough in their eternity to

---

[2] World Christian Trends AD 30 – AD 2200, David B. Barrett and Todd M. Johnson, 2001

endure any present persecution or torture. Christians in the west are often spoiled, lazy, and deceived. Some define persecution as a shop clerk saying "Happy Holidays" in mid-December or a 60-minute church service that drags out an extra ten minutes.

Middle East Christians have more in common with the first century church than western Christians who enjoy the safety and comfort of a society that promises more of the same if they will compromise just a wee bit. *Be tolerant. Be loving.*

Satan is an expert theologian, twisting the Word upon itself to those willing to be *reasonable*. The second greatest commandment, to love others as we do ourselves, is the most effective weapon in Satan's arsenal. What is ignored is the first and great commandment; love the Lord with all you have. How are Christ-followers to show love?

> *Jesus said to him, "'You shall love the Lord your God with all your heart, with all your soul, and with all your mind.' This is the first and great commandment. And the second is like it: 'You shall love your neighbor as yourself.' On these two commandments hang all the Law and the Prophets"—Matthew 22:37-40*
>
> *"If you love Me, keep my commandments."—John 14:15*

There is no middle ground between God and Not God, between Jesus Christ and Satan. The challenge to Christ-followers in the 21st century is to separate from the world enough to recognize truth but remain close enough to serve as called. Temptation and distractions leap out at every turn. Most followers of Christ may never face attack by conventional weapons, but guns and swords have never proven as effective as an insignificant lie left unchallenged.

Human sin nature believes the lie that we are the center of the universe. Whatever we experience, for good or ill, is filtered through the arrogant and distorted lens of ME. Young folks today are being taught that their success is not entirely their own and failure is not just their fault. There's nothing better than blaming others for our poor outcome.

"Be sober, be vigilant; because your adversary the devil walks about like a roaring lion, seeking whom he may devour."— 1Peter 5:8

The ruler of this world (Satan) seeks to separate as many from the herd as possible, leaving them vulnerable to predation. You cannot focus on Christ if you're consumed by self-interest.

"Beware of dividing up your life by the influence of friends or circumstances; beware of anything that is going to split up your oneness with Him [Christ] and make you see yourself separately. Beware of allowing self-consciousness to continue because... it will awaken self-pity, and self-pity is Satanic."—Oswald Chambers, My Utmost for His Highest

The tiny book of Jude perfectly summarizes our place on the timeline of human history. The church on earth suffers a crisis of faith caused by false teaching and deception. It is time to "contend earnestly for the faith" (Jude 1-2). Jude reminds believers that judgment awaits the sexually immoral who corrupt themselves as brute beasts, like clouds without rain, trees without fruit, drowning in waves of shame reserved for blackness and darkness forever (Jude 7, 10, 12, 13). Mockers and sensual persons walk in the filth of their own lusts; using impassioned and inspirational rhetoric to flatter you to gain advantage, cause division and your eternal demise (Jude 16, 18-19).

"I will no longer talk much with you, for the ruler of this world is coming, and he has nothing in Me."—John 14:30

Uncompromising Christians are in short supply. Existing on the fringes of *religious* conviction, the worldly accuse Christ-followers of extremism. The world is correct. God is unbending in His requirements and we must be unyielding in our obedience. Any compromise is as good as total surrender. One iota of sin or compromise with the ruler of this world prevents an eternity spent in God's presence.

We are in the final push toward the last day. The King is coming. Where will you be fifteen minutes into eternity? It depends on whom you listen to, whom you believe, and whether your faith is real or imagined. You are approaching the door to eternity regardless of your religion or age. Where you find yourself fifteen minutes into eternity is a matter of what IS, not what you believe "is" is. How can you choose wisely unless you can separate truth from deception?

> *"[God] is immutable, which means that He has never changed and can never change in any smallest measure. To change He would need to go from better to worse or from worse to better. He cannot do either, for being perfect He cannot become more perfect, and if He were to become less perfect He would be less than God."—A.W. Tozer, The Pursuit of God*

Apart from God there is nothing; no reason, no morality, and no future. Apart from God there is chaos. God's elect recognize the truth which accords with godliness, providing the sure *hope of eternal life which God,* **who cannot lie***, promised before time began* (Titus 1:1-2).

Culture Clash—Society and God

God's plan makes perfect sense and is easier for humans to live under than the ones we imagine ourselves. One promoted by most western societies condemns young people to a task equal to swimming the English Channel with quarter-ton ankle weights.

Would you join a group that required prospective members to swim a mile shackled to a 500-pound ankle weight? It isn't possible, and anyone who considers such a group needs to have his head examined. What Western societies demand of young people isn't much different from this hypothetical group of lunatic swimmers.

God's Word calls each man and woman to remain chaste until married. That means no experimentation, no sowing of wild oats, and no friends with benefits. Few people can live up to such strict standards. Children are expected to finish their educations and get good jobs before getting married. Many teenagers fall in love while still in high school. Donny Osmond's 1972 hit *Puppy Love* lamented the assumption that young love cannot be true love. It can. Hormones start bubbling during teen-age years by design. The urge young people feel to marry and start a family is natural. Society, not God, expects young people to either indulge such urges or deny their natures.

God's plan keeps kids at home until they learn to respect His word, develop the skills necessary to keep a home, produce food, and live peaceably and productively within the boundaries of community, marriage, and parenthood. In traditional societies, the age of consent for a sexual union was tribal custom or a matter for families to decide. In most cases, it coincided with signs of puberty, menstruation for a woman and pubic hair for a man. Telling young folks to ignore natural yearnings only sets them up for frustration and failure.

How can it be sinful to do what is natural? Why would you worship some God who expects you to do the impossible? It's natural to want to engage in sex. It's natural to want to play house. The lie, of course, is that God asks the impossible. In the case of family life, God offers what is natural and rewarding. God doesn't want young people to play house; He wants them to establish homes and families. What is unnatural is telling kids they aren't grown up enough for such activities until ten or more years later.

> *"It is good for a man not to touch a woman. Nevertheless, because of sexual immorality, let each man have his own wife, and let each woman have her own husband. Let the husband render to his wife the affection due her, and likewise also the wife to her husband."—1 Corinthians 7:1-3*

The deception of modern society has destroyed biblical marriage and the natural relationship between men and women, parents and children, neighbors and strangers, men and Nature. Deception separates man's soul from fulfillment, peace, and the One who created it all.

How did we move from truth to delusion? Mankind has been off track for so long that most people don't know that there used to be a different track. Intellectuals and liars have convinced the masses that science and humanity itself prove God to be either myth or monster.

And Satan grins. The purpose of *Fifteen Minutes into Eternity* is to shine the light of truth on the lies that bind the world to darkness. From Eden to Evolution, apart from God's Word, all is deception.

> *"Sin has many tools, but a lie is the handle which fits them all."*—Edmund Burke, 18th century Irish statesman

Two Doors to Eternity

> *"When enough insane people scream in harmony that they really are healthy, they can actually start to believe themselves. Or put even more simply: people with overlapping delusions get along wonderfully."*—Daniel Mackler, Toward Truth: A psychological guide to enlightenment

Since the dawn of time, men have struggled to separate truth from falsehood. The challenge has never been as difficult as it is today because we have all been deceived. Imagine two closed doors to eternity before you. One door opens to eternal goodness and the other to eternal badness; one to eternal darkness and the other to eternal Light. You must choose which door to open. Identical signs hang on both doors stating, "This door is TRUE, the other is a LIE."

Which door you choose depends on the sum of your life experience. Everything you see, hear, touch, read, learn, or feel contributes to your perception of truth. The fact is, one sign is correct. If the God of the Bible exists it is of eternal consequence to choose rightly. *"Jesus said to him, 'I am the way, the truth, and the life. No one comes to the Father except through Me'"* (John 14:6).

One door *does* lead to eternal goodness and Light. Determining which door is which is a function of what you believe and if what you believe is fantasy or reality. Your personal thoughts about truth have no impact on what is or is not true.

One precious toddler I know was taught that butterflies roar. His parents thought it was cute to ask, "How does the butterfly go?" to which the little boy most emphatically responded, "ROAR!" It was cute, but I have often wondered how he felt when he learned that butterflies do not roar. Did he feel foolish? Did he question what other lies his parents may have told him? Did he find it an innocent joke or a betrayal?

Eternity becomes a crapshoot if you discover that God lied even once. If one verse of God's Word is untrue there is no reason to believe any verse and that mansion in heaven is nothing but a pipe dream.

> *"The Spirit of truth, whom the world cannot receive, because it neither sees Him nor knows Him; but you know Him, for He dwells with you and will be in you."—John 14:17*

Truth matters. You want to choose the correct door. You want your loved ones to choose the correct door. The innocent and gullible believe lies told by people in positions of authority. Perhaps you never believed that butterflies roar, but how can you know if what you were taught is really true? How can you know for certain which camp you're in and if fellow campers are friends or foe?

If everyone lined up in front of one of the two doors you would notice one very long line and one that is painfully short by comparison. People at home in a world that prefers darkness to Light are driven by human nature. That shouldn't be a surprise to anyone – it's natural.

The line in front of the door that Human Nature chooses will be long, loud, and wide. People in the other line wait patiently, peaceful countenances glowing with anticipation. The crowd in the longer line mocks and jeers these whom they consider ignorant, irritating, or intolerant. *You will know them by their fruit.*

Lynn Baber

Separating truth from deception is of vital importance if eternal destiny is of interest to you. Of all you know or think you know, what is really true and what is the product of calculated deception? The complicating factor for all humans is how we lie to ourselves–and others–without being aware that we lie. Humans are far easier to deceive than dogs or horses. Animals are far more honest than people because no species except humans ever examined God's plan and rejected it in favor of its own.

"The human soul is the only thing we cannot properly study, because it is at once both the study and the student." – G.K. Chesterton, Lunacy & Letters

1859

ω

"Jesus did not say, 'Go into all the world and tell the world it is quite right.'"—C.S. Lewis [3]

Individual fingers of late winter sunlight pierced the gloomy university classroom as I read the first of twenty essay questions on the History of Psychology midterm exam. I confess, my memory has always been somewhat selective, burying with creative abandon many particulars of both childhood and education. Yet one essay question remains vivid more than thirty years later.

From Kindergarten through two excursions in post-graduate study, only a handful of teachers and fellow classmates are easily retrieved from memory. Yet one essay question remains evergreen. I don't remember the professor's name. I don't remember question number two or any of the eighteen others. What question was so impactful that it remains front of mind decades later?

Here is that first question–verbatim:

"Trace the history of science from 550 BC to 1859."

As a Christian writer, equine clinician, and student of all things related to relationship, leadership, and discipleship, I spend a lot of time on research. I read a lot, I write a lot, and I certainly talk too much. That silly essay-question took center stage when I started investigating the antagonism between evolution and creation theorists.

Darwin's theory of evolution thrust itself into the humanities, sciences, and drawing rooms in 1859. *How curious*, I thought. *There's 1859 again.* A short time later I delved into dispensationalism so I could credibly address charges that rapture is a concept no one thought about until dispensationalism was introduced. *Only cult-followers of John Nelson Darby believe in*

---

[3] cbn.com/special/narnia/articles/ans_lewislastinterviewb.aspx

rapture. You may not be surprised to learn that John Nelson Darby introduced Dispensationalism in 1859.

They say the third time is the charm. 1859 was a hat-trick of either design or coincidence, and I don't believe in coincidence. Surely others connected these dots. I searched for any book, report, or study documenting the amazing "coincidental" events of 1859.

Apparently, no one else from my History of Psychology class does the same kind of research I do. I found nothing. Nada. Zilch. So, I looked deeper. The more subjects I examined, the more 1859 popped up.

My husband is brilliant. Whenever I mention some interesting factoid or bit of trivia and ask, "What year did _____?"

He knows the answer every time I ask. 1859.

The Best and Worst of Times Collided in 1859

"It was the best of times, it was the worst of times, it was the age of wisdom, it was the age of foolishness, it was the epoch of belief, it was the epoch of incredulity, it was the season of Light, it was the season of Darkness, it was the spring of hope, it was the winter of despair, we had everything before us, we had nothing before us, we were all going direct to Heaven, we were all going direct the other way - in short, the period was so far like the present period, that some of its noisiest authorities insisted on its being received, for good or for evil, in the superlative degree of comparison only."—Charles Dickens, A Tale of Two Cities (1859)

Deception became an art form in 1859, forever changing the status and standards of relationship between one person and another, one nation and another, and most importantly, the relationship between God and man. The foundation of human existence split into two camps in 1859. The issue at stake was control; who had it and who wanted it. What you believe to be true is, ultimately, an issue of control. Events of 1859 split mankind into one camp willing to let

God manage the world and everything in it, and another relentlessly seeking to know, to explain, to rationalize, and to bring God down to its own level.

Deception enjoyed exponential growth in 1859, creating global confusion about which camp was which. Did events of 1859 ring in the best of times or the worst of times? For much of human history society, culture, government, and religion were impossible to separate into discretely different elements of experience. All drew, built, influenced, and were changed by the others.

"Those who don't know history are doomed to repeat it."—
attributed to Edmund Burke and George Santayana

Throughout history, people believed that someone or something greater than themselves was in control. Prior to 1859 people habitually yielded power to one or more gods. In the years since, devotion to deity has largely been replaced by an intellectual faith in random chance. Mankind has been demoted from the crown jewel of creation to an accident of time and circumstance.

All the greatest esoteric questions plaguing mankind throughout history have simple answers. The only reason great mysteries remain is because people don't want to accept any truth that takes control, power, value, or freedom away from them.

The midterm question suggests that the whole of pre-1859 scientific history can reasonably be covered in a single essay. One essay question, much less one lifetime, isn't sufficient to summarize evolution, DNA, computers, aircraft, nuclear fission, and space travel. The scope of topics covered in one 24-hour news cycle today is too vast for any one question, discussion, or academic discipline.

Humanism, sexism, racism, communism, fascism, gender issues, immigration, religious persecution, economics, free speech, abortion rights, global conflict, assisted suicide, and dozens of other debates heat up the bits and bytes of personal smart devices.

Most folks speed-read headlines to keep up with the news. News is no longer news, but opinion. Regardless of the subject material, journalists now report truth that is first filtered by personal experience and prejudices. If a reporter believes butterflies roar, that news will appear in banner type somewhere on the web.

Science changed forever in 1859. The trajectory of every topic listed in a previous paragraph changed in 1859. For some people, the worst of the old was replaced with the best of the new. For others the best of the old was rejected and the worst of the new barged in without apology.

> *"Modern scientists in general lived, thought, and worked in the framework of rejecting human authority, while respecting what was taught in the Bible in regard to the cosmos – right up to the time of Michael Faraday and James Clerk Maxwell in the second half of the nineteenth century."—Frances Schaeffer, Whatever Happened to the Human Race, Complete Works vol 5, p 362*

Science Notes:

Michael Faraday (1791-1867) an Englishman with little formal education, but one of the most influential scientists in history who contributed to the fields of electromagnetism and electrochemistry. He discovered electromagnetic induction, diamagnetism, and electrolysis. Faraday also established that magnetism can affect rays of light.

James Clerk Maxwell (1831-1879) Scottish scientist who formulated the theory of electromagnetic radiation, bringing together for the first time electricity, magnetism, and light as manifestations of the same phenomenon. Maxwell's equations for electromagnetism have been called the "second great unification in physics" after the first one realized by Isaac Newton.

Maxwell was awarded the Adams Prize in 1859 for his essay, *On the stability of the motion of Saturn's rings*. When George Biddell Airy read it he commented, "It is one of the most remarkable applications of mathematics to physics that I have ever seen." Maxwell's prediction was confirmed by direct observations of the Voyager in the 1980s.

Sir George Biddell Airy (1801-1892) English mathematician and Astronomer Royal from 1835 to 1881 noted for his work on planetary orbits, measuring Earth's mean density, and establishing the prime meridian in Greenwich.

Why 1859 is a Pivotal Year

Satan launched his greatest attack in 1859 with Darwin's theory of evolution. Science, medicine, physics, mathematics, energy, education, and theology abandoned what they had been throughout the history of mankind and veered into a new direction. Most hot topics in the first two decades of the 21st century were also hot topics in 1859.

The Supreme Court of the United States kicked prayer out of public schools in 1962. In 1980 the Supreme Court doubled down and evicted the Ten Commandments as well. The foundations for those transformative decisions were laid in 1859.

Whet your curiosity whistle with these 1859 events:

- Charles Dickens published "A Tale of Two Cities."
- Charles Darwin published "On the Origin of Species."
- Karl Marx published the preface to A Contribution to the Critique of Political Economy.
- *Harper's Weekly* featured a cartoon about childhood drug addiction
- Dan Sickles was acquitted of murder in the first use of the insanity plea in a US court.
- Elizabeth Blackwell, first woman medical school graduate
- John Brown's raid on Harpers Ferry initiated the American Civil War
- John Stuart Mill published *On Liberty*. It has never been out of print and is still passed from hand to hand in government today.
- The first self-help book is published, entitled *Self-Help; with Illustrations of Character and Conduct*, published by Samuel Smiles. It has been called the bible of mid-Victorian liberalism. *Self-Help* sold 20,000 copies in its first year of

publication. When the author died in 1904 it had sold over a quarter of a million.

- Southern Baptist Theological Seminary was founded.
- John Nelson Darby introduced Dispensationalism.
- Horace Greely, founder and editor of The New York Tribune, interviewed President of the Mormon Church, Brigham Young.
- Civil ceremony replaced religious marriage in Mexico.
- Syrian Revolt: Muslim-Christian mid-east conflicts heat up.
- John Tyndall introduced issue of climate change due to atmospheric gases.
- Edwin Drake drilled the first oil well (Titusville, Pennsylvania.)
- R.C. Carrington & R. Hodgson first observed a solar flare.
- G.R. Kirchoff described the chemical composition of the sun.
- London's Big Ben chimed for the first time over the Houses of Parliament in Westminster, England.
- Ground was broken for the Suez Canal.

If you consider God's design as linear, it would be made up of straight lines, in precise and efficient order. In 1859, man decided that straight lines were too rigid and began to force the straight lines of God's design into bends, curves, and squiggles with no relationship between one and another.

Straight lines and right angles are the basis of strong buildings and orderly interaction. A level foundation is, by definition, straight on the top. How many stories can you add if the foundation surface resembles a piece of over cooked spaghetti?

Of course, God *did* design curves. He designed certain curves to precisely match others. God called one curve man and the other woman. *"He created them male and female, and blessed them and called them Mankind in the day they were created"* (Genesis 5:2).

Satan lured Eve into sin by promising that forbidden fruit would make her as God—and that God wouldn't really mind the change. She fell victim to delusion and committed the original sin: self-indulgence. From creation to astronomy, anything men can understand they think they can control. At least that's the lie that's been gaining ground since 1859.

"For where envy and self-seeking exist, confusion and every evil thing are there."—James 1:16

1859 Trivia

ω

Publishing:

- Samuel Smiles publishes the first Self Help book entitled *Self-Help; with Illustrations of Character and Conduct* also called the bible of mid-Victorian liberalism
- *The Base Ball Player's Pocket Companion*, the first book about baseball published
- *The Home Review* became the first women's magazine in Nordic countries
- Isabelle Beeton pens the first cookbook for educated American women
- Charles Dickins publishes *A Tale of Two Cities*
- Charles Darwin publishes *On the Origin of Species*
- Karl Marx publishes Preface to A Contribution to the Critique of Political Economy
- Pony Express Bible published. Riders had to swear to and sign the frontier pledge of loyalty, honesty, and sobriety printed on the inside front cover.
- Søren Kierkegaard published posthumously, *The Point of View For my Work as an Author: A Direct Communication, Report to History,* an autobiography contrasting Christian writing under his own name and more humanistic thoughts under pseudonyms.
- Ethology: the science of animal behavior introduced by Isidore Geoffroy Saint-Hilaire, *Histoire Naturelle Générale des Règnes Organiques* (2nd volume).
- Sir Arthur Conan Doyle was born, the English author who brought Sherlock Holmes to life.
- Mildred J. Hill was born. She wrote *Happy Birthday to You,* the best-known song in the English language.
- The 1859 Merriam-Webster edition was the first American dictionary to include pictorial illustrations; also featuring a supplement of new words and explanations of the distinctions among synonyms.

- John Stuart Mill published *On Liberty* in 1859. The ideas presented in *On Liberty* remain the basis of much liberal political thought. Mill also contributed to the theory of the scientific method.

Other authors publishing famous works in 1859:

- Alfred Lord Tennyson
- George Sand
- Harriet Beecher Stowe
- Fyodor Dostoevsky
- Leo Tolstoy
- Washington Irving
- George Eliot's first full-length novel, *Adam Bede*, published in the United Kingdom. Some reviews were positive while others described it as the "vile outpourings of a lewd woman's mind." Libraries refused to stock it or kept it hidden under the counter

Sports:

- The first book about baseball published.
- May 31–Philadelphia A's organize to play "town ball" which became baseball 20 years later
- July 1–First intercollegiate baseball game; Amherst beat Williams 66-32 under Massachusetts Game rules. The first collegiate ball game under New York rules occurred on November 3 when the Rose Hill Baseball Club of Fordham (St. John's) defeated St. Francis Xavier prep school 33-11.
- July 20–Baseball fans were charged admission for the first time. Spectators bought 1500 tickets for 50 cents apiece to watch Brooklyn play New York.
- Aug. 15–Charles A. Comiskey, namesake of Comiskey Park, born in Chicago; first and only player to later own a team.
- Oct. 29–Charles Ebbets born, (namesake of Ebbets Field, Brooklyn)

- Umpires reportedly sat in padded rocking chairs behind the catcher until 1859.
- May 17–Australian Rules Football first 'laws of the game' published
- June 28–First dog show held at Newcastle-on-Tyne, England
- The first game of lawn tennis is played by Major Harry Gem and his friend Augurio Perera on a croquet lawn in England.
- April–Walter Camp, father of American football (Yale) is born.
- April 18–Montreal Canadiens win their 4th straight NHL Stanley Cup

It's All About Me

ω

"One of the penalties of sin is acceptance of it. It is not only God who punishes for sin, but sin establishes itself in the sinner and takes its toll. The penalty of sin is that you gradually get used to it, until you finally come to the place where you no longer even realize that it is sin." – Oswald Chambers, My Utmost for His Highest

How many differences of opinion or outright arguments did you witness this week? Were you a party to any? Did you leave a contrary comment on Facebook or Tweet something snarky about a person or news story? Was this a week of perfect agreement with your spouse, your children, your boss, the preacher, and the world? Or was it the usual; disputes, protests, battles, or just being misunderstood?

Current events describe endless conflicts, but few instances of solidarity. Whether the friction regards family, government, law, economics, race, religion, politics, social justice, property, or international affairs—everyone seems to be riled up over something or someone. Demands or outright threats abound while offers of true compromise are scarce.

Civil, criminal, and international laws are disputed daily. The basis of law itself is under attack on every side. Law divides, condemns, separates, judges, and sits above us. Depending on who you are, it's okay to ignore laws you viscerally disagree with because, "It's a bad law." One frequent excuse used by lawbreakers when charged today is…

Discrimination! Victimization! I am not subject to those who are not like me. Even the law guarantees me the right to be judged by my peers.

If I am a certain skin color, I can only be judged by peers who look like me. If I am a drug addict, I can only be judged by peers who understand me. If I am an atheist, I can only be rightly judged by peers with no silly belief in some deity. If I am uneducated, I can only be judged by uneducated peers. We not only demand our cake, but further demand unlimited cake refills because *no one's plate should be empty*!

The Apostle Paul confirms that total obedience to God's law is impossible. The purpose of the law is to convict us of our imperfections and drive us to Christ for resolution. We are inadequate and deserve censure. Our opinions, our power, and our judgment are sub-par, unacceptable, selfish, foolish and ignorant.

Followers of Jesus Christ know the only path to eternal life is through the Cross. We bring nothing of value to the table. Our key won't open the right door to eternity. On our own, we can't even tell which door is the right door.

Fewer people are willing to sit under the law, demanding instead to stand over it. People are unwilling to have God judge them. The world encourages us to believe that God is subject to the personal preference and uniqueness of each person. The reason many believe God simply shakes His head and smiles like a doting grandpa is delusion. In plain language, the world lies and we believe it.

God knows us better than we know ourselves. We are no different from little kids performing clumsy magic tricks for grownups. They smile and offer words of encouragement though the sleight-of-hand is completely obvious. *See what I did! Bet you can't figure out how I did that.*

All our posturing and protest against God is as blatantly obvious as little Bobby's first attempt to produce a quarter from Aunt Lucy's ear. There's no magic, just an awkward kid hoping to amaze his elders. The difference is, we foolishly believe in our powers of reason and intellect and expect God to respect them.

Where do folks get the crazy idea that they are sufficient? All wise? All important? All deserving? Ignorance of the law is no excuse in the courts of men; how much less will it matter before the judgment throne of God?

All sin is original sin because there is only one sin. From Adam and Eve onward, every sin is functionally the same. All sin is self-indulgence; believing the lie that we are as good as God, as high as God, as deserving as God, and as powerful as God. When you are unsure whether you are right or wrong on an issue, where do you go for confirmation or correction? According to the world, the best place to look is in the mirror.

Whether in politics or religion (both institutions of men) people conduct internal audits to resolve concerns about possible mistakes. Most times the verdict is, "Nope. All is well. I checked on myself just to be sure." The political question of whether or not Hillary Clinton handled emails correctly while Secretary of State was addressed seriously and responsibly.

You may remember that Mrs. Clinton used a private server and decided which emails were relevant. Her response to the call for clarity and transparency was to audit herself. She found her behavior perfectly correct and legal. End of story. Her behavior confirmed her behavior. Sin confirms itself.

Humans have imperfect perspective because our field and depth of vision is limited. We can evaluate our appearance in a set of mirrors yet not see everything others see. The very act of turning around or moving eyes up, down, or sideways changes the angle and shadow of our reflection.

It is impossible to be objective about ourselves.

Primary Identity Dictates World View

Every sentient being (able to perceive or feel) has an identity that defines its perceptions, decisions, and loyalties to which all judgments are subject. Primary identity is the core definition of self.

Every person has some identity or allegiance that molds his or her vision. *Who you are* is like a pair of contact lenses. Every visual image your brain processes first passes through the contact lens. *Who you are* can't be removed like contacts. Your brain processes each thing you see, taste, smell, think, or hear through a prism of personal primary allegiance before it consciously registers.

Decisions about what you do, where you live, and with whom you associate are driven by primary identity. How you occupy your time, spend your money, or exert energy is based on your primary identity. What makes you joyous or angry, how you vote, how you love, and how you worship are determined by *who you are.*

People without core identities are conflicted, insecure, unstable, inconsistent, and often fearful. When every man is an island to himself there is no constancy; there is no rule; all direction comes from self, and that self is confused.

> *Everywhere I go, there I am. – unknown*

The artfulness of rationalization and compartmentalization reached epic proportions in the late 20th century when society adopted egocentricity as the norm; evaluating everything with the perspective that *I am the center of the universe.* It became fashionable in the 1970s to leave the old life and relationships behind to "find myself." In 1966 Timothy Leary[4] made the phrase, *"Turn on, tune in, drop out"* famous.

> *"Drop out" suggested an active, selective, graceful process of detachment from involuntary or unconscious commitments. "Drop Out" meant self-reliance, a discovery of one's singularity, a commitment to mobility, choice, and change."—Timothy Leary, Flashbacks*

I wonder if Mr. Leary would be shocked by his contribution to the downfall of western society. Self-indulgence is no longer selective or graceful. Perhaps President Nixon was right when he pegged Leary as "the most dangerous man in America."

Why would someone believe another person would lie about one thing but not about another? Usually it's because the lie didn't affect him directly. This is an example of deception. A liar is a liar. Someone who cheats on his income tax will cheat elsewhere because he is a cheat. If someone you know lies to others, he will lie

---

[4] Timothy Francis Leary (1920 – 1996) an American psychologist and educator known for advocating psychedelic drugs; most notably LSD. During the 60s and 70s, he involuntarily visited 29 different prisons throughout the world.

to you. If he has lied to you about one thing, he will lie to you about anything.

Many politicians lie. People continue to support known liars for the reasons cited in the previous paragraph–plus one more. The liars on *my* team are more acceptable than the liars on *your* team. Folks often find familiar liars more acceptable than truthful members of another tribe.

Every person has a primary association. You may describe yourself by race, gender, marital status, citizenship, age, family status as parent or grandparent, profession, avocation, religion, doctrine or ideology.

Every person is a complex amalgam of characteristics, relationships, experience, preferences, and philosophy, but you have only one *primary* perception of self that trumps all others. This concept of identity dictates how you evaluate, process, define, and order everything in your life.

People tend to associate with others like them. Collective Identity is the shared sense of belonging to a group. Groups establish rules, social mores, and doctrines. Leaders are given the power to define membership and guide group members. Every group competes in some way with every other group. Without some major commonality or unifier, disparate groups cannot live together in harmony and peace because differences will eventually lead to conflict.

In present western cultures one group has been identified as a common enemy by all others; those whose primary allegiance is to the Lord Jesus Christ. In God's opinion a lie is a lie is a lie. It doesn't matter who told it or why. Is it so difficult to understand why God insists that members of His family adopt His rules, social mores, doctrines, and leadership? Team loyalty and tribalism is hardly a new concept.

Decades ago, friends from Illinois visited my husband and me in Omaha, arriving with six precious football tickets. Formerly a resident of Minnesota and Michigan, where major-league football is the norm and no university without an instate rival, the attention

Nebraskans lavish on one college football program struck me as oddly excessive.

On late summer and autumn Saturdays, the University of Nebraska warm-up and play-by-play is broadcast in grocery stores and shopping malls, which is why I paid any attention at all.

To provide context, this was in the mid-1980s with coaching provided by the legendary Tom Osborne. Victory was the norm.

You couldn't escape fans who bled and breathed Red. Adding injury to curiosity, the fans were often ugly to those who didn't share their passion.

I was teased, lectured, even ostracized, for not being a rabid fan of the erstwhile Bugeaters (the original team name), which didn't warm my heart one degree toward Big Red.

That Saturday, six of us went to the Illinois-Nebraska game on the Cornhusker's home field. Mr. Baber's business colleague, and proud graduate of Illinois, brought gorgeous team jerseys for both of us. I wore mine to the game.

Our group was evenly divided; three in red and three in white with orange and blue accents.

Four of the six tickets were in the Illinois section and two in the higher elevations of Nebraska's bleachers. My husband and I spent the first half of the game with Illinois fans and the second half with the folks in red.

During the second half, my enemy colors infuriated the lady sitting directly in front of me. Dressed in a red sweater, red poodle skirt, red beret, red boots, and red earrings with red lipstick smeared all over her front teeth (true), she spit her gall at me, "You shouldn't have a ticket to this game!"

I suspect she was warmer toward the visiting fans who stayed where they belonged. Pity the fool who dared to wear the offensive colors to her territory!

If college football people are that exclusive, why should God be less so?

The history of mankind is fraught with irreconcilable conflicts and competitions of every type and description. But sooner or later everyone chooses membership in one of two camps: the one ordered by God and the one not. God does not change. He is ever honest, faithful, and the same today as He was yesterday and will be tomorrow.

"If we say that we have no sin, we deceive ourselves, and the truth is not in us."—1 John 1:8

Many of us are not who we think we are. Perhaps an acquaintance tells others that he is generous, kind, and thoughtful. After you observe him slapping a baby, kicking a puppy, and shoplifting a sixpack, he admits to his foolishness but argues that "underneath I am still a good person!"

Do you believe it? Do you think he believes it? How can we know if what other people think or presume about themselves is correct? People not only lie to each other, but they lie to themselves without any awareness at all.

Throughout much of history people did not primarily think of themselves as individuals, but as members of a clan, family, caste, nation, order, or religion. Hunter-gatherers were families or clans with their own societies and culture. As people gathered into villages more societal systems, cultures, and organized governments evolved.

People no longer lived within self-sufficient family units. Neighbors no longer held identical principles or morals. The more diverse the customs, traditions, or religious observances of people in a society, the greater the competition for resources, privilege, and control. The result is always compromise or battle.

"But there are some people, nevertheless—and I am one of them—who think that the most practical and important thing about a man is his view of the universe."—G.K. Chesterton, Heretics

Battle for Grazing Control

One of the most famous feuds of the American Old West was what has come to be known as the Pleasant Valley War, a years-long vendetta between two ranch families in Arizona. The trouble started in the 1880s, when differences arose between the Tewksburys, a family of sheepherders, and the cattle-raising Grahams. The two families regularly argued over the borders of their two properties, and both claimed that the other's animals tore up their land and left it useless for grazing. Eventually, the conflict escalated into an outright war that claimed the lives of as many as 20 people.[5]

Dinosaur Wars

In the 19th century, Edward Drinker Cope and Othniel Charles Marsh turned the hunt for new dinosaur species into a cutthroat game of one-upmanship. The two scientists started out on friendly terms—each had once named new fossils after the other—but they had a falling out in the late 1860s, after Marsh bribed workers into helping him acquire bones from one of Cope's dig sites. The "Bone Wars" would eventually ruin both men professionally and financially, but it left paleontology all the richer. By the 1890s, Cope and Marsh's competition led to the discovery of thousands of fossils and 136 new dinosaur species including the Triceratops, the Stegosaurus and the Apatosaurus.[6]

People have long considered folks from other nations, sects, clans, or religions dangerous, inconvenient, or less-than-human. Human nature fears what it does not understand. Common interests create common ground, but sometimes there is no common ground. Since Cain slew Abel, existential battles have waged between deities and

---

[5] toptenz.net/top-ten-famous-feuds-and-vendettas.php
[6] history.com/news/history-lists/6-vicious-rivalries

men, between deity and deity, and between men and men. We have come full circle. The battle today is the battle for your eternity.

By the late 1920s the collectivist perspective had all but disappeared from mainstream social psychology. Instead of God, country, or family first, western cultures encouraged and rewarded policies of "Me: first, last, and always."

Today, sharing common ideologies creates social categorization as much as anything else. The most important question has become, *"Who agrees with me?"*

Henri Tajfel (1919-1982) survived multiple concentration camps during World War II while most of his family perished. The experience inspired his study of prejudice and social identity theory. He wrote that "Social categorization is a haphazardly floating independent variable which strikes at random as the spirit moves." Simply stated, folks seek a more collectivist or group approach when it is in their own best interest. People are conditioned to declare that "you're not the boss of me", unless they need back up and security is best found within a larger group.

From Philosophy to Communism

Considered the father of modern political theory, Niccolò Machiavelli (1469-1527) abandoned religion and classical philosophy, choosing instead to advise rulers of his day using the basics of human nature proven throughout history. He wrote *The Prince*, a handbook for politicians on the use of ruthless, wily, and self-serving tactics that inspired the term "Machiavellian." His tools? Deceit and fear.

> *"Never attempt to win by force what can be won by deception." -attributed to Niccolò Machiavelli*

German philosophers Georg Hegel (1770-1831) and Karl Marx (1818-83) classified politics as the inevitable result of historical processes. They argued that groups (collectives) should be thought of as more real and of greater value than individual members.

Hegelianism suggests that only the rational is real. His goal was to reduce reality to a system of absolute idealism. In other words, reality becomes unreality. Further, Hegelianism holds that whatever truth there is in art and in religion is contained in a philosophy free from all limitations. Philosophy is *"the highest, freest and wisest phase of the union of subjective and objective mind, and the ultimate goal of all development."*

Hegel would have appreciated personal success guru Napoleon Hill's (1883-1970) now famous quote. *"Whatever the mind can conceive and believe, it can achieve."*[7] Hill taught principles and method while Hegel thought everything was pretty much a matter of personal experience.

The other massive difference between the two deals with power and human limitations. Hegel considered humanity the sum of all things. Hill openly gave credit to other-worldly spirits and the Masters who revealed secrets and knowledge to him.

Whether you agree more with Hegel or Hill, both suggest that destiny rests in the hands of the individual. Hill defined the secret of success as (1) helping others create value and personal benefit, and (2) having a *Definite Major Purpose.*

What you believe is material. What you believe determines where you will be fifteen minutes into eternity. The important question remains; *is what you believe actually true?* Hegel might argue that truth is what you think. Hill said you must think precisely, have deep faith in what you think, and then be nice. I wonder what door to eternity Napoleon Hill chose.

Georg Hegel got the ball rolling; Karl Marx picked it up and ran with it. Marx morphed from a drunk and disorderly university student and spendthrift into a Georg Hegel fan. From there he graduated into socialism. Banished from Germany, France, and Belgium, Marx ended up in London where he played a pivotal role in the birth of modern Communism.

---

[7] "Think and Grow Rich" published in 1937

A prolific critic of Capitalism, Karl Marx organized, published, and worked as a journalist. Although he was born into a wealthy middle-class family, Marx never earned enough to support himself; living off the largesse of Friedrich Engels, co-author of *The Communist Manifesto*. The extended Marx family continued to be very successful with connections to major corporate players still known today.

As is still the case, privileged children receive private educations rich in liberal humanist doctrine. The Marx family owned wineries and Karl's father was a successful lawyer. Business paid for his private education, but the content of that private education turned Karl against the very hand that provided it.

Napoleon Hill might suggest that the sole reason for Marx's longevity was the strength of his beliefs. He was committed to tearing down the fabric of western society that denied him what he wanted but didn't want to work for within the current system. Marx spent his life trying to figure out why some people get rich and others do not.

This is a simplistic observation, but despite starting life with great resources Marx seemed to tick off most of the people around him, including his family. Napoleon Hill would tell him that was a huge part of the problem right there.

Human nature resists looking in the mirror when searching for someone to blame. Marx thought that people who owned businesses must somehow be guilty since they had more than he, a *nouveau* member of the working class, and a failed one at that.

God was no longer the basis and reason for human morality and the arbiter of truth. From the earliest days of humanity, political authority was based on a shared belief in God (or other deities) and divinely instituted natural laws.

The new world of science, philosophy, medicine, economics, gained strength throughout the 19th century as traditional social, religious, and foundations of political authority were examined and determined to be unfair to the individual. *Me* was quickly replacing

Thee. The shift in power and control was well underway. The Tower of Babel was largely repaired.

Events of 1859 marked the transition from a world explained and powered by God to one explained and powered by individual personality and reason.

Defining Primary Identity

Everyone has an identity that defines them. As Tajfel noted, identity is changeable by circumstance or whim. People in western societies are obsessed with who they are, how they feel, and pursuing validation from others. Differences among friends, neighbors, and family members crop up because of misunderstandings, failures to communicate, and flat out competition for space or control.

Some people have a primary identity based on family relationships or commitments. Many of my friends might say their primary identity is Grandmother. Others say they are members of a particular religion, church, or denomination. Still others self-identify as members of an organization or political party.

Primary identity can also be based on a particular cause or ideology. People exchange one identity lens for another when it's beneficial to join a larger group (collective.) This philosophy is shared by Georg Hegel and Karl Marx. The difference between their ideology and the west today is consistency. Hegel and Marx were committed, while folks today pick up or put down ideologies based on the benefit of the moment.

Examples of ideological identification:

- Illegal Immigration
- Race
- Climate Change – Environmentalism
- Abortion rights
- Gender/ Sexuality issues
- Socio-economic status or perceived inequity

Primary identification is inextricably linked to issues of control, power, value, and morality. What someone believes to be true often depends more on his or her allegiances than what *is*.

> *"Domination by researchers with any narrow outlook, moral perspective, worldview, or political perspective risks creating a social psychology riddled with blind spots, biased interpretations, and distorted and unjustified claims and conclusions." (Haidt, 2012; Jussim, 2012a; Prentice, 2012; Tetlock, 1994[8])*

All opinions, philosophies, decisions, and behaviors are driven by how one's personal identity or world view interprets and orders the world around them. In ages past, worldview was shared by entire populations. Over time it has become a completely individual matter. This resulted in duality or split personalities as traditional religion tried to share the path with emerging humanism. Eventually one must bow to the other because God (the belief in any deity) and humanism are mutually exclusive.

---

[8] rci.rutgers.edu/~jussim/IdeologicalBiasinSocial.pdf pg 91

What Do You Believe?

ω

"Most assuredly, I say to you, he who believes in Me has everlasting life."—John 6:47

*W*here you think you will be fifteen minutes into eternity depends on *what* you believe. People fall into one of two camps when it comes to belief; they believe in something or they believe in nothing. Except that it is impossible to believe in nothing. The absence of everything defines a vacuum. If there was anything in the vacuum that recognized it as a vacuum, as nothing, it couldn't really be a vacuum.

Even the practice of non-belief is fracturing into different denominations, because people demand the freedom to believe in nothing in their own unique way. Proving again that truth is stranger than fiction, even the broad religious category of No Religion now produces discontent and doctrinal division among faithful non-believers. Christians and Atheists alike squabble over the details of how to properly practice their beliefs (or lack thereof.)

Christian sects and denominations have played doctrinal one-upmanship for centuries in an endless argument over whose rules for worshiping Jesus Christ are most correct. Humanists now insist on the same right to have it their way. Humanism is becoming a full-fledged religion.

Doctrine is not exclusive to religious discussions. It is defined as a specific (or group) principle, position, or policy advocated or taught. Doctrine is often synonymous with ideology or creed, a set of beliefs, ethics, morality, or world view.

Historically, religion was defined as "an organized system of beliefs, ceremonies, and rules used to worship a god or a group of gods" (Merriam-Webster). The definition of religion evolved until it now recognizes any "interest, belief, or activity that is *very* important to a person or group" as a religion.

Odd Religions

Lest you think Humanism is the strangest religion, let me share a few of the more interesting religions in the world.

The **Prince Philip Movement** is a cargo cult of the Yaohnanen tribe on the southern island of Tanna in Vanuatu. The Yaohnanen believe that Prince Philip, Duke of Edinburgh, consort to Queen Elizabeth II, is a divine being, and that ritual worship of the Duke will one day bring a load (cargo) of material wealth. When the cult formed is unclear, but it is likely that it was sometime in the 1950s or 1960s. Prince Philip is aware of the religion and has exchanged gifts with its leaders and even visited them.[9]

Originating as a New York Black Muslim group in the 1970s, the **Nuwabians** have gone through many changes since. White people, explains Nuwaubian myth, were created as a race of killers to serve blacks as a slave army–a plan gone awry.

Some of its more creative doctrines teach:

- Some aborted fetuses survive abortion to live in the sewers, where they are being gathered and organized to take over the world
- Women existed for many generations before they invented men through genetic manipulation
- *Homo sapiens* are the result of cloning experiments that were done on Mars using *Homo erectus*, and the most creative of all,
- The Illuminati nurtured a child, Satan's son, born June 6, 1966 at the Dakota House on 72nd Street in New York to Jacqueline Kennedy Onassis of the Rothschild/Kennedy families. The Pope was present at the birth and performed necromantic ceremonies. Raised by former U.S. president Richard Nixon, the child now lives in Belgium, where he is connected to a computer called "The Beast 3M" or "3666".[10]

---

[9] Listverse.com

[10] Listverse.com/2009/09/10/10-extremely-weird-religions

Started by the Reverend Chris Korda in Boston, Massachusetts, **the Church of Euthanasia's** website shares its one commandment: "Thou shalt not procreate". The CoE further asserts four principal pillars: suicide, abortion, cannibalism (strictly limited to consumption of the dead), and sodomy (a sexual act not intended for procreation).[11]

Based in Japan, **Panawave** is an exceedingly odd group scared witless by electromagnetic waves, blaming them for climate change, environmental destruction and other worldly ills.[12]

The **Aetherius Society** combines a bit of Christian dogma with Hindu, Buddhist and Jewish beliefs, mixing them all together with a healthy dose of UFOs and extraterrestrials, hoping to prevent the total annihilation of the Earth.[13]

Zoroastrianism is one of the world's oldest monotheistic religions, sharing many tenets with Judaism and Christianity. Founded in Iran by the Prophet Zoroaster around 1500 BC, it was one of the most powerful world religions for the next 1000 years. Now one of the world's smallest religions, the New York Times reported less than 190,000 followers in 2006. Yazidis share elements with Zoroastrianism. In 2014, the Islamic State (ISIS) in northern Iraq drove Yazidis from their homes and remain refugees in 2016. In practice, modern Zoroastrianism has a positive outlook. It teaches that mankind is ultimately good and that this goodness will finally triumph over evil.[14]

The Persians and ruling class during the time of the book of Esther were most likely Zoroastrians. Freddy Mercury of the band Queen was a Zoroastrian.

---

[11] Listverse.com/2009/09/10/10-extremely-weird-religions

[12] indiatimes.com/news/weird/13-religions

[13] indiatimes.com/news/weird/13-religions

[14] bbc.co.uk/religion/religions/zoroastrian

Religion of Humanism

Primary identity can be complicated when one's religion clashes with other personal ideologies or preferences. Christian denominations that differ on material issues don't have a corner on that problem. Now, even non-believers quibble about how to non-believe on an individual level while still clinging to some semblance of group unity.

> *"While this age does owe a vast debt to the traditional religions, it is none the less obvious that any religion that can hope to be a synthesizing and dynamic force for today must be shaped for the needs of this age. To establish such a religion is a major necessity of the present." – A Humanist Manifesto (1933)*

The "needs of this age" are of interest only to those who don't believe in eternity. Faith, not in human potential, but in God, is a matter for all ages. Eternity is neither impressed by, nor subject to, the needs of this age.

In the past 150 years, two major humanist ideologies have overtaken every aspect of public and private life:

1. In advanced (progressive) cultures the individual is of primary concern, emphasizing the desires, individuality, and rights of every unique person. Each is a god unto himself.
2. Humans have little intrinsic worth, with no special place in the world and universe. Which means, humanists promote a deity without value.

When tactically expedient, individuals create power and safety by banding together. Group ideologies or demands aren't formulated to promote a cause or set of principles as much as to validate and benefit the individuals. Personal benefit is the highest goal of most current ideologies. Without God, however, nothing has any ultimate meaning.

Secular humanists believe that we are accidents of time and chance on a never-ending road to the next accident. What is the eternal meaning of a dandelion or earthworm? Evolutionists believe humans share a common ancestor with both.

Matters of Faith

Many people claim that the Bible is filled with inconsistencies or contradictions. It is not. Separating any verse from the whole is error. Where and what you worship isn't a matter of fellowship or camaraderie, but a matter of eternity. Worship men or worship God. Worship the creation or the Creator. Obedience to the still small voice of the Holy Spirit always brings peace–regardless of external circumstances.

People who speak truth live truth. People who live truth speak Christ.

> *"Many of us prefer to stay at the threshold of the Christian life instead of going on to construct a soul in accordance with the new life God has put within. We fail because we are ignorant of the way we are made, we put things down to the devil instead of our own undisciplined natures."—Oswald Chambers, My Utmost for His Highest*

Do your interests define your faith or does your faith determine your interests?

Do your opinions define God or does Christ define you?

Do you stand in judgment over God or willingly yield to His judgment?

Do you hold something apart from Christ or *surrender* all?

Faith fails when the object of faith is unworthy or imaginary. The power of Jesus Christ as master, savior, friend, and as God, is in the truth of Christ, not what people choose to believe He is or is not.

> *"We [demons] must picture hell as a state where everyone is perpetually concerned about his own dignity and advancement, where everyone has a grievance, and where everyone lives with the deadly serious passions of envy, self-*

importance, and resentment."—C.S. Lewis, The Screwtape Letters

You can't fool God, mock God, or manipulate God. Petulant and spoiled people accuse, "If you really loved me you would do as I ask!" People routinely pout before God, but He is not moved.

God does not accept guilt trips. A mocking voice is no more powerful to God than the smallest breeze on a blade of grass 100 miles away. Nothing requires God to give us what we want. It's popular to quote, "Ask and ye shall receive." What isn't so popular is the companion verse, "Ye receive not because ye ask amiss." Ask in the will of God and you will receive.

The world encourages us to pigeonhole God, accusing Him of wrongdoing when we don't get what we want. Many people protest that "my God" would do such and such, as opposed to the intolerant God of the Bible. The truth is, any god conjured up in the imagination of man has only as much power as the imagination that dreamed it up. If the person who creates a pleasant convenient god has enough personal power to transform eternity, then it's a good choice. Otherwise, fifteen minutes into eternity, the error is irreversible.

Present Christ AS HE IS. Only Jesus Christ, the literal man who was born of a virgin, died on a Roman cross, and walked from the tomb into glory, has the power to save. One day the world is going to end in a great ball of fire.

Choose the world and prepare to burn. Choose God and enjoy eternity.

Choose wisely.

Christianity and Social Justice

ω

"The little "I am" always sulks when God says do. Let the little "I am" be shriveled up in God's indignation – "I AM THAT I AM... hath sent me." He must dominate. Is it not penetrating to realise that God knows where we live, and the kennels we crawl into. He will hunt us up like a lightning flash. No human being knows human beings as God does."—Oswald Chambers, *My Utmost for His Highest*

The battle between God's Word and the world intensifies by the moment. God created everything and reserves the right to sit in judgment over all of it. Ever since the serpent offered Eve forbidden fruit the world has preached the lie of self-importance. Human nature inclines to the pretty thought that we can sit in judgment over our surroundings, our circumstance, and all the folks who pass through our lives.

Human nature has no secrets from God because He created order and purpose. Humans considered His plan and discarded it for one of their own. Unfortunately, not all humans share the same plan. The bad news is that there is no resolution to disputes among humans regarding property, ideology, or behavior. The more perfectly one believes he has defined perfection, the further his vision strays from that of his neighbor.

My truth is the truth. I will tolerate your truth until is impinges upon mine. In that case, my truth rules.

How are disputes settled and peace established among men competing for scarce resources or operating under different plans?

The same options have existed for all post-Eden human history.

1. Steal or conquer by force
2. Greater generosity
3. Agree to principles, rules, and laws applicable to all

Generosity is rare. Jesus preached it and the Apostles practiced it. Much of the world, however, considers generosity a sign of weakness. It's easy to convince ourselves that it is somehow just to take everything someone is willing to give. *They deserve to lose all they have because they're too weak or lazy to fight to keep it.*

Both warfare and law require some limitation on individuals. Stealing is always an option, but when an angry victim or law enforcement catches you, the price you pay may exceed the value of what you stole. That leaves one viable option for peace: society with others under law. This basic truth has been proven throughout every human era. History also proves that unless laws are enforced, the only beneficiary is the lawbreaker. Accepting the benefits of orderly society requires people to sit under established judges or leadership.

People who lived before the 18th century believed they were at the mercy of the Creator God (Jehovah) or other gods. Most folks preferred to obey the rules rather than face the consequences for breaking them. People today don't think they should be under the law of anyone or anything except what is approved by their own intellect and is in their best interest.

Human ears have itched since the moment Adam and Eve were evicted from Eden. Cain killed his brother because he thought God dissed him in favor of Abel. Social justice theories do little more than describe the human condition and conclude that some are innocent and others guilty. Yet most social justice ideologies share a common goal–denouncing Jesus Christ. Perhaps they aren't aware of what they're doing, but isn't that precisely what they say about others?

"Preach the word! Be ready in season and out of season. Convince, rebuke, exhort, with all longsuffering and teaching. For the time will come when they will not endure sound doctrine, but according to their own desires, because they have itching ears, they will heap up for themselves teachers; and they will turn their ears away from the truth, and be turned aside to fables."—2 Timothy 4:2-4

The only real difference between humanists, socialists, communists, and critical theorists is who or what they worship. Every philosophy and -ism establish a divide between right and wrong, the innocent and the guilty, and those who deserve consideration from those who deserve condemnation.

The end game is separating Biblical Christians from society. It's been a long time coming. It's here.

The Battle for Control

People want a vote on what happens to them today, tomorrow, and forever. Deep in every human heart lurks the sin of self-indulgence and the desire to be master of one's fate. Where you find yourself fifteen minutes into eternity depends on who controls your destiny.

Destiny is determined by one of the following:

1. God
2. Humans
3. Nature
4. No one

If God is in control, the only rational course is to repent your sins and get right with Him. If humans are in control, you need to figure out who has the most power and make friends. If Nature is the arbiter of your fate, study up on botany, astronomy, geology, climatology, and every other -ology you can think of. Take your best shot at making nice with Mother Nature. I've heard she has a bit of a temper.

Then there are those pesky atheists and nihilists who believe that no one is in control, that there is no order, and that there is no eternity. Everything is random and temporary, so eat, drink, and be merry for tomorrow you will be nothing more than an evaporated drop of dew.

In this age of darkness, where trophies are given for participation rather than achievement, the concept of standards has morphed from describing ideals and goals into something punitive, divisive, and ugly. Those who seek to control others insist that standards are only as good or bad as the fruit they produce. How could a Bible-believing person argue that point? Before answering that question, we need to answer this one:

Who determines what fruit is good and what fruit is not?

Sometimes Even Good Fruit Stinks

God is found behind one of the two doors to eternity. Lying in wait behind the other door is Not God. In this book the use of God refers solely to God, Jehovah and Creator, who reveals Himself through His written Word and in the person of Jesus Christ. It's a pretty simple either/or choice.

Anything other than total and glorious submission to God is the total and complete rejection of God. There is no third option. Some folks will argue that middle ground exists. And it may, but only in their imagination. Some folks believe in unicorns. That doesn't mean unicorns exist.

Jesus Christ is a take it or leave it proposition. He is unchanging and unchangeable. He is everything the Bible says He is or He is nothing. People who choose what parts of the Bible to believe and which to reject create new religions based on personal preferences and ideologies. None of those personal religions have a savior that offers eternity with Christ.

People believe a variety of things and even self-labeled Christians disagree vehemently over what is true and what is not. Some people who profess Jesus as Lord don't appear to produce as much sweet fruit as others who insist they never met Him. G.K. Chesterton, the apostle of common sense, once said that *"to criticize religion because it leads people to kill each other is like criticizing love because it has the same effect."* All the best things, when abused, can cause bad things to happen; the common element is human nature.

Truth and perspective are not synonymous, but the devil and progressive humanists work diligently to spread that lie whenever and wherever possible. In order for something to be true it must be true in all circumstances, in all places, and at all times. Truth is defined as the *actual state of a matter, or conformity with fact or reality.* In other words, truth is neither a consensus of opinion nor a description of the present cultural mood. Truth is what IS.

Perspective is a way of regarding circumstances and judging their relative importance. Truth describes what IS. Perspective is an opinion about what someone thinks and whether or not what IS has any value.

A diamond may be of great value to the jeweler who sets it into a beautiful ring, but nothing more than a nasty tooth-breaking irritant to the hungry man who discovered it in a stale hunk of bread. Diamonds are minerals; that's the truth. Whether a diamond is a thing of beauty or a nuisance is a matter of perspective. Value, like beauty, is often in the eye of the beholder.

Every Christian is flawed. If you're still breathing earthly air you are flawed. Some have flaws so minute that they are visible only under a spiritual loupe while others wear their cracks and refurbishments out front for all to see.

Some really good-looking fruits and vegetables will kill you. Ask the families of the four people who died from eating fresh packaged spinach contaminated with E coli in 2006. More than 200 people in 26 states were affected by triple-washed organic spinach packaged by Dole.

Man's fall from grace originated with the ripe juicy fruit of the Tree of the Knowledge of Good and Evil. Adam and Eve sure thought that fruit looked good, but by it death was introduced into the world.

> *"Men occasionally stumble over the truth, but most of them pick themselves up and hurry off as if nothing had happened."—(attributed to) Winston Churchill*

There is only one Truth that is true in all instances, places, and times. That is the truth God shares with His people through His Word under the tutelage of the Holy Spirit. Anything apart from God's truth is an opinion, someone's perspective, or a lie. Which door you open to eternity is determined by what you believe to be true, and if it is actually true or not.

"A man who lies to himself, and believes his own lies, becomes unable to recognize truth, either in himself or in anyone else, and he ends up losing respect for himself and for others. When he has no respect for anyone, he can no longer love, and in him, he yields to his impulses, indulges in the lowest form of pleasure, and behaves in the end like an animal in satisfying his vices. And it all comes from lying — to others and to yourself." —Fyodor Dostoyevsky, The Brothers Karamazov

Humanism is the religion of the enlightened. 1859 was a banner year for humanistic theory. Humanism denies the supernatural by elevating humanity to deity while simultaneously reducing it to a product of time and chance. Humanism believes there is nothing in eternity except eternity.

H.J. Blackburn shared his humanist worldview with this illustration:

"On humanist assumptions, life leads to nothing, and every pretense that it does not is a deceit. If there is a bridge over a gorge which spans only half the distance and ends in mid-air, and if the bridge is crowded with human beings pressing on, one after the other they fall into the abyss. The bridge leads nowhere, and those who are pressing forward to cross it are going nowhere... It does not matter where they think they are going, what preparations for the journey that they may have made, how much they may be enjoying it all. The objection merely points out objectively that such a situation is a model of futility." [15]

Humanists may be kind, enlightened, proud, or self-important. But humanism has no depth of joy because it neither offers nor believes that life goes somewhere, has purpose, and is without ultimate meaning. Humanists believe that nothing exists beyond the material, the natural, the mundane, and the pointless.

---

[15] Francis Schaeffer's "Whatever Happened to the Human Race" vol 5, pg 355

Control

Humans are always looking for a better deal, an upgrade or greener grass. That's why married people stray, why folks with great jobs are always on the lookout for another, why people in cozy homes stretch emaciated budgets to buy something a bit grander, and why people seek a more convenient god. Isn't it odd that the biggest shopping day of the year is the day after Thanksgiving?

> *"Black Friday: because only in America will people trample others for sales exactly one day after being thankful for what they already have."—Unknown*

Control is a function of power. Power is a function of value. Value is a function of both utility and morality. Whoever establishes utility and morality gains control.

Nominal Christians continue to live as if their works will produce meaningful merit in the hereafter, clinging to the fantasy that their work product correlates with their eternity, grasping one last shred of control. *If I control my effort, I control my eternity.* Jesus Christ did all that was necessary to insure your eternity. Let Him insure yours, because you can't insure your own.

Master of Your Destiny

You have been deceived. The world suggests that everyone is the master of his or her own destiny. Many believe the lie because it contains an element of truth. You are the master of your destiny to the extent that you decide which eternal door to open. The problem we all face is choosing the right door.

Society and goodwill among men erode daily because of the lie. The only way you can be the master of your universe is if you're the only one in it.

When two masters in one universe collide the worldly believe that:

- Your truth is only true to the extent it agrees with my truth.
- What you consider rational is only as sensible as what I consider rational.

- Your values are always less virtuous than mine.
- Your judgment is always less discerning than mine.
- Your desires are never as commendable as mine.
- What you think will never trump what I think.

Every –ism, special interest group, and social justice theory or movement uses human nature as justification. Social justice theories are built on disputed facts. Disagreements flare over what is real, true, moral, equal, or relevant to establishing justice. The difference between objectivity and subjectivity is usually decided by personal opinion. Who defines what is just, generous, shameful or equal?

Liberal humanists insist that every man and woman is entitled to freedom of expression with complete equality. People want freedom and they want control. The heart of such teaching is a lie. The extent to which any individual can control his or her personal circumstance is limited to the power held by each individual. Can he or she defend ideology or property from the guy next door who wants to control it himself?

Control is a function of power. Governments who give freedoms to people can also take them away because the power of the government dwarfs the power of the individual. The United States Declaration of Independence recognizes freedom as bestowed from our Creator, not the government. When governments confer entitlements and value to citizens it removes all real control and power from them, which explains why the Creator has been removed from the public square in recent decades.

Whoever holds power controls conversations, draws conclusions, and enforces judgment. Like the two doors to eternity, humans either base their concept of justice on (1) self-benefit, or (2) God's standards.

Unless people submit to a higher authority, whether temporal or divine, there is anarchy and an endless battle for power, position, and benefit. The only authority powerful enough and faithful enough for eternity is Jesus Christ. All else is temporary and stands apart from reality that *is*.

Familiarity Breeds Contempt

ω

And they said, "Come, let us build ourselves a city, and a tower [of Babel] whose top is in the heavens; let us make a name for ourselves."—Genesis 11:4

Belief in miracles assumes that human power has limits and that something or someone bigger and more powerful than self exists. The goal, since 1859, is selling natural explanations for everything, eliminating any consideration for the supernatural or miraculous. None of mankind's yearnings, falsehoods, creeds, beliefs, theorems, or postulations have the power to change one iota of what truly *is*.

Knowledge vs Obedience

"All of God's revealed truths are sealed until they are opened to us through obedience. You will never open them through philosophy or thinking. But once you obey, a flash of light comes immediately. Let God's truth work into you by immersing yourself in it, not by worrying into it."—Oswald Chambers, My Utmost for His Highest

If Jesus walked beside a lake today and said "Follow Me" to (a modern) Peter and Andrew, wouldn't you expect them to ask for more information before making such a huge commitment? Who in his right mind would follow some guy without knowing the details of message, mission, expectations, and negotiating an attractive compensation package for his time and effort?

Followers of Christ settle in behind Jesus to walk in His footsteps. When they hear "Follow" their feet begin to move. Christians obey first. The disciples didn't ask questions before making decisions. Many times Jesus knew they had questions; offering answers because the disciples feared to ask. On other occasions Jesus refused to answer questions but still expected obedience. Peter, after hearing that his ministry would end in martyrdom, nodded in John's direction and asked Jesus, "But Lord, what about this man?" Jesus said to him, "If I will that he remain till I come, *what is that to you? You follow Me*" (John 21:21-22).

> *"But I fear, lest somehow, as the serpent deceived Eve by his craftiness, so your minds may be corrupted from the simplicity that is in Christ. For if he who comes preaches another Jesus whom we have not preached, or if you receive a different spirit which you have not received, or a different gospel which you have not accepted—you may well put up with it!"—2 Corinthians 11:3-4*

Jesus began His ministry expecting obedience first. Knowledge was imparted when it was necessary to teach His followers what they needed to succeed in the tasks ahead. Somewhere along the line mankind flipped the order, seeking knowledge before deciding if obedience was a rational choice.

The world suggests that only weak-minded people obey Christ without doing due diligence. The jesus the world heralds is not Jesus of Nazareth, but some progressive liberal myth who wants to be friends and serve as a blessing machine. This is the jesus appealed to by those preaching Prosperity in worldly terms and tolerance for anything people naturally prefer, even when God's Word condemns. This lie of another jesus has been a huge success because it's what itching ears want to hear, making it palatable and easy to tolerate.

Anyone insisting that Christ explain Himself and provide an itemized list of everything He expects in exchange for obedience and followership has an unfortunate surprise coming. Obedience isn't a transaction. True obedience must be offered. If there is no option to disobey, acquiescence is by domination, not choice. Jesus never makes you do anything.

Sometimes we pray, "Lord, make me generous. Make me wise. Make me do what you want. Make me obedient." Jesus says, "Come." The choice is yours.

The lie spread; *Knowledge* first, then *Obedience*. With passing centuries deception exploded. In 1859 the weight of error finally surpassed that of rectitude. Followers of Christ don't approve the route in advance. Instead, we obediently follow like Peter and Andrew, because we love Him.

> *"Trust in the Lord with all your heart, and lean not on your own understanding; In all your ways acknowledge Him, And He shall direct your paths."—Proverbs 3:5-6*

Successfully Selling Deception

> *"God is light. Therefore, to engage in fellowship with Him we must walk in the light and not in darkness. Two major roadblocks to hinder this walk will be falling in love with the world and falling for the alluring lies of false teachers." – Introduction to 1 John, Thomas Nelson NKJV, 1994*

The most successful way to sell a lie is to wrap it with incontrovertible truth. The two most successful methods of deception are (1) telling what is 99.5% true mixed with a wee smidgeon of lie, and (2) speaking only what is true but not the whole truth.

Have you ever wondered why rats eat rat killer? When you examine the list of ingredients you discover that most of the box is chock full of yummy rat food. Rats eat it because it's good stuff–sweet rat fruit–except for the itty-bit of poison mixed in with the otherwise scrumptious and nutritious food. Most rat poison is 99.95% really good food with a dash (.05%) of warfarin (anticoagulant.)

Doctrine that is 99.95% true means the remainder, no matter how small, is a lie. Satan has been wrapping poison with just enough truth to convince people to swallow it. What and who you believe matters a great deal. The fruit on the Tree of the Knowledge of Good and Evil must have looked delicious to Eve, just like a box of yummy rat food.

"Just because something isn't a lie does not mean that it isn't deceptive. A liar knows that he is a liar, but one who speaks mere portions of truth in order to deceive is a craftsman of destruction."—Criss Jami

Everything you see and hear must be examined for origin and context and then confirmed by God's Word. Accepting anything of importance at face value is negligent, ignorant, or deceitful in itself. Deception is rampant in politics, law, education, religion, the media, and in your neighborhood. Eve blamed the serpent for deceiving her. God didn't accept an excuse from her, and He won't accept an excuse from me or you.

The battle over what is true, what is factual, and what matters is one of control. Even where there is a meeting of minds on what is *is*, it is possible to agree on the facts of a matter yet draw completely different conclusions.

In his book *Telling Lies,* Dr. Paul Ekman writes: "There are two primary ways to lie: to conceal and to falsify. In concealing, the liar withholds some information without actually saying anything untrue. In falsifying, the liar takes an additional step. Not only does the liar withhold true information, but he presents false information as if it were true."

"Like a madman who throws firebrands, arrows, and death, is the man who deceives his neighbor, and says, 'I was only joking!'"—Proverbs 26:18-19

A little leaven affects the whole dough and one little falsehood sours every bit of the otherwise delicious fruit of truth. It matters what books you read, which preachers you listen to, which homes your children visit, and how well you know your Bible.

Most effective deceptions occur over time. The greatest lies begin with what is mostly true and transition ever so slowly until the distance from where you began to where you are is as great as that from Milwaukee to the far side of the planet Neptune.

Object of Worship

ω

"Elijah came to all the people, and said, "How long will you falter between two opinions? If the Lord is God, follow Him; but if Baal, follow him.""—1 Kings 18:21

Where you find yourself fifteen minutes into eternity depends on who or what you worship. There are only two options; either you worship the God of the Bible or you worship something else. All who follow the Lord Jesus Christ will be unimaginably blessed in eternity. Fifteen minutes into eternity all who chose someone or something else to worship will awaken to endless regret.

"Jesus Christ is the same yesterday, today, and forever." – Hebrews 13:8

Jesus is a take it or leave it proposition, He doesn't come in sizes, styles, colors, or characters that vary from person to person. Jesus is God. He does not change. For that matter, humans do not change unless reborn as New Creations in Christ. Humans haven't change materially since the Garden of Eden.

People worship God (Jehovah, Yahweh) or they don't. This simple division between true worshippers and critics began in Genesis 3. Events from recent centuries, and particularly 1859, obliterated what were once clear boundaries between the two. It is far more difficult to look around today and know which side is which.

Where you are fifteen minutes into eternity depends on your choice. Making the right one depends on knowing where you are today and how you got here.

Did you hear the one about the man who walked into the psychiatrist's office thinking he was a duck? Maybe he really thought he was a duck. People might have assured him he was indeed a duck. Maybe he even convinced a judge to change his name to "A. Duck." No matter the terminology, legal status, or personal conviction; no man is a duck.

Did you hear the one about the man who walked up to heaven's gate believing he was a Christian?

He may have thought he was a Christian. Highly credentialed people may have assured him he was. Maybe a judge even ruled that his beliefs were acceptable as Christian. No matter the terminology, legal status, or personal conviction, unless one is born again in Christ he will not spend eternity with Jesus.

> *"And if it seems evil to you to serve the LORD, choose for yourselves this day whom you will serve, whether the gods which your fathers served that were on the other side of the River, or the gods of the Amorites, in whose land you dwell. But as for me and my house, we will serve the LORD."—Joshua 24:15.*

King of the Hill

People either (1) believe in something bigger than they are or (2) believe that nothing is bigger than they are. All religions, cults, and god- or idol-based systems fall into the first group. The second includes every denomination of humanist. Humanism, atheism, and agnosticism are adjacent religions on the wheel of human belief.

Nihilists reject all religious and moral principles. Nihilists don't believe there is any material continuity after death. They believe that fifteen minutes into eternity is endless nothingness and are a type of humanist.

Buddhists believe that the dead either pass into nothingness (nirvana) or return to bodily life in some new incarnation. Heaven and Hell are not eternal places. Nirvana is liberation from the endless cycle of birth, death, and rebirth. Buddhists consider *nothingness* the highest and best achievement; neither existence nor non-existence.

Muslims believe that the soul remains in a kind of soul sleep until Judgment Day when Allah will judge everyone according to their deeds in life. The dead remain in the grave until the world is destroyed and Allah calls all to account.

Hindus consider reincarnation an unwelcome circumstance because life means suffering. *Moksha* is the traditional Sanskrit term for release or liberation from the endless chain of death and rebirth. In southern Asian religious traditions moksha represents the supreme goal of human strivings. The highest human achievement is Self-knowledge. One who dies possessing it bypasses the four courses and his soul is absorbed into Brahmin. The self no longer exists.

One **Atheist** described where he believes he will be fifteen minutes into eternity; "I do not think people have souls or anything supernatural that transcends our physical selves therefore when a person dies that is it, they are dead and nothing else."[16]

Mormons believe that much of the physical realm continues on in the spiritual realm in similar ways. Service and ministry remain important elements in life after death. *"Think of the order and the organization there—men and women engaged in the work of the Lord, blessing lives and bringing people closer to our Father in Heaven."[17]* Additional instruction is required before the spirit eventually reunites with its body.

Christians believe human spirits live on in eternity in one of two states, in the presence of God (Jesus Christ) or outside of the presence of God. Differences exist among Christians as far as the specifics of where, when, and how eternity plays out, but the basics are fairly uniform.

What distinguished the place where one crucified thief awoke at 24:15 from where the other found himself? The soon-to-be resident of Paradise rebuked the blaspheming thief saying, *"Do you not even fear God, seeing you are under the same condemnation? And we indeed justly, for we receive the due reward of our deeds; but this Man has done nothing wrong."* Then he said to Jesus, *"Lord, remember me when You come into Your kingdom. Jesus said to the*

---

[16]tn-atheist.com/2009/03/atheist-explains-what-happens-when-we-die/

[17]ldsliving.com/Life-After-Death-6-Insights-into-the-Spirit-World/s/77329

thief on the cross beside him, "Assuredly, I say to you, today you will be with Me in Paradise" (Luke 23:43).

Where you believe you will be fifteen minutes into eternity is not the most relevant issue. What matters most is what you will see once you arrive and discover if what you believed was accurate. Francis Frangipane wrote that people remain in their deceptions until their faith for their deception is all used up.

It is what it is.

Humanists don't believe in God. The doctrine of humanism is built on the foundation of "I am God" with no plan or prospect for eternity. Humanists may believe that yesterday actually happened, but they profess to live exclusively in the now. Dog training guru, Caesar Milan teaches people that dogs live in the now, neither live in the past nor projecting into the future. If that is an argument for the lack of soul in animals, then humanists have no greater claim to soul than the companion animal under your desk.

The most powerful religion in the United States is Humanism.

Humanism

ω

"And in vain they worship Me, teaching as doctrines the commandments of men."—Mark 7:7

Humanism is the unofficially official religion of the United States of America. Humanism tolerates the existence of other religions but not their practice. The only public religious expression either supports or endorses the doctrines and ideologies of Humanism.

Our world is circling the drain, threatening to disappear into the sewer of human history. The most intelligent and tolerant among us (so they claim) have determined that theistic religions are best practiced in private. These same most-deserving-of-esteem folks have successfully elevated atheism, the religion of personal opinion, to center stage. It has become the *de facto*[18] national religion of the USA.

The Establishment Clause of the First Amendment states that Congress shall make no law respecting the establishment of religion or prohibiting the free exercise thereof.

The US Constitution forbids the establishment of any national religion. In recent years interpretations of the First Amendment changed from protecting the free right to practice religion to the specific legal rejection of deity-centric religion.

Ironically, the First Amendment today isn't used to prevent the establishment of a national religion, but to impose one. Humanism is the new national religion of non-religion.

Humanists are atheists. Religious Atheists are active and organizing.

Consider that:

---

[18] *De facto*: In fact, or in effect, whether by right or not

- Atheist groups receive IRS non-profit status as *churches.*
- Atheist mega-*churches* gather their faithful non-believers weekly.
- Atheists now squabble with one another in a-theological doctrinal debate.

"...that we should no longer be children, tossed to and fro and carried about with every wind of doctrine, by the trickery of men, in the cunning craftiness of deceitful plotting."—Ephesians 4:14

Scarcely a day passes without some new protest against Judeo-Christian norms. Do these norms really trample the freedom of others, or do protests against historical norms imperil the freedom of Jews and Christians?

Have religious communities wrongly strayed into the political arena or has politics invaded the pulpits, pews, and sanctuaries of US religious communities? Based on recent events, the infamous wall of separation (a phrase penned by Thomas Jefferson in his 1802 epistle to Danbury Baptist[19]) is not really a wall at all, but a one-way street. Traffic flows freely in one direction while those attempting to go the opposite way face increasing legal penalty.

What Humanists Believe

How complex can a religion of personal opinion be? After all, there is no synod, scripture, or text. I'm not a Humanist so figured I'd best let them speak for themselves.

The sort of answer you get to the question "What is humanism?" depends on the sort of humanist you ask! The word "humanism" has a number of meanings. And because authors and speakers often don't clarify which meaning they

---

[19] "The now well-known expression lay dormant for nearly a century and a half until Supreme Court Justice Hugo Black, in the 1947 case *Everson v. Board of Education,* that *any* government support or preference for religion amounts to an unconstitutional establishment of religion."-Heritage.org

intend, those trying to explain humanism can easily become a source of confusion. —American Humanist Association (AHA)[20]

No matter the subject material, folks are just folks. Muslims do not agree on the finer points of Islam. Christians don't agree on precisely what constitutes Christianity and Atheists can't agree on how to properly believe in nothing. Sooner or later every major religion seems to fracture into denominations. Humanism is no exception.

Humanists are atheistic, denying deity, because no evidence proves the existence of supernatural forces. Humanists believe in evolution. Saying *God created everything* to a humanist begs the question, *Who created God?* Humanists are nihilists, believing that *"the very idea of an afterlife is really just wishful thinking.* Humanists *"strongly object to schools teaching children about religion as if it were established fact."*[21]

Humanists believe that religion should be studied using the same methodology as science and history. Critically speaking, there is far more proof that God exists than proof that He does not.

Humanists are moralists, believing people need a moral code to live together in peace. [W]e believe that morality comes from within ourselves, not from "God."

Humanists have two particular responsibilities here:

1. We must share with others our view that the highest human values and ideals come from people and not from "God."
2. We must seek to influence society for the best, along the lines that we ourselves have worked out. (AHA)

Humans have practiced slavery for most of human history and murder is almost uniquely human. Abortion is uniquely human. Same-sex marriage is as natural as a corn beef and concrete

---

[20] AmericanHumanist.org

[21] American Humanist Association (AHA)

sandwich. Nature doesn't allow same-sex spouses to procreate and prevents fathers from nursing babies.

How might humanists explain sociopaths? Perhaps they are the most evolved of all, truly interested in nothing but themselves. Even Solomon said to *"eat, drink, and be merry"* (Ecclesiastes 8:15) if there is nothing more important in eternity than self-indulgence.

How do humanists agree on what is best for society? Obviously, they don't, which explains why Humanism is dividing into denominations of non-belief.

Humanism and Social Issues

> *"We accept our responsibility for the society in which we live but we will resist those who wish to re-impose the prejudiced and intolerant morals of the past. We tackle sensitive issues-from abortion to capital punishment, from medical ethics to religious and moral education. Our approach is based on a concern for the welfare and happiness of both individuals and communities".* —AHA

> *"The humanist has faith in man's intellectual and spiritual resources not only to bring knowledge and understanding of the world but to solve the moral problems of how to use that knowledge. That man should show respect to man irrespective of class, race or creed is fundamental to the humanist attitude to life. Among the fundamental moral principles he would count those of freedom, tolerance and happiness."* —Pear's Cylopaedia

If a moral code was good enough for society yesterday, what makes it prejudiced and intolerant today? Does morality evolve? Abortion is good for individuals and communities? Human nature believes that morality equates to whatever benefits *me*. How can ethics of any kind be defined by committee? Hitler was pretty sure his ethics were far superior to the Poles and Jews he murdered.

Freedom appears to be a foundational principle of Humanism. Few in western society would argue against freedom as a good thing.

The issue is, has been, and will always continue to be, establishing the line where my freedom ends and yours begins. Exercising my freedom to use your car may tick you off. Placing a dam in the river to create a lovely lake on my property may condemn your fields to drought. Total freedom is only possible when you play Solitaire.

Margaret Sanger inspired Adolf Hitler's goal to exterminate the weaker and less desirable elements of humanity. Margaret Sanger founded Planned Parenthood predominantly to abort babies of African extraction. As a fellow atheist, would Humanists consider Sanger one of their own? Is genocide moral? Who decides?

The Theory of Evolution is largely about survival of the fittest. Morality either transcends survival of the fittest or it does not. Teaching ideologies that weaken humanity by making procreation a laboratory event must, by definition, deny evolution or judge it errant.

Macro-evolution considers man nothing more than a high order animal, descending from lower order animals and even inanimate materials. Imposing ideological morality into any animal population would result in disrupting the natural process of evolution.

Humanists seem to be big on morality. If religion, say Humanists, must be studied within the same constraints as science and history, what about morality? How's that working out for us? The more the intellectual is affirmed and the spiritual denied the worse human relationships become. There is always someone more fit, more greedy, more dominant, more punitive, more opportunistic or more evil. Evil will always triumph over good unless good has a secret weapon.

"Unquestionably it is a very common phrase of modern intellectualism to say that the morality of one age can be entirely different to the morality of another. And like a great many other phrases of modern intellectualism, it means literally nothing at all. If the two moralities are entirely different, why do you call them both moralities? It is as if a man said, "Camels in various places are totally diverse; some have six legs, some have none, some have scales, some

have feathers, some have horns, some have wings, some are green, some are triangular. There is no point which they have in common."...Of course, there is a permanent substance of morality, as much as there is a permanent substance of art; to say that is only to say that morality is morality and art is art." –G.K. Chesterton, Heretics

Humanist Doctrine

Non-believers now quibble about how to *not believe* as unique individuals while still clinging to some semblance of group unity. Perhaps that's because they want the power, protection, and influence of a larger clan and voting bloc.

Major Ray Bradley was assigned to readiness support for the Army Reserve's medical staff at Fort Bragg when the preference code for the humanist religion took effective for all members of the US Army on April 12, 2014. Major Bradley finally had the ability to "self-identity the belief system that governs my life."

"The real importance of this change is that our official military records can reflect humanists now," said Bradley, who initially was listed under the broad category of "no religious preference."

In practical terms, the change means that humanists could face fewer hurdles in trying to organize within the ranks, military brass would have better information to aid in planning a deceased soldier's funeral, and it could lay the groundwork for eventually adding humanist chaplains.

"Although he doesn't believe in God, Bradley determined that the term atheist was not sufficient for him." –Religion News [22]

Apparently, Humanism is similar to Christianity in the myriad of ways people choose to practice their preferred religion.

---

[22].religionnews.com/2014/04/22/army-approves-humanist-religious-preference/

The Genesis of Humanism

Where did Humanism begin? How did it become stronger in western cultures than the God of the Bible? The rampant spread of humanism must surely be based on serious, sober, and well-investigated foundations, or is it?

The foundation of modern culture and evolved "progressive" human society is based on the ideology, opinion, and authorship of the Father of Sociology, Auguste Compte[23] (1798-1857.) Comte's social theories culminated in the Religion of Humanity which influenced the development of religious humanist and secular humanist organizations in the 19th century. Comte likewise coined the word *altruism*.

Altruism is an ethical doctrine suggesting that the moral value of an individual's action depends solely on its impact on other people regardless of the consequences to the individual himself. Auguste Comte's version of altruism calls for living for the sake of others. One who holds to either of these ethics is known as an altruist.

Regrettably, although most of Compte's ideology has come through unscathed, it seems his concept of altruism, as it affected humanism, was hi-jacked not long after his death– right about 1859. Today's humanistic culture is based on Compte's writings, but somewhere along the line its central doctrine shifted from altruism to self-indulgence. Folks tend to pick and choose what they like about most religions, customizing them to suit their personal tastes. As a religion, Humanism is no exception.

Who was the famed Mr. Compte? Surprisingly, he was not a beloved statesman or educator, but a rejected suitor and, to put it bluntly, a highly unbalanced personality.

August Comte married Mademoiselle Caroline Massin in 1825. In 1826, he was taken to a mental health hospital, but left "without being cured"–simply stabilized by French psychiatrist Jean-Étienne Dominique Esquirol–so that he could work again on his plan. He

---

[23] en.wikipedia.org/?title=Auguste_Comte

would later attempt suicide in 1827 by jumping off the Pont des Arts. In the time between this and his divorce in 1842, he published the six volumes of his *Cours.*

Comte became close friends with John Stuart Mill (1806 - 1873.) Compte and Mill developed radical philosophies elevating thoughts, feelings, and whatever promotes happiness above such mundane considerations as fact, history, logic, mathematics, and observations based on actual experience. Mill proposed the principle of utility; that *"actions are right in proportion as they tend to promote happiness; wrong as they tend to produce the reverse of happiness."*

Unrequited love caused Compte's detestation of religion and spurred on his research. He fell deeply in love with Clotilde de Vaux in 1844, a married woman and devout Catholic. Compte's love for her was never consummated. After her death in 1846, his love became quasi-religious, and Comte, working closely with Mill (who was refining his own such system) developed the new Religion of Humanity.

Compte described three stages of societal development. From the beginning of human history until the end of the middle ages men did not question the existence, impact, and power of supernatural deities on their lives.

Humans believed in the existence of spirits and that Powers greater than their own were at work in the world around them. The next stage involved thinking in abstractions; God became impersonal and changeable. Total dependence on *greater powers* began to shift to greater emphasis on the power of humans.

Finally, in the Scientific stage, Compte suggests that observation and science could eventually explain and order the world and those who inhabit it. In his own time, Auguste Compte was considered mentally ill, eccentric, and even unscientific. And yet his work is the basis and inspiration for much of the mess western societies experience today.

Later in his career Comte recognized that removing traditional worship would leave human society without the necessary commonality to hold it together. So, he imagined a Religion of Humanism.

Compte's system was largely unsuccessful, but its combination with Darwin's *On the Origin of Species* (1859) resulted in the 19th century proliferation of various secular humanist organizations. The combination of Charles Darwin and August Compte's influence effectually destroyed the basis of relationship between man and God. Ironically, the two weren't distraught because God didn't exist, but because of their intense anger at Him.

> *"Here we must distinguish between Darwin the scientist and Darwin the unbeliever. Darwin, who was raised Anglican and even considered becoming a clergyman, did eventually relinquish his Christian faith. But he did not do so because of evolution.*

> *"The story is told in Adrian Desmond and James Moore's authoritative biography, Darwin: The Life of a Tormented Evolutionist. When Darwin's daughter Annie died at age 10, Darwin came to hate the God he blamed for this. This was in 1851, eight years before Darwin released Origin of Species.*

> *Around the time of Annie's death, Darwin also wrote that if Christianity were true, then it would follow that his grandfather Erasmus Darwin and many of his closest family friends would be in hell. Darwin found this utterly unacceptable, given that these men were wise and kind and generous. Darwin's rejection of God was less an act of unbelief than a rebellion against the kind of God posited by Christianity. A God who would allow a young girl to die and good people to go to hell was not anyone whom Darwin wanted to worship." - Dinesh D'Souza ,The Two Faces of Darwin (2009)*

Good, moral, and pious folks elevate man-made ideology and self-religion above what is historical, natural, and heirloom out of self-indulgence. *The best for my body. The best for my world. My opinion over God's, because God loves me and wants me to be happy.*

The world and the worldly argue that placing self above all else is actually the best way to please God. *After all, aren't you made in His image?* Those who quote Genesis 1:27 never do so when the subject is "Where did we come from?" because evolution and "made in God's image" cannot coexist in any coherent/rational world view.

The liturgy of the world chants that THEE = ME = THEE and therefore it's really all about ME.

How did we get here? The lies have piled up for so long that even old beliefs were built on deception. A brief historical review of Christian religion is required to properly address the deceits of our day. Mankind bases its rejection of God on the theories, philosophies, and arguments of men who were nuts, eccentric, unscientific, rejected suitors, and vehemently angry with God for personal disappointments and sorrows.

> *"The further society drifts from the truth, the more it will hate those who speak it."—attributed to George Orwell*

Spirits of confusion and deception press the point that man somehow evolved, and in the process overcame his need for God. Those who still profess some measure of faith suggest that God has changed to keep up with the latest trends and desires in human culture, science, fashion, scholarship, and personal preference. Not only, they argue, has man evolved, but so has God. Man has gotten bigger and smarter and God smaller and less powerful.

According to Compte, it's more important to be nice than to recognize and submit to God's authority. Isn't it curious, how both Mr. Compte and Mr. Darwin suffered from deep emotional pain they blamed on God?

Original Sin

ω

"Our systems, perhaps, are nothing more than an unconscious apology for our faults, a gigantic scaffolding whose object is to hide from us our favorite sin."—Henri Frederic Amiel, Journal Intime (1882)

As a rule, only those folks who believe that there is a difference between heaven and hell are concerned with sin. Where you find yourself fifteen minutes into eternity depends on sin; what it is and how it is resolved. Most dictionaries define sin as *an amoral act of transgression* which begs the question; who determines what is moral and what is not?

One online biblical dictionary begins the definition of sin in this very unhelpful way, "Sin is a riddle, a mystery, a reality that eludes definition and comprehension."

Sin is not a riddle or mystery. If the editors of that dictionary believe sin eludes definition and comprehension, they might do a bit more research. Simply put, the genesis of all sin is original sin. Every tension and imbalance in the world is the result of Adam's fall in the Garden of Eden.

The history of man, from Eden to the day Christ returns, is the tale of every human's struggle between God and self. Conversations about sin tend to generate angst, conflict, and confusion because the topic is usually limited to sin *behavior* and not sin *nature*.

Do people do wrong? Of course, but defining wrong is a debate making both headlines and enemies. Is taking a life a sin? The answer depends on the life and the manner by which it is extinguished. To some, capital punishment is a criminal act by the state, yet many of these same folks consider the slaughter of unborn babies basic women's healthcare.

One cannot argue definitions of what is or is not criminal without first resolving the issue of the existence of man's sin nature.

There is some debate of course, but most folks agree that all people do bad things. God doesn't send folks to hell because Adam sinned. Adam's contribution to humanity is the heredity of a sin nature. What is sin nature? It is the human desire to be one's own god. *My truth is my truth and yours is yours. You're not the boss of me. I have a right to control my body, my life, and my eternity.*

The crux of the problem is the question of who controls eternity. The new religion of Humanism promotes the lie that sin is a weapon used to control religious populations. Many preachers today shy away from the topic of sin nature. Instead, they sell a wholesale forgiveness by Jesus Christ that excuses every past, present, or future behavioral misstep from eternal judgment, eliminating all human accountability.

Jesus Christ paid the price of sin once and for all. Being born in sin isn't a death sentence, but a string of sorts is attached. All who insist they are entitled to the gift without acknowledging the Giver will be barred from eternity in God's presence. *Jesus who?*

Original sin was the first deceit perpetrated on humanity. It worked so well that Satan never found a reason to come up with another. Every time "God said" isn't enough to elicit obedience, the devil wins again.

Another way to think about sin is as infidelity to God; breaking our commitment to reverence, obey, and follow Jesus Christ and Him alone, no cheating allowed. I am mystified by the confusion and passionate debate that goes on about sin. If you want to know what is or is not cheating, what constitutes infidelity or adultery in your marriage—ask your spouse. Sitting down over coffee to discuss the finer points of infidelity with your buddies will only get you in hot water at home.

If you want to know what is or is not cheating, infidelity, or adultery in your relationship to Christ, ask Him. God's Word is explicit, and the Holy Spirit is willing and able to convict you on the matter. Don't ask friends or colleagues to define sin unless you're curious about what they believe. They are not the authority on the matter.

One day the church will be the Bride of Christ and He expects her to make entrance to the marriage feast wearing spotless white.

> *"Sin is a fundamental relationship; it is not wrong doing, it is wrong being."—Oswald Chambers, My Utmost for His Highest*

Modern Christians agree on plenty of behaviors that are wrong but few that are right. This inability to identify correct action and to discern between right and wrong and good and evil is of eternal consequence. The problem is sin and the remedy is Jesus Christ.

Original sin (ancestral sin) is the doctrine that mankind's state of sin resulted from the choice Adam (and Eve) made in Eden. Much is written about original sin and whether or not it is logical or fair to make all men culpable for what one man did. There is a lot written about what is written, but I find little that discusses, in any meaningful way, what original sin is and why it continues unabated.

All sin is original sin because there is only one sin. Sin, from the Garden of Eden onward, is man engaging in self-indulgence, believing the lie that we are as good as God, as high as God, and as powerful as God.

> *"For the Christian dogmatists were trying to establish a reign of holiness, and trying to get defined, first of all, what was really holy. But our modern educationists are trying to bring about a religious liberty without attempting to settle what religion is or what is liberty. Let us leave all these arbitrary standards and embrace liberty." This is, logically rendered, "Let us not decide what is good, but let it be considered good not to decide it." He says, "Away with your old moral formulae; I am for progress." But because the North Pole is unattainable, it does not follow that it is indefinable."—G.K. Chesterton, Heretics*

History of the Christian Church

ω

"And He put all things under His feet, and gave Him to be head over all things to the church."—Ephesians 1:22

The Word of God was made flesh in the person Jesus Christ and recorded for humanity in the Holy Bible. The Word of God to man has not varied, evolved, mutated, or changed from the instant Adam took his first breath to the moment you read these words.

A concise overview of the history of the church follows. The dates used are either precise or those most widely accepted. Additional notes are included to provide context or information not universally known. It is noteworthy that the Catholic Church was the only representative of Christianity for many centuries.

Significant Events

4 BC—Jesus born in Bethlehem (Luke 2:11)

30 AD—Jesus crucified and rose from the dead (Matthew 28:5-6)

35 AD—Saul encounters Christ on the road to Damascus (Acts 9:5-6)

49 AD—Council of Jerusalem. The Jews accepted Gentiles into the church "when they saw that the gospel for the uncircumcised had been committed to me [Paul], as the gospel for the circumcised was to Peter."–Galatians 2:7

64-67 AD—Peter and Paul martyred (John 21:18-19)

Peter was given the gospel for the Jews and Paul for everyone else. How did Rome become the seat of Christianity? God's Word places Paul in Rome, not Peter. Tradition suggests Peter may have been martyred in Rome but there is no evidence that he ever preached there, let alone ruled as the undisputed leader of whatever church was in Rome in the first century. Paul writes both from Rome and to Roman Christians but never mentions Peter's role, if indeed he had any.

Rome became the seat of Christianity in 500 AD when competition for power and control was centered, not in local churches and local bishops as the Bible directs, but in the Bishopric of Rome. It was a political decision, not one based in scripture. Centuries after the fact the Roman church decreed that local leaders of the Roman Church directly succeeded Peter.

> *In practical terms, each local church had control only over itself, and over no other church. There were no organizational ties between local churches and one set of elders in a local church never had any control over any other local churches. Each local congregation was self-governing under Jesus Christ as its head.*

> *The concept of a diocese (groups of local churches ruled by one bishop) and even more so "mother churches" (patriarchs), simply did not exist in the Bible. Historically, it wasn't until about 150 AD that we first see a single bishop ruling over the local church. But even in 150 AD, he had no control over other local churches. It wasn't until about 250 AD, when the first diocese began to develop, that these solo bishops began to exercise power outside the domains of their local congregations.*[24]

95 AD—Apostle John wrote the Book of Revelation

100 AD—Apostle John's death

Official Vatican (w2.vatican.va) records reveal that (what eventually became) the Roman Church was already on its fourth pope at the time of John's death. John, the last surviving apostle, never mentions Peter (or anyone else) as the singular head of the church (or its official successors) in his gospel, 1, 2, or 3 John, or in the Book of Revelation. He does, however, write at length about false teachers and false prophets.

------

[24].bible.ca/ntx-organization-historical-development-papal-patriarchal-systems-33-150AD.htm

120 AD—*Didache* (Did-eh-key). The document local churches used to order day-to-day affairs and teach basic doctrine. Composed from various New Testament scriptures, it provided instruction as well as tests for itinerant or visiting preachers and prophets, including how much to feed them, limiting stays to three days or less, and how to deal with requests for money.

Excerpts from the *Didache*[25]

- 1:1 There are two ways, one of life and one of death, and there is a great difference between the two ways.
- 4:14 For He comes, not to call men with respect of persons, but He comes to those whom the Spirit has prepared.

Regarding baptism:

- 7:3 But if you do not have running water, then baptize in other water;
- 7:4 And if you are not able in cold, then in warm.
- 7:5 But if you have neither, then pour water on the head three times in the name of the Father and of the Son and of the Holy Spirit.

Within twenty years of the Apostle John's death baptism by sprinkling was acceptable. Heated arguments about the manner of baptism escalated as divisions within the body of Christ tried to carve out places of power and control. Paul instructs believers to resist disputing that which is disputable.[26] Good advice.

- 11:5 Let every apostle, when he comes to you, be received as the Lord;
- 11:6 But he shall not abide more than a single day, or if there be need, a little more.
- 11:7 But if he abide three days, he is a false prophet.
- 11:8 And when he departs, let the apostle receive nothing except bread, until he finds shelter;

---

[25] J.B. Lightfoot translation

[26] Romans 14:1, 1 Timothy 6:4, 2 Timothy 2:23, and Titus 3:9

- 11:9 But if he asks for money, he is a false prophet.
- 16:6 For in the last days the false prophets and corrupters shall be multiplied, and the sheep shall be turned into wolves, and love shall be turned into hate.
- 16:7 For as lawlessness increases, they shall hate one another and shall persecute and betray.

The *Didache* required the Lord's Prayer be recited three times each day.[27]

230 AD—The first known public Christian church, Saint Georgeous, was built in northern Jordan.

New threats to the church emerged in the second century. Attacks from outside Christianity came from 1) Pagan philosophers attacking Christianity for religious or philosophical reasons and 2) the Roman Empire that persecuted Christians for legal and political reasons. Other self-proclaimed Christians threatened the body of Christ by teaching doctrine at odds with the apostles; "a different gospel" (Galatians 1:6).

Gnostic Christians believed that only an elite few could discover the secret knowledge required for salvation. Gnostics also taught dualism. Dualism states that what is spirit is, by definition, good, and what is material is, by definition, evil. Gnostics believed God to be spirit and perfectly good, rendering Him incapable of creating anything material or being involved in an imperfect world.

Irenaeus,[28] an early apologist, considered Gnosticism foolish yet a significant potential threat to Christianity. Irenaeus was also one of the first to speak of the documents that make up our New Testament as *scriptures* with equal authority to the Hebrew Scriptures (Old Testament). Iranaeus was first to refer to them as the "New" covenant or testament.

----

[27].web.archive.org/web/20090325022304/http://ministries.tliquest.net/theology/apocryphas /nt/didache.htm

[28] Irenaeus (Bishop of Lyon) studied under Polycarp who studied under the Apostle John.

350 AD—*Codex Vaticanus* – the first complete Bible.

380 AD—Christianity becomes Rome's official religion.

449 AD—Pope Leo asserts papal supremacy.

500 AD—The title Pope, formerly applied to all bishops, was now reserved for the Bishop of Rome.

625 AD—Mohammad begins to write the Quran.

1382—First English Bible published by John Wycliffe.

1455—The Gutenberg Bible (2-volumes in Latin) became the first bible printed with moveable metal type. Personal access to the written word of God spread rapidly afterwards. Of the original 180 sets printed, 49 complete or partial Gutenberg Bibles survive.

1517—Martin Luther posts 95 Theses on the University of Wittenberg's chapel door. The printing press made it possible for copies of the Theses to spread across Germany in two weeks and across Europe in two months.

While preparing a lecture on Paul's Epistle to the Romans, [Luther] read, "The just will live by faith." He dwelled on this statement for some time. Finally, he realized that the key to spiritual salvation was not to fear God or be enslaved by religious dogma, but to believe that faith alone would bring salvation. [29]

Luther didn't believe that the Roman pope or the Catholic Church had the sole authority to interpret scripture. Accepting no testimony other than the Word of God, Luther was quickly excommunicated. After conviction for heresy in 1521, Luther holed up in Wartburg Castle to translate the Bible into German, the language of the people.

1528—Ulrich Zwingli published further details of reformation.

The main theses Zwingli put forth were (1) that the church is born of the Word of God and has Christ alone as its head, (2) that its laws are binding only insofar as they agree with the Scripture, (3) that

---

[29] biography.com/people/martin-luther-9389283

Christ alone is man's righteousness, (4) that the Holy Scripture does not teach transubstantiation, Christ's corporeal presence in the bread and wine at the Lord's Supper, (5) that the mass is a gross affront to the sacrifice and death of Christ, (6) that there is no biblical foundation for the mediation or intercession of the dead, for purgatory, or for images and pictures (iconography), and (7) that marriage is lawful to all. [Britannica.com]

1536 – John Calvin published *Institutes of the Christian Religion* in Basel, Switzerland.

Calvin rejected Roman Catholicism before founding the presbyterian system of church government in his attempt to organize protestant Christianity. He believed that men are unable to choose God unless first chosen by God. Calvin also taught that the church and state should operate independently of one another, and that one reward for diligent work was the accumulation of wealth. [30]

1609—John Smyth founded the Baptist church in Holland based upon (1) believer's baptism by immersion, (2) rejecting liturgy and books of worship as inventions of sinful men, (3) permitting only spontaneous worship that excluded reading from the Bible because it was translated by men, and (4) restricting church leadership to pastor and deacon (eliminating elders, bishops, and lay-leaders.) Smyth later regretted that he had baptized himself.[31]

1620—Pilgrims formed Plymouth Bay Colony in America. They did not reject their English heritage but sought a place where it was possible to practice new political and spiritual identities. Individual righteousness before God was a primary consideration for Pilgrims.

1628—Puritans formed Massachusetts Bay Colony in America, believing in (English) covenant theology. Unlike the Pilgrims, Puritans emphasized *the corporate righteousness of their entire community before God.*[32]

---

[30] theopedia.com/john-calvin

[31] Wikipedia, John Smyth Baptist minister

[32] puritansermons.com/banner/logan1.htm

1648-1789—The Age of Enlightenment. Men began to look away from superstition and religion toward scientific, political, and social advances. Religion was becoming tiresome, limiting, and unworthy of the enlightened human intellect.

Events during this Age of Reason made possible the massive 1859 transition from faith in God to faith in the world. As John the Baptist prepared the way for Christ, so philosophers, scientists, and neo-humanists of the Enlightenment cleared the path to make way for the religion of humanism and the retirement of God as Creator and Authority over human behavior.[33]"

Advances in science joined with growing opposition to a dogmatic Roman Catholic Church and monarchal rule in general. Central to the theme of reason were tolerance, progress, liberty, and breaking the hold both church and state had on the people. The more men believe they understand the world around them the less respect is reserved for God.

"It was also a time of religious (and anti-religious) innovation, as Christians sought to reposition their faith along rational lines and deists and materialists argued that the universe seemed to determine its own course without God's intervention. Secret societies—the Freemasons, the Bavarian Illuminati,[34] the Rosicrucians[35]—flourished, offering European men (and a few women) new modes of fellowship, esoteric ritual and mutual assistance. Coffeehouses, newspapers and literary salons emerged as new venues for ideas to circulate.[36]"

---

[33] unattributed

[34] Bavarian Illuminati – secret sect (anti-Jesuit and anti-Catholic) purportedly teaching happiness by illuminating the mind, thereby eliminating prejudice and superstition

[35] Rosicrucian – secret Christian sect based on enlightenment, intellect, healing, and mysticism- including alchemists and sages.

[36] history.com/topics/enlightenment

1729—John Wesley, Anglican minister and theologian, founded Methodism. He served as both Anglican priest and pastor of an American church in Savannah, Georgia. Wesley returned to England after legal and relationship setbacks in America. With good reason, because critics of Methodism objected to the sole power and authority Wesley held over his new denomination. At one point, Wesley hand wrote tickets to members in good standing, renewable every three months. Those deemed unworthy received no ticket and dropped out. Wesley greatly narrowed the definition of who was, or was not, a true Christian.[37]

1845—Methodists and Baptists split over slavery.

1859—Belief in the intellect of man surpasses belief in the power of God.

1859—John Nelson Darby, Father of Dispensationalism, began preaching in the USA. He believed that God's Word speaks to both Christians and Israelites - though not in parallel. Darby also advanced the study of eschatology.

Dispensational premillennialists (Darby) interpret scripture literally, believing Jesus Christ will physically return to the earth after a 7-year period of tribulation and before the millennium. Unlike previous theological teachings, premillennialists believe that Christ will reign for 1000 years rather than simply "a long time." Postmillennialism teaches that Christ returns after a 1000-year period of peace, which was the dominant Protestant eschatological position from the Reformation until 1859.

Albrecht Ritschl (1822-1889) was considered the most influential liberal theologian of the nineteenth century. His theology of the kingdom of God birthed what is known in America as the "social gospel," that is, the task of Christianity to "transform not just individuals but the whole of society through justice, morality, and love. "[38]

---

[37] Wikipedia
[38] Wikipedia

"Ritschl rejected such doctrines as original sin, the miraculous birth of Christ, the Trinity, and the Incarnation. His attempt to apply the tenets of Kantian philosophy to Protestant Christianity was typical of an era that had little feeling for the mystery of religion and no dread of a divine judgment." [39]

1870—The dogma of papal infallibility was formally accepted at the First Vatican Council. Popes are not without error or sin as men, but when speaking about moral or theological issues as the direct successor to Peter (*ex cathedra*) the views of the Pope are considered infallible.

1882—German philosopher Friedrich Nietzsche (1844-1900) declared that God is Dead. The declaration's meaning was not that God had existed and did no longer, but that the idea or myth of God no longer had power over the lives and morals of the people. In the absence of God, Nietzsche believed that mankind needed to come up with another way to divide right from wrong and morality from immorality, lest chaos result.

1925—Scopes Monkey Trial in Tennessee, a case that tested whether modern science regarding the creation–evolution controversy should be taught in schools. Prosecuting attorney William Jennings Bryant was called to testify by defense attorney Clarence Darrow. *Bryan, gauging the effect the session was having, snapped that its purpose was "to cast ridicule on everybody who believes in the Bible". Darrow, with equal vehemence, retorted, "We have the purpose of preventing bigots and ignoramuses from controlling the education of the United States."* (Wikipedia) The 1925 verdict gave the win to God - all the way to the Supreme Court.

1946-1956—The Dead Sea scrolls were discovered in eleven Qumran caves in the West Bank of Israel. Dating from 300BC-100AD, the scrolls contain the third oldest surviving manuscripts of biblical scripture.

---

[39] Britannica.com/biography/Albrecht Ritschl

1948—World Council of Churches formed. The WCC works for the unity and renewal of the Christian denominations and offers them a forum in which they may work together in the spirit of tolerance and mutual understanding. [40]

1948—Israel became a nation.

1967 – Israel recaptured the city of Jerusalem.

Events Leading to the Coming Implosion

Followers of Jesus Christ cannot walk the same path as humanists. They try, but the ruse can't be maintained for long before one must bow to the other. The basic concepts of deity and humanism are mutually exclusive. Richard Niebuhr's (1894-1962) critical description of liberal theology in general has become a classic: "*A God without wrath brought men without sin into a kingdom without judgment through the ministration of a Christ without a cross.*" The latest significant events for the Christian church in America involve the official rejection of God from education and social morality.

1962—Engel v Vitale. The Supreme Court ruled that all prayer in school is unconstitutional.

1973—Roe v Wade. The Supreme Court legalized abortion.

2015—Obergefell v Hodges. Supreme Court legalized gay marriage.

Scripture

From the day of Pentecost (Acts 2) until now, God's Word remains unchanged. The message is the same and His Word still true. Men and women have read the same words for over 2000 years.

Just imagine:

The same message has been read from Irenaeus (130-202) to Francis of Assisi (1182-1226), Martin Luther (1483-1546) to George Washington (1732-1799), and from my great-grandfather,

---

[40] Britannica.com

Daniel Christian, to succeeding generations. Regardless of age, God's Word has not changed nor was there any great attempt to argue otherwise until the mid to late 19th century; specifically, 1859. Like many families, we still have the very Bible used by my great-grandfather. The Word is unchanged.

Apart from God there is nothing eternal; no reason, no morality, and no future. Friedrich Nietzsche was right, apart from God there is only chaos.

Absolutes, Truth, and Science

ω

"In passing we should note this curious mark of our age: The only absolute allowed is the absolute insistence that there is no absolute."—Frederick Moore Vinson, former Chief Justice of the United States Supreme Court [41]

Progressive society and the *intellectually evolved* suggest that there is no such animal as an absolute. New generations learn that everything is relative and that your truth and my truth don't have to be the same truth. Denying absolutes is a ridiculous position.

Consider a rock. My truth is that the rock is inanimate. Your truth is that the rock is animate; maybe even somebody's mother. In theory, the world suggests such mutually exclusive truths are both valid and equally true. In other words, we must agree that the rock has no life but could well be a mother.

The Bible is God's Word to mankind. The God Who speaks through the Bible claims the sole right to determine truth, establish absolutes, judge behaviors, and dispense justice or salvation based upon relationship to Him. The world admits few, if any, absolute truths. The ruler of this world is Satan and the last thing he wants is for God's truth to be accepted or His justice served. Enter human self-indulgence and self-worship. Humanism, the national religion of the United States, is preached throughout the world as the Religion of Me.

"The man who refuses to judge, who neither agrees nor disagrees, who declares that there are no absolutes and believes that he escapes responsibility, is the man responsible for all the blood that is now spilled in the world. Reality is an absolute, existence is an absolute, a speck of dust is an absolute and so is a human life. Whether you live

---

[41] Quoted by Frances Schaeffer, *How Should We Then Live*

or die is an absolute. There are two sides to every issue: one side is right and the other is wrong, but the middle is always evil."—Ayn Rand, Atlas Shrugged

The Lie of Common Historical "Facts"

Many fables are accepted as truth. The Great Chicago Fire of 1871 was not caused by Mrs. O'Leary's cow kicking over a lantern. A newspaper reporter invented the story to make colorful copy. Is today's news any less fanciful?

Albert Einstein did not fail mathematics in school as is widely reported. Upon seeing a column making this claim, Einstein said "I never failed in mathematics. Before I was fifteen I had mastered differential and integral calculus." Einstein did however fail the Swiss Federal Polytechnic School entrance exam on his first attempt in 1895, although he was two years younger than his fellow students at the time and scored exceedingly well in the mathematics and science sections.

Medieval Europeans did not believe the Earth was flat. From the time of the ancient Greek philosophers Plato and Aristotle, belief in a spherical Earth remained almost universal among European intellectuals. As a result, Christopher Columbus's efforts to obtain support for his voyages were hampered not by belief in a flat Earth but the reasonable concern that the East Indies were farther than he realized. If the Americas had not existed, he would surely have run out of supplies before reaching Asia.

Napoleon Bonaparte wasn't short. Perhaps his enemies liked to paint him as an angry midget. The confusion probably originates in the difference between French and English measurement: the pouce, a pre-revolution unit is slightly longer than a British inch. So, 5'2" in pouce is 5'6" in feet and inches, a normal height for a man of Napoleon's era.

No witches were burned at the stake as a result of the late 17th century Salem witch trials. Twenty people were condemned according to English law; 19 met their fate at the gallows and one was crushed by rocks.

I hoped to share big myths about black holes, something every science fiction movie seems to include. While separating what is known about black holes from what is assumed, I learned one thing: nothing is truly known about black holes. Lists of facts from numerous sources contain such qualifiers as: *equations suggest; likely exist; theorize the existence, seems to, could, appear to, not really sure.* Aside from the definition itself, there is no other fact about black holes to share.

"A black hole is [defined as] a mathematically defined region of spacetime exhibiting such a strong gravitational pull that no particle or electromagnetic radiation can escape from it. The theory of general relativity predicts that a sufficiently compact mass can deform spacetime to form a black hole."[42]

Well then, that clears it up nicely.

And lest you believe the Supreme Court of the United States rules on the basis of scientific fact; in Nix v Hedden (1893) justices unanimously ruled that tomatoes are vegetables in the legal sense for the purpose of taxation. Science classifies tomatoes as fruits in the botanical sense, but the law of the land insists they're vegetables. You'll find this same legal split-personality in the discussion of gender in a later chapter.

Science, the Bible, and Algebra

"It is the mark of an educated mind to be able to entertain a thought without accepting it."—Aristotle

The Scientific Method designs experiments using constants and variables. Laboratories are scrupulously ordered so all parts of an experiment remain the same except for the ONE variable being tested. It isn't possible, scientists say, to assign causality to a change of circumstances unless everything else remains the same.

---

[42] The Cosmic Compendium: Black Holes, Rupert W. Anderson, pg 1

Algebra is a mathematical operation used to solve for variables. A very simple algebraic equation is x + 1 = 5. Algebra seeks to reduce every equation to its simplest form. In this case it would be x+1-1 = 5 − 1, which simplifies to x = 4. There is only one variable, so finding the correct answer isn't all that difficult.

If you were asked to solve this equally simple equation, $x+y-z = f^2 (r)$, how long would it take you to arrive at the correct answer?

I'll wait.

You'll never get the answer because the equation contains no absolute values. Mathematicians could restate and reorder the equation but never figure out what x, y, z, f, or r mean. Such equations are the stuff of philosophy, politics, protest, and legend. They look formidable and can be discussed *ad nauseum*, but without absolutes, they can never be resolved in a meaningful way because they don't represent anything real.

Scholars could ruminate on similar equations for decades and be no further along that when they began. The exercise is meaningless and hopeless. Multiple theories or hypotheses might be offered suggesting possible solutions, but that's all they are. None could ever be proven.

Settled Science

If you are confused about the definition or intent of the phrase *settled science*, any Egyptian Pharaoh, five-star general, Pope, or even my German grandmother could clear it up in a heartbeat. *Settled* means it's over. No more discussion, input, or lip. "It is settled" literally means, "I have spoken."

Settled science is a form of decree, a judgment made with the power to punish all who disagree. Scientific foundations of climate change and evolution are much like cosmic black holes; nothing but assumptions and variables subject to change and further change. Like most religions, when you read about *settled science* it means someone got to decide what constitutes acceptable doctrine and what is heresy. *Settled science* is little different from religion; go along or face excommunication. Not because the evidence is incontrovertible, but because someone "has spoken."

Is it true that 97% of scientists concur on man-made climate change? Absolutely not. The details are covered in the discussion of climate change.

Is it true that Darwin's Theory of Evolution has been scientifically proven? Absolutely not. You'll find the facts in the discussion of Evolution in a later section.

Science and Eternity

Few scientists argue the existence of life and death. Most agree on what distinguishes one from the other but the answer to "What happens before life and after death?" based on anything other than assumption remains a mystery.

"Scientists at the University of Southampton spent four years examining more than 2,000 people who suffered cardiac arrests at 15 hospitals in the UK, US and Austria. [Reporting in 2014] they found that nearly 40 per cent of people who survived described some kind of 'awareness' during the time when they were clinically dead before their hearts were restarted.

"We know the brain can't function when the heart has stopped beating," said Dr. Sam Parnia, a former research fellow at Southampton University, now at the State University of New York, who led the study.

"But in this case, conscious awareness appears to have continued for up to three minutes into the period when the heart wasn't beating, even though the brain typically shuts down within 20-30 seconds after the heart has stopped."[43]

---

[43].telegraph.co.uk/news/science/science-news/11144442/First-hint-of-life-after-death-in-biggest-ever-scientific-study.html

I confess to some curiosity about these two declarative statements from Dr. Parnia. Scientists *know the brain can't function* once the heart stops beating, yet *conscious awareness continues*. Giving science the win, one must conclude that consciousness is not exclusive to brain function.

Unless you are a nihilist, you believe that you will be somewhere fifteen minutes after your mortal body dies. For those who place faith solely in what may be observed or proven, new scientific research may soon put their belief that nothing exists after death into question.

If faith in something beyond this life is illogical and unsupportable, how do they explain Dr. Parnia's research? Logic and science contradict one another, unless you add faith in something or someone outside of earthly time to the equation.

1859 Trivia

ω

Inventions and Discoveries:

- Jan. 5—First Steamboat sails, Red River
- Feb. 16—The French Government passes a law to set the A-note above middle C to a frequency of 435 Hz, in an attempt to standardize the pitch.
- March 26—First sighting of Vulcan, a planet thought to orbit inside Mercury
- May 15— Pierre Curre born on this day in history in France, physicist (Nobel Prize 1903)
- May 26—Geologist Joseph Prestwich reports to the Royal Society of London the results of Somme valley gravel-pit investigations, extending human history back to what will become known as the Paleolithic Era.
- June 11—Comstock silver load discovered in Nevada
- July 1—Balloon covers a record 809 miles over St Louis
- July 5—Capt. N. C. Brooks discovers Midway Islands
- July 12—William Goodale patents a paper bag manufacturing machine
- Aug. 9—Otis Tufts patents the elevator
- Aug. 17—First balloon air mail took off from Lafayette, Indiana
- Aug. 27—First successful oil well drilled by Edwin Drake, Pennsylvania
- Sept. 1—First Pullman sleeping car placed in service
- Sept. 2—Gas lighting introduced to Hawaii
- Sept. 16—Lake Nyasa, which forms Malawi's boundary with Tanzania & Mozambique, is discovered by British explorer David Livingstone
- Sept. 20 —George Simpson patents the electric range
- Nov. 1st—The current Cape Lookout, North Carolina, lighthouse was lit for the first time.

- Dec. 15—G.R. Kirchoff describes the chemical composition of the Sun
- Marian A. Kowalski publishes the first usable method to deduce the rotation of the Milky Way
- Etienne Lenoir of Paris, produces the first single cylinder two-stroke gas engine with an electric ignition system
- George Washington Ferris was born, who developed the first Ferris Wheel for the Columbian Exposition in Chicago, Illinois (1893).
- Michael Joseph Owens was born. He invented a revolutionary automatic glass bottle making machine and founded Owens Bottle Machine Co.
- James and E. P. Monroe were issued a patent for the eggbeater
- Ferdinand Carre invented the ammonia vapor-compression system for refrigeration, which became the most widely used. Vapor compression is still the system most used today.

Rise and Fall of the United States

ω

"America is finished. We as a nation have turned our back on God. We have kicked Him out of our schools and out of the public arena. We have declared Him to be off-limits. We have given the boot to the very One who made us great and showered us with blessings. We are in the process of becoming a thoroughly secular and pagan nation. And in the process, we are courting the wrath of God. Many professing Christians have deceived themselves into believing that there is hope for our nation if we can only elect the right President or elect the right political party to control Congress. If that is your view, then you have set yourself up for certain disappointment."—Dr. David Reagan, A Prophetic Manifesto 2012.

Pastors haven't overreached into the political realm as much as politicians and activists seek to limit and control the free speech of Christians. God's Word is increasingly unlawful in the United States, threatening the free practice of Christian worship and lifestyle with negative social, economic, political or judicial consequence. Pastors aren't invading politics; politicians are occupying Christian houses of worship.

USA—The Crumbling Foundation

Traditional Judeo-Christian values established and anchored the foundation of the United States; *values* not *religion*. In 1782 the US Congress endorsed the first complete English Bible produced in the United States. Printed by Robert Aiken, official publisher for the congressional journal, it was edited and reviewed by Congressional chaplains. Public schools opened to teach people how to read the Bible for themselves. Most Ivy League bastions of liberal progressivism today began as divinity schools.

- 1636—Harvard originally trained Congregationalist and Unitarian clergy though it was never formally part of any denomination.
- 1699—Early Yale students were required to read Scriptures morning and evening at times of prayer. Yale was founded in New Haven circa 1640 to preserve the tradition of European liberal education in the New World. This vision was fulfilled in 1701, when the charter was granted for a school *"wherein Youth may be instructed in the Arts and Sciences [and] through the blessing of Almighty God may be fitted for Publick employment both in Church and Civil State."* (Yale.edu)
- 1740—Evangelist George Whitfield founded what became the University of Pennsylvania. Benjamin Franklin's 1750s attempt to secularize it failed, returning to its traditional religious beginning soon after.
- 1746—Princeton, formerly the College of New Jersey, was founded by Presbyterians.
- 1754—Columbia was founded as King's College by Anglicans. After a hiatus during the Revolutionary War, the college reopened in 1784 under its present name, Columbia.
- 1764—Brown was the first college in the United States to accept students regardless of their professed religion or denomination.
- 1769—Dartmouth was chartered by Congregational minister Rev. Eleazar Wheelock primarily to educate Native Americans.
- 1865—Cornell University was founded by Ezra Cornell and Andrew White. Cornell did not have a religious origin, being dedicated by Cornell with this statement, *"I would found an institution where any person can find instruction in any study."*

Though not considered an Ivy League institution, Episcopalians established the College of William and Mary in 1693. The school was destroyed by fire in 1859. After several mishaps, it returned to continuous service in 1888.

Like most institutions of higher learning originally dedicated to religious instruction, these schools have progressed to what they are today; bastions of secular progressive thought. *Progress* simply states the movement from one thing to another. One progresses in age or development from childhood to adulthood to elder status. The United States has progressed from a culture based on the truth of God to one based on "*My truth and your truth can both be true, even if they are mutually exclusive.*"

God no longer rules in academia. Apparently, He no longer rules western religion. Imitating a British trend, dozens of atheist mega churches have sprouted in the United States. Religion is no longer supernatural, but "It's the community. It's Sunday school, it's the seeing people afterwards in the foyer or in the courtyard, and it's enjoying coffee. They want that kind of [religious] moral community that is about connecting with others and is about celebrating life, celebrating morals, and ethics in a non-supernatural context."[44]

Humanism has replaced the former ideal of justice based on equality under the law. The focus of law, lawyers, and judges has changed from "the truth and nothing but the truth" to the artsmanship of jurisprudence and controlling the narrative.

Justice is no longer blind, but a priestess of humanistic relativity. What matters under the law isn't so much what you did, but whom you did it to. Politically correct speech and behavior aren't based on equity or truth, but on the doctrine of self-serving ideology. Absolutes and observable facts are of themselves considered discriminatory. Reality itself is discriminatory.

"The LORD, the God of their fathers, sent word to them again and again by His messengers, because He had compassion on His people and on His dwelling place; but they continually mocked the messengers of God, despised His words and scoffed at His prophets, until the wrath of the

---

[44] .cbn.com/cbnnews/world/2013/november/atheist-mega-churches-becoming-global-phenomenon/?mobile=false

LORD arose against His people, until there was no remedy."—2 Chronicles 36: 15-16

What Happened to God in America?

For nearly 200 years the social and legal institutions of the United States recognized God's omnipotence. The founding document of our nation, the Declaration of Independence, affirms the Creator as the source of inalienable human rights.

Apostasy isn't found only in secular populations. Even those professing and preaching Christ have fallen away from adherence to God's Word, favoring adherence to the doctrines of humanism.

Surveys by the Barna Group reveal that among those claiming to be *Evangelicals* today:

- 19% are living with a partner outside of marriage.
- 37% do not believe the Bible to be totally accurate.
- 45% do not believe Jesus was sinless.
- 52% do not believe Satan is real.
- 7% do not believe Jesus is the only way to eternal life.
- 57% believe that good works play a part in gaining eternal life.

"As you can see from these survey results, the term, Evangelical, has lost its meaning."—Dr. David Reagan, A Prophetic Manifesto, 2012

Did God move out of the universe? Was Friedrich Nietzsche right; is God's influence dead? When did people become smarter, more powerful, and more righteous than God? How can anyone believe in God yet stand against His Word? Did He clock out leaving secular humanists in charge? Has He abandoned us to the mob? Or have humans evolved beyond God, with power and intellect not only greater than His, but wise enough to stand in judgment over Him?

God didn't die. He didn't clock out and people certainly haven't surpassed His knowledge and ability. We're simply seeing prophecy playing out in the headlines. Nothing is happening that wasn't foretold in scripture. Folks just want what they want and are pleased to shout down or figuratively (for the moment) martyr all who pledge sole allegiance to God's throne.

Politics has invaded the churches and left a slimy residue of sin. False preaching is becoming the norm. Adherence to God's Word has become the textbook definition of intolerance. I can't argue with that, because God's Word does include definitions and sets standards. Willfully violating those standards comes with a price. Consequences and penalties are, by definition, punitive and discriminatory. The question each reader needs to answer is, "Who has the right to establish standards and administer justice?" God or men?

Nations will pass away without notice from God. Institutions of man only truly exist in the shared imagination of the men who, for a brief moment, agreed on their existence. Constitutions and the geo-political legalese of nations are no more significant to God than the Book of Methodist Discipline, the Book of Mormon, or the Philadelphia telephone book.

Relationship with God is complete and exhaustive. It is all; every fiber, cell, and thought of being. The Bible is an introduction to God; who He is, His vision, and the past, present, and future story of our relationship with Him.

Unless God is first and only in your life, you may not find yourself where you hope to spend eternity.

Rule of Law

The United States of America has been brought to its knees. Civilization, constitutional government, and Christianity as we knew them have passed away. The older you are the more you recognize the massive change between the United States as founded and the United States today. Younger folks may not appreciate the drastic changes over the past 60 years because public education quit teaching them. In fact, American History as it actually happened continues to be revised to support the new socially relevant doctrine of Humanism.

How did the US go from one nation under God to a nation where:

- Children habitually share nude selfies like trading cards.[45]
- Two brides (or grooms) walk down the aisle to be joined in marriage to each other.
- One person in a black robe can strike down the will of the people of an entire state.
- 60 million unborn children have been legally slaughtered, primarily for convenience.
- Nearly 40 percent of able people ages 16-24 don't want to work even when work is available.[46]
- Toddlers, middle-schoolers, and teens are encouraged to batter one another, creating fight videos for social media.
- American flag shirts are legally banished from American public schools on Mexican holidays.
- In 2008, the USA elected a President unwilling to answer the most basic questions about his background.
- The military promoted Major Nidal Hasan, a known Islamic jihadist (Fort Hood massacre) to senior military rank yet Chaplains who speak the name of Jesus are censured or worse.
- The most likely candidate to be elected President in 2016 has so many skeletons in her closet that opening the door sounds like the percussion section of an orchestra.
- Law enforcement officers are considered guilty until proven innocent while criminals are often considered heroes.
- Politicians threaten ministers for no greater wrong than preaching the Bible from their own pulpit.[47]
- An Army deserter (Bowe Bergdahl) was exchanged for five notorious enemy operatives in 2014.

---

[45] Lower Cape May, NJ, 2015

[46] Pew Research, 11-14-2014

[47].washingtonpost.com/national/religion/houston-subpoenas-pastors-sermons-in-gay-rights-ordinance-case/2014/10/15/9b848ff0-549d-11e4-b86d-184ac281388d_story.html

- The scientific community at large believes it is more credible that man descended from a rock than that God created man.
- Foreign lawbreakers are granted higher ranks of privilege and protection under the law than law-abiding citizens.
- Displaying the Ten Commandments is deemed *a noxious attack on human sensibility,* yet a Satanic Temple can erect a display at the Florida Capital in celebration of the 2014 Christmas holiday.
- The gifts, gluttony, excess, music, time off from school and work, decoration, public celebration, noise and glitter of the Christmas holiday became officially Christ-free. Christian symbolism and Jesus Christ are banned from—let's be clear—a 100% Christian celebration.
- The issue of sex and gender is considered so complex that two simple options of *male* and *female* are considered unfairly limiting and intolerable. How did it become possible for 5-year olds to know they were born the wrong gender, but 2-year olds have insufficient self-awareness to merit life?
- The highest court ruled that gender is nothing more than opinion.[48]
- The majority of the members of Congress believe that borrowing money saves money.
- Sloth, avarice, deceit, and manipulation became virtuous work and God's Word became inane and repugnant?
- The world devolved into a place where tolerance for murderous zealots is regarded more highly than tolerance for people who believe marriage involves a man and a woman.
- The United States of America, established by Congress and upheld by the Supreme Court as a Christian nation, has now officially declared it never knew Christ.

---

[48] Obergefell v Hodges, 14-556, 2015

- "I, me, and mine" became more important than *We the People* or the Creator who endowed them with inalienable rights.

How did good become evil and evil good?

Once the first breach of the law, both civil and moral, passed without penalty the dam representing the rule of law began to leak. Each successive step was so small that all who objected were treated, without consequence, as ill-willed intolerant folk.

All dams eventually rupture unless the drip-drip-drip is stopped. No repair crews were called in and the dam was systematically allowed to weaken. The very concept of a dam, separating one thing from another, is evidence of intolerance. Humanists need the rule of law to collapse in order to weaken the rule of God.

There are only two commanders: God and Not God. Everyone serves one or the other. Where you find yourself fifteen minutes into eternity depends on which standard you choose to salute.

The Line in the Sand

In April 2015, Baltimore riots law enforcement officers were ordered to stand idly by as private and public property was destroyed and looters and arsonists ran free. *"The city's top cops now acknowledge they repeatedly ordered officers not to engage rioters at all, even as they looted stores, burned buildings and attacked police.[49]"* What will it take to reverse the process and get peace officers back to enforcing the law?

The steps that brought us to this dangerous place happened so gradually that efforts to reverse it are next to impossible. Few people seemed concerned and the few who spoke up were shamed into silence. Would you be willing to pitch a fit every time someone breaks a rule *just a little*?

---

[49] New York Daily News, Jason Silverstein, 7-1-2015

Satan is an expert on scripture, citing fragments that support his argument while conveniently dropping those that do not. When Jesus invited the sinless to cast the first stone at the adulteress they left. The next recorded thing He said to her was, "Go and sin no more."

When would you object to a rule breaker? How much *gimmee* ought there be when it comes to the rule of law. Where do you draw a line in the sand? What about speed limits? If the posted limit is 65 mph, do you scrupulously stay at or below the limit?

Would you holler if a friend drove 66 mph in a 65-mph zone? "*Slow down! You're breaking the law. Back it down or let me out.*" People speed all the time. I doubt many are harangued for driving a mile or two over the speed limit. *It's okay, everyone knows there's a three to five mile per hour gimmee.*

Most will agree that driving one mile an hour over the limit isn't a big deal. Why be critical? What about two miles an hour over the limit? Three? Four? Five? Many people think that driving five miles over the posted limit is not too bad. Sure, technically illegal, but no one is going to care about five measly miles an hour.

What about six? Seven?

If one mile per hour over the limit isn't an issue, what's the problem with six? It's just one more mile than five, which most would agree isn't a federal offence. And seven is just one mile more than six. If one mile over the limit is okay, then seven is just ONE MORE mile over the previous acceptable limit.

What about fifteen miles per hour over the limit? Twenty? Fifty?

Everyone should agree that this is a problem. Driving 85 or 115 mph when the posted limit is 65 is simply not acceptable. *Give that moron a ticket!* Driving 20 or 50 mph over the limit is just wrong. It can't be allowed. It's just too fast.

Where is the line in the sand? If the legal limit is 65 mph, when do drivers deserve a penalty? How much wiggle room do you figure God built into His laws? Did Moses tell the Israelites it was okay to push the limits just a bit, but not too much?

How specific is God? God's attention to detail is often overlooked. God instructed Moses on how to build His altar. The stone was not to be hewn because tools would "profane it." There were specifically to be no steps. Would God really care if Moses added a step or two for convenience?

> *"Nor shall you go up by steps to My altar, that your nakedness may not be exposed on it."—Exodus 20:25.*

If steps had eyes they would get an up-skirt view. God requires holy. There is no wiggle room in obedience, reverence, or righteousness. People play fast and loose with rules, laws, relationships, and truth. They do so at their peril. The lie has been told that "it doesn't matter; chill."

Where you find yourself fifteen minutes into eternity depends on whether or not you believe that lie.

Tolerance and Enforcement in Opposition

Would even the most devout Jew or Christian publicly protest speeders going 66 mph in a 65-mph zone? Do you ever drive one mile over the limit? Most folks do. Take a moment and figure out why you speed. It seems a trivial matter, but whatever your excuse for speeding, that's the same voice telling you that God built *gimmees* into His rule. He did not.

The United States and the world at large suffer under the death sentence of tolerance. In order to get along shouldn't we all give just a little. What could be wrong adding one little bitty step to God's altar if it makes it more accessible to folks with handicaps?

In the United States, the rule of law fell victim to tolerance and a purposefully apathetic system of enforcement. Even worse, law enforcement officers are now held to an impossible standard.

- Protesters break the law because there is no penalty.
- Presidents break the law because there is no penalty.
- Cabinet members break the law and there is no penalty.

- Elected representatives break the law and there is no penalty.
- Students break the rules because there is no penalty.
- People thumb their nose at the law because there is no penalty.

People dismiss God because experience proves that there is no penalty for breaking the rules. Where is the line in the sand? What will be the straw that breaks the camel's back? It may be too late for the laws of men to set our nation and world aright.

What action (or failure to act) of government or religious leadership might motivate you to draw a line? Under what circumstance will you draw your own line and stand firmly behind it, refusing to cross regardless of the penalty? Christians do not take up arms or do violence in the Name of Christ, but is there a line beyond which you will reject the world in favor of heaven and live (or die) with the consequences?

Prophetic Supreme Court Decisions

During the first 150 years of nationhood, the Supreme Court of the United States consistently upheld the Creator God and the Bible as the foundational supports of the USA and her Constitution. In approximately 1859 the drip-drip-drip began as the law began to reflect a more progressive ideology.

Humanists convinced even professed Christians that new moral and legal standards are more loving, tolerant, and progressive than the old. In other words, humans are more loving, tolerant, and righteous than the Creator God. How did the United States go from being one nation under God to a nation dedicated to banishing Him completely?

A handful of Supreme Court decisions changed the world.

Engel v. Vitale, 370 U.S. 421 (1962) – Ruling: Prayer in public schools is unconstitutional

A New York state law required public schools to begin each day with the Pledge of Allegiance and non-denominational prayer acknowledging shared dependence on God. Students were free to "absent themselves." The majority ruled the activity endorsed a specific program of belief and was therefore unconstitutional. Ruling: 8 Yes, 1 No.

Roe v. Wade, 410 U.S. 113 (1973) – Ruling: Abortion is legal until a fetus becomes viable

Texas law denied abortion except when the mother's life was in jeopardy. A class action suit was brought by an unidentified pregnant woman, *Jane Roe*. The majority ruled that abortion is legal up to fetal viability as a right to privacy. Ruling: 7 Yes, 2 No.

Stone v. Graham 449 U.S. 30 (1980) – Ruling: Posting the Ten Commandments in public schools is unconstitutional

Merely hanging privately provided copies of the Ten Commandments in public schools has "no secular legislative purpose" so therefore violates the Establishment Clause of the First Amendment. The majority opinion expressed clear concern that posting the Ten Commandments might encourage student "to read, meditate upon, and perhaps venerate and obey" them. Ruling: 5 Yes, 4 No.

Lawrence v. Texas, 539 U.S. 558 (2003) – Ruling: Same-sex activity is legal

Reversing a Supreme Court decision made just seventeen years earlier, morality laws were rendered baseless. The case was choreographed from beginning to end. Being heard before the Supreme Court was the goal from the moment the defendants were arrested. Defendants and activist counsel sought and received additional criminal charges and negotiated higher fines in order to qualify the case for the Supremes. Ruling: 6 Yes, 3 No.

Obergefell v. Hodges, 576 U.S (2015) – Ruling: Legalized same-sex marriage throughout the U.S.

From the opinion syllabus: "The history of marriage is one of both continuity and change. Changed understandings of marriage are characteristic of a Nation where new dimensions of freedom become apparent to new generations. Finally, this Court's cases and the Nation's traditions make clear that marriage is a keystone of the Nation's social order." Ruling: 5 Yes, 4 No.

How did multiple SCOTUS decisions uphold the Constitution for centuries before new rights important enough to reverse every precedent were discovered? Did foundational documents or their intent change? Have humans changed? What led to decisions that, for most folks over 50, would be considered the stuff of lunatics?

> *"In the late 20th century, following substantial cultural and political developments, same-sex couples began to lead more open and public lives. The generations that wrote and ratified the Bill of Rights and the Fourteenth Amendment did not presume to know the extent of freedom in all of its dimensions, and so they entrusted to future generations a charter protecting the right of all persons to enjoy liberty as we learn its meaning."—Majority opinion by Justice Kennedy, Obergefell v Hodges*

Five Supreme Court justices evidently believe that the extent of what is possible is the most accurate definition of freedom and that liberty cannot be constrained by morality, tradition, or nature itself. Men have not changed, nor has God. However, what is or is not natural, what is or is not moral, and what is or is not legal is now a question for culture and politicians.

Two things are guaranteed to change with time; culture and politics. The very things that are eternal are held in less regard than what is temporary.

In addition to serving as the basis for Common Law practices, traditional religious doctrine was discarded in favor of popularity. I doubt you remember what the number one song on the pop chart was February 18th, 2014[50]? What is popular and what is politically correct change with the wind. And like popular music, what is hot and what is not depends on your genre of choice.

---

[50] *Dark Horse* by Katy Perry

Thousands of babies are murdered daily. If Roe v Wade didn't provide enough motivation to draw a line and defend it, what will? Marriage is now undefined. Gender is now undefinable. The government no longer trusts in God but seeks to remove every reference from public view just as some Egyptian pharaohs used to obliterate all likenesses or references to their predecessors.

Like it or not, there is a line in the sand. There is a set of rules that cannot be broken without penalty. If you aren't familiar with them, may I suggest you read Genesis beginning with Chapter One. Continue reading all the way to the end of Revelation Chapter 22.

No one can keep all the rules perfectly. The penalty isn't just a life sentence, but an eternal one. There is a zero-tolerance policy for error, but God has a plan for that. His name is Jesus Christ.

"The grace of our Lord Jesus Christ be with you all."— *Revelation 22:20-21*

Mobs Are Made Up of Good Citizens

"The dead man disposed of, and the crowd being under the necessity of providing some other entertainment for itself, another brighter genius (or perhaps the same) conceived the humour of impeaching casual passers-by and wreaking vengeance on them. Chase was given to some score of inoffensive persons in the realisation of this fancy, and they were roughly hustled and maltreated. The transition to the sport of window-breaking, and thence to the plundering of public-houses, was easy and natural."—Charles Dickens, A Tale of Two Cities

Whether pre-revolution France or Ferguson, Missouri, mob mentality hasn't changed. Whenever mobs are given license to act the result is carnage and grief. Monday-morning quarterbacks (though it was actually a Tuesday) flooded every existing medium with the question, "Where was the leadership in Baltimore?" after the death of Freddie Gray. Before that it was, "Where was the leadership in Ferguson, Missouri?" after the death of Michael Brown.

Good citizens animate every mob as well as occupy every position of authority. Where was the leadership in Baltimore and Ferguson? What could have been done to quell the unlawful mob trashing neighborhoods, destroying property and violating the rule of law with impunity?

It has since been confirmed that Baltimore law enforcement was ordered to stand down.[51] Federal leadership not only turns a blind eye to unlawful entry into the United States but offers freebies and get-out-of-jail-free cards to the lawbreakers. Border control agents and others charged with defending the law and upholding the peace have been ordered to *Stand down.*

Should law enforcement be situational? Which mob deserves a pass and which should face the nightstick, water cannon, or more lethal response? Which *good citizens* need to be reformed or punished and which held up as heroes?

> *"A mob's always made up of people, no matter what. Mr. Cunningham was part of a mob last night, but he was still a man. Every mob in every little southern town is always made up of people you know–doesn't say much for them, does it?"—Harper Lee, To Kill a Mockingbird*

The United States is under siege by many mobs. Like every other mob, each is made up of *good citizens*. Once part of a mob, formerly *good citizens* over-ride the rule of law with demands that it accommodate them.

Mobs infest the United States with activism in the name of racial equality, unlimited access to abortion, rights for illegal aliens, normalization of gay and non-specific gender status issues, and even the demand to *feel safe* anywhere at any time. These mobs may also be made of *good citizens*. Most believe they are on the right side of their issue and will eventually be on the right side of history.

---

[51].thegatewaypundit.com/2015/07/baltimore-officials-admit-they-gave-police-stand-down-order-during-violent-riots/

Mobs will never be on the right side of history. The Nazi mob was comprised of *good citizens*. The endless trail of blood spilled by Madame Guillotine was the act of *good citizens*. Human nature has not changed since the Garden of Eden. After World War I the German people were dispirited and felt victimized. Hitler played to that social weakness, laying fault at the foot of the Jews.

An outraged mob of *good citizens* fought to regain what they had lost. Mobs seldom care if the object of their ire is actually the guilty party. Sometimes the best view of who is most accountable is seen in a mirror. The Holocaust was nothing more than mob behavior of *good citizens*.

Baltimore Riot and the Nation of Islam

A group of imposing men dressed in suits with white shirts entered the wild streets of Baltimore on the overcast afternoon of April 25, 2015. News video cameras caught their entry. I watched as the men created order and peace wherever they went. These men stood against the protestors and rioters, driving them back with nothing more than the power of their presence. Suited men linked arms to protect the line of police from the growing crowd. They were men from the Nation of Islam. I was impressed.

The folks in the neighborhood knew them, respected them, listened to them, and obeyed them. Until…

Eventually even the men from the Nation of Islam yielded to the mob. Once the people they addressed changed from "me" to "we", they were finished. Mobs yield to no one. Mobs yield only to force. But what leader is ever willing to order the use of force against *good citizens*?

> *"Hush. Don't ask any questions. It's always best on these occasions to do what the mob does. But suppose there are two mobs?" suggested Mr. Snodgrass. Shout with the largest," replied Mr. Pickwick. Volumes could not have said more"*—Charles Dickens, The Pickwick Papers

Devolution of Society

ω

"And it came to pass, when the judge was dead, that they reverted and behaved more corruptly than their fathers, by following other gods, to serve them and bow down to them. They did not cease from their own doings nor from their stubborn way."—Judges 2:19

Cultures and societies across the globe are devolving by the day. Mobs do not seek common ground. Pursuing relief from perceived victimization, mobs destroy everything in their path. Any complaint or cause triggering an emotional response can create a new class of victims. Little effort is needed to get a protest underway, and because every protest needs a guilty party, eventually no class remains to blame except other victims.

Then, as Charles Dickens wrote, *the transition from sport to plundering is easy and natural.*

Mobs never mete out justice because they behave without conscience. Mobs serve evil and *good citizens* become pawns serving the wishes of the devil. They certainly are not ministers of God, yet some will argue that they are. Which god then, do they serve?

"A moderated religion is as good for us as no religion at all—and more amusing."—C.S. Lewis, Screwtape Letters

Morality, culture, politics, and religions may change but God does not. That opinion infuriates many *good citizens* today. Humanists believe we have evolved past the need for any god who establishes rules, laws, standards, and reserves the right to judge. Religions have moderated to accommodate the will of the people in the same way and for the same reasons as the Supreme Court in recent ground-shifting rulings.

God has not moderated, nor will He accommodate.

"Every way of a man is right in his own eyes, but the LORD weighs the hearts."—Proverbs 21:2

Current secular and spiritual leaders stand on shiftier foundations than a house of cards. Leaders fail because our nation serves the wrong god. Of course, nations don't really choose a god. Nations are not individuals. Leadership fails because *good citizens* chose the wrong god to serve.

The Bible is not just multi-topical, but all-topical. God's Word includes all of human history, the principles and process of war, and the creation and destruction of culture and societies. Little has changed since the Exodus. The Israelites were the drama queens of the Sinai Desert. They wailed about manna and wanted to go back to slavery. Back in Egypt they had no worries as long as they were obedient little slaves.

Humans are doomed to repeat history. Moses' laws kept the complaining people busy. God is smart. Since then, governments and would-be dictators learned that they can kill creative and free productivity if they keep the people so busy obeying the rules and regulations that they have no time to recognize that they are slaves.

Deception is the strategy Satan uses to separate you from the safety and security of family, friends, congregation, the body of Christ, and from God Himself. There is safety in numbers and security in the "herd."

Gathering together isn't exclusively for worship. Assembly is necessary to keep the Enemy at bay; to protect the vulnerable; to be reminded of what is true and what is not. None of us can be totally objective about ourselves. We need the perspective of like-minded brothers and sisters to help us see the bigger picture. As the second coming of Christ grows nearer, it is even more important to avoid being alone in the world.

"And let us consider one another in order to stir up love and good works, not forsaking the assembling of ourselves together, a is the manner of some, but exhorting one

another, and so much the more as you see the Day approaching."—Hebrews 10:24-25

Propaganda hasn't appreciably changed since Genesis 3. Humanism teaches the lie that each person is an island of self-importance—and therefore ALONE. It is far easier to conquer an individual separated from others than a cohesive committed group.

Events of 1859 radically changed human society, culture, faith, and behavior. To properly appreciate and react to the changes we must know where we came from. No subject is more prone to error or argument than truth and no battle more fierce than the one for control.

Crumbling Foundations

Structures are only as good as the foundation upon which they are built. The rule of law in the United States is as strong as a block of cheap Swiss cheese; full of air holes so large rats could use it as a maze before devouring the walls.

Political correctness requires that *good citizens* be given a fair deal, even if the law must yield in the process. Educators, legislators, activists, and atheists have been crying foul over legal outcomes for decades. What is the result? Victims have become victors and victors the victim. Which is which depends on media bias and who has the most political juice.

> *"This is the age in which thin and theoretic minorities can cover and conquer unconscious and untheoretic majorities."—G.K. Chesterton ILN, 12/20/19*

Law is disappearing in the United States. First God was evicted from the schools, then from government. The problem, of course, is that the Bible begins with law and ends with salvation through Jesus Christ. The same folks who charge the law with creating classes of privilege and victim use the same accusation to justify their own exemption from the law. *Any law that's good for me is a good law. But any law that's bad for me is a bad law. I don't have to submit to bad laws.*

Personal interests don't always converge. The concept of common ground is fast disappearing. The result is politics of division. The limit of freedom used to be where mine ends and yours begins. Now every *good citizen* claims the right to total freedom. Since that isn't possible, the first mob to act usually gets its way.

Fantasy of Equal Outcomes

ω

"Socialism is a philosophy of failure, the creed of ignorance, and the gospel of envy, its inherent virtue is the equal sharing of misery."—Winston Churchill, 1948 House of Commons address

The framework established by the US Constitution requires that both law and opportunity be equally applied. Recent social change rests on the doctrine of Equal Outcomes, the lie that good policy, law, and morality deliver equal outcomes for all protected under their umbrellas.

Equal outcomes for all is not biblical, rational, desirable, or even possible. It is, however, the basis for Socialism. Socialism always fails once people believe they can receive all they want without cost or effort. Eventually no one does anything because there is no motivation to work or contribute.

Consider Socialism at work in the real world. A class of university economics students insisted that under Socialism no one would be poor and no one would be rich, giving everyone an *equal outcome*. Opting to test rather than debate the hypothesis, the professor replied; "In this class all grades will be averaged and everyone will receive the same grade."

After the first test, the grades were averaged and everyone got a B. The second test average was a D. The average for the third was an F. As testing proceeded, the scores never improved as bickering, blame and name-calling resulted in hard feelings because no one would study for the benefit of others. Every student failed. The students learned that when a reward is great the effort to succeed is great, but when Socialism removes the reward for achievement, no one tries to succeed.[52]

---

[52].danieljmitchell.wordpress.com/2011/11/16/does-socialism-work-a-classroom-experiment/

Reducing God to human level denies His qualities of being *other* or *more* than we. Sinful human nature seeks to bring God down to our level rather than being inspired to move closer to His. How many preachers and teachers today insist that Jesus is your friend, that Jesus needs you, and that Jesus thinks and makes decision the same way you do?

Did your favorite teacher try to match your level of ignorance the day you set foot in the classroom for the first time? Do you define education as becoming equal in knowledge by dumbing down the teacher? Do you seek instruction in order to bring others down to your level or to move closer to theirs?

The equality demanded by varied protest groups today is *equal outcome*; everyone sharing in the same mediocrity; no one rising above and no one falling below. Many public-school classrooms teach to the least common denominator. In other words, the abilities of the least able (or willing) limit the most able and motivated. The result is failure for all.

How was Adam's fall engineered? Satan pitched the concept that a loving God would surely not deny them something good. Eve agreed that God was good. She agreed that the fruit was good for her. Therefore, it was only logical that God couldn't have meant what He said.

> *"The serpent said, "For God knows that in the day you eat of it your eyes will be opened, and you will be like God, knowing good and evil. So when the woman saw that the tree was good for food, that it was pleasant to the eyes, and a tree desirable to make one wise, she took of its fruit and ate. She also gave to her husband with her, and he ate."—Genesis 3:5-6*

Satan covered his lie that "Surely, God hath not said!" by convincing Eve that (1) she was mistaken that God would withhold something wonderful or (2) if God did He was a rotten selfish meanie. It was far easier for Eve to believe she misunderstood God than to think He would deny her and Adam something wonderful "just because." It made perfect sense to believe the lie that "Surely, God hath not said." And so she ate.

Eve believed that God was not so far above her that a piece of fruit couldn't level the playing field. Satan is all about leading gullible and willful humans to over familiarity with God. The best weapon in Satan's arsenal is contempt for God.

Once God is reduced to human level He loses His other-ness and more-ness. Being *other* and *more* produces respect, awe, and fear. Take them away and God tumbles from His throne in the opinion of men. Whether forbidden fruit, the Tower of Babel, free love, abortion, same-sex marriage, or any other lust humans wish to indulge in, the result is either "God DID say" or *God didn't really mean* to say what He did.

Familiarity breeds contempt. Students of history discover the pains victors took to humiliate and savage the vanquished. It was easy to kill deposed monarchs or famous warriors once they were reduced to bits of frail flesh, bone, and human-ness. Tear them down to the lowest level of the victor's tribe and both fear and fame evaporate.

The flesh always seeks to demean that which opposes it. That is precisely what the intellectual, the worldly, and false preachers seek to do today—reduce God to human level. If you can understand Him, there ceases to be anything supernatural or *more*. His Word loses its power to restrain, inspire, or elevate. Once God becomes too familiar, He is God no more.

Value

We need to address the concept of value before getting deeper into the quagmire of equal outcomes. Every object and living thing has (1) no value (2) some value or (3) great value. How is value determined? Do all like objects or living things have equal value?

Things can have more or less value in comparison to other like objects (or living things.)

- Is one cow more valuable or desirable than another?
- Is one automobile more valuable or desirable than another?

- Is one diamond more valuable or desirable than another?
- Is one acre of property more valuable or desirable than another?
- Is one person more valuable or desirable than another?

If folks can agree that each question can be answered yes, don't you have to wonder why?

- Isn't every cow equally bovine or dog canine?
- Isn't every car equally automotive?
- Isn't every diamond a mass of pressed carbon?
- Isn't one plot of dirt equal to every other?
- Isn't every person equally human?

It's easier to argue the relative merits of cars, diamonds, and property than it is cows, dogs, or people. There is something about any living being that separates it from every other. Every individual is unique, with differences usually identified in terms of personality, spirit, or soul.

People seeking to take power away from others press the fantasy of equal outcomes. The best way to successfully argue in favor of anything is to frame it as a matter of equality or social justice. Even if a request is met with willingness to share assets, power, or voice, there will never be a place of resolution because equal outcome is *not possible*.

The spirit of the demand for equal outcomes is one of pure deceit because equal outcomes can never be realized. That's the beauty of deceptive strategy. All who agree that equality is the goal of moral, wise, kind, and reasonable people swallowed the same bait Satan used in the Garden to lure Eve into sin.

Are you horrified by the thought that one human is considered intrinsically more important or valuable than another? The basis for most social protest paired with predictable outrage originates with a demand for justice; for equal outcomes.

Each issue in the following list of cultural and moral battles finds its foundation in the demand for equal outcomes. Every item on the list is discussed in detail in later chapters.

- Abortion
- Economics
- Education
- Evolution
- Global Warming/Climate Change
- Racism and Slavery
- LGBT (Lesbian, Gay, Bi, Transsexual)

God's Word not only fails to preach equal outcomes, it specifically warns against the lie. The result? Once equality becomes the measure of good, God's Word becomes the foulest source of evil. Pretty effective deception, wouldn't you agree? It worked in Genesis 3 and still works today.

"You shall do no injustice in judgment. You shall not be partial to the poor, nor honor the person of the mighty. In righteousness you shall judge your neighbor" (Leviticus 19:15).

> *"The rich and the poor have this in common; The LORD is the maker of them all."—Proverbs 22:2*

Deception is the currency of Satan

From Genesis 3 until today, God's message has not changed. You must choose between Light and darkness, good and evil, God and Not God. Jesus is coming again and Satan will be put down. Many who deny the change of seasons we're experiencing challenge believers to *Show me where things have ever changed.* Mankind has not evolved since Adam and Eve were evicted from the Garden; with a single exception, the indwelling of the Holy Spirit in new creations in Christ.

> *"Scoffers will come in the last days, walking according to their own lusts, and saying, "Where is the promise of His coming? For since the fathers fell asleep, all things continue as they were from the beginning of creation."—2 Peter 3:3-4*

In 1859, the face of every believer was figuratively slapped with a glove of challenge as the greatest era of deception in human history unleashed its fury. A new era of revival and persecution began. Satan has been busy, but so have the people of God through the ministry of His Holy Spirit.

Hold fast to what you have.

> *"As many as I love, I rebuke and chasten. Therefore be zealous and repent. Behold, I stand at the door and knock. If anyone hears My voice and opens the door, I will come in to him and dine with him, and he with Me. To him who overcomes I will grant to sit with Me on My throne, as I also overcame and sat down with My Father on His throne."—Revelation 3:19-21*

Prior to Genesis 3, there was one pathway for man and woman; God. Once Eve fell for Satan's deception a second road opened; Not God. Every person must choose which road to walk. Any argument, philosophy, or scholarship that suggests a third option is nothing but more deception paving the path leading away from God, to eternity with Not God.

1859 Trivia

ω

Politics and Conflicts

- Oregon is the only state admitted with a constitution forbidding black people from living, working, or owning property. Black people couldn't legally move to Oregon until 1926.
- The first land-grant university bill introduced in Congress in 1857 and passed in 1859. Vetoed by President Buchanan it was ultimately enacted into law in 1862.
- Arkansas legislature requires free blacks to choose exile or slavery.
- Texas-Mexico border – series of raids by Juan Cortina began.
- Hungarian campaign for independence from Austrian Empire began.
- The border between the United States and British North America was set at the 49th parallel.
- Australia: Queensland is established as a separate colony from New South Wales.
- Pig War: Ambiguity in the Oregon Treaty leads to the "Northwestern Boundary Dispute" between U.S. and British/Canadian settlers.
- South Carolina declared an independent commonwealth.
- The Indiana General Assembly convened a special joint session to consider a petition calling for women's rights.
- United Hebrew Relief Association founded.
- John Brown leads twenty-one men in a raid on a federal arsenal at Harper's Ferry, VA.
- Spain declares war on Morocco.
- The 1859 Njambur revolt marked a change in Islamic jihad. Although the revolt failed, the underlying factors causing Muslim leaders to fight among themselves and with the state was not resolved.

- The Koi revolt is an important mass uprising among the tribal people in the region of Bastar, India. The rebellion formed to stand against the autocratic and domineering British rule.
- Italy, Risorgamento. Italians revolted against Austrians, Bourbons, and the Pope. Leadership coalesced in 1859 under King Vittorio Emanuele II. Success came in 1870 after five decades of war.

Politics in 1859

ω

"That which has been is what will be, that which is done is what will be done, and there is nothing new under the sun."—Ecclesiastes 1:9

The 36ᵗʰ Congress in 1859 had a majority Democratic Senate and majority Republican House. The fifteenth president, James Buchanan, served from 1857 to 1861. His victory was due in great part to support in the South. Buchanan believed that slavery was an issue for the states to decide, not the federal government. During the campaign Buchanan suggested that the problem of slavery could be resolved "speedily and finally." Buchanan was wrong.

Conditions and concerns in the United States of 1859 are similar enough to what we face today to recognize the hand of God in what is certainly not mere coincidence. The countries giving the USA grief today are the same one's that plagued the Buchanan administration. There was also a similar absence of fiscal control in 1859 as politics of special interest threatened to dis-unite the nation. The threat became real when South Carolina became the first state to secede in December 1860.

Buchanan on the State of the Nation

December 1859

Our deep and heartfelt gratitude is due to that Almighty Power which has bestowed upon us such varied and numerous blessings throughout the past year. The general health of the country has been excellent, our harvests have been unusually plentiful, and prosperity smiles throughout the land. Indeed, notwithstanding our demerits, we have much reason to believe from the past events in our history that we have enjoyed the special protection of Divine Providence ever since our origin as a nation.

NOTE: Rhetoric hasn't changed much since 1859. President Buchanan assured everyone that the "general" state of the nation is excellent although war looms on fronts both foreign and domestic.

> *Whilst it is the duty of the President from time to time to give to Congress information of the state of the Union, I shall not refer in detail to the recent sad and bloody occurrences at Harpers Ferry. Still, it is proper to observe that these events, however bad and cruel in themselves, derive their chief importance from the apprehension that they are but symptoms of an incurable disease in the public mind, which may break out in still more dangerous outrages and terminate at last in an open war by the North to abolish slavery in the South. Whilst for myself I entertain no such apprehension, they ought to afford a solemn warning to us all to beware of the approach of danger. Our Union is a stake of such inestimable value as to demand our constant and watchful vigilance for its preservation.*

NOTE: The President says he isn't personally worried about civil war yet warns of a potential civil war within the nation. *Things are looking really bad – but it's all good!* (Insert smiley face.) The State of the Union speech made in January 2016 is much the same; the nation faces serious challenges but there's no need for concern! Delusion is the preferred capital of both Satan and politicians.

> *... On the other hand, when a market for African slaves shall no longer be furnished in Cuba, and thus all the world be closed against this trade, we may then indulge a reasonable hope for the gradual improvement of Africa. The chief motive of war among the tribes will cease whenever there is no longer any demand for slaves. The resources of that fertile but miserable country might then be developed by the hand of industry and afford subjects for legitimate foreign and domestic commerce. In this manner Christianity and civilization may gradually penetrate the existing gloom.*

... I need not repeat the arguments which I urged in my last annual message in favor of the acquisition of Cuba by fair purchase. My opinions on that measure remain unchanged. I therefore again invite the serious attention of Congress to this important subject. Without a recognition of this policy on their part it will be almost impossible to institute negotiations with any reasonable prospect of success.

NOTE: In an eerie parallel to the state of the nation today, Cuba, Africa, and the debate about bringing jobs to other parts of the world made it into Buchanan's 1859 speech.

... In my last annual message I communicated to Congress the circumstances under which the late minister of the United States suspended his official relations with the central Government [of Mexico] and withdrew from the country. It was impossible to maintain friendly intercourse with a government ... under whose usurped authority wrongs were constantly committed, but never redressed.

U.S. Ambassador to Mexico Robert McLane presented his credentials to President Juarez, "pronouncing the Government of Juarez to be the only existing government of the Republic." Unhappily, however, the constitutional Government [of Mexico] has not been able to establish its power over the whole Republic. It is supported by a large majority of the people and the States, but there are important parts of the country where it can enforce no obedience.

NOTE: Mexico was as much a problem in 1859 as it is today with corruption and law enforcement issues plaguing the United States. President Buchanan believed that the only thing keeping the US from military action against Mexico was its disarray. The same inability (or unwillingness) to enforce the law created the border and drug cartels working the US southern border in the 21st century.

... The Thirty-fifth Congress terminated on the 3d of March, 1859, without having passed the "act making appropriations for the service of the Post-Office Department." This act also contained an appropriation "to supply deficiencies in the revenue of the Post-Office Department for the year ending 30th June, 1859." I believe this is the first instance since the origin of the Federal Government, now more than seventy years ago, when any Congress went out of existence without having passed all the general appropriation bills necessary to carry on the Government until the regular period for the meeting of a new Congress. This event imposed on the Executive a grave responsibility. It presented a choice of evils.

... We have yet scarcely recovered from the habits of extravagant expenditure produced by our overflowing Treasury during several years prior to the commencement of my Administration. The financial reverses which we have since experienced ought to teach us all to scrutinize our expenditures with the greatest vigilance and to reduce them to the lowest possible point.

... Public expenditures during the fiscal year ending June 30, 1859, amounted to $83,751,511.57. (2014 total: $3,504,000,000,000.) Of this sum $17,405,285.44 (2014 total: $271,000,000,000) were applied to the payment of interest on the public debt and the redemption of the issues of Treasury notes.

... The expenditures of the Post-Office Department during the past fiscal year, ending on the 30th June, 1859, exclusive of payments for mail service specially provided for by Congress out of the general Treasury, amounted to $14,964,493.33 and its receipts to $7,968,484.07, showing a deficiency to be supplied from the Treasury of $6,996,009.26, against $5,235,677.15 for the year ending 30th June, 1858.

NOTE: Congress didn't pass a complete budget for fiscal year 1859, relying instead on appropriations bills as we do today. 1859 opened the door to fiscal insolvency and the USA boldly stormed through. Lest we think it a new strategy to blame previous administrations for the failures of the present, it happened in 1859 the same way it happens today.

Men never change. Neither does God.

Politics of Division

ω

But Jesus knew their thoughts, and said to them: "Every kingdom divided against itself is brought to desolation, and every city or house divided against itself will not stand."—Matthew 12:25

There is safety in numbers. There is also greater opportunity to gain control when the power of one becomes the power of many. However, groups aren't necessarily right or beneficial simply because they're big.

"In her essay, *The Arts of The Contact Zone*, Mary Louise Pratt, a member of the Modern Language Association, relates the challenges of politics to the concept of a social space where "cultures meet, clash and grapple," accordingly termed contact zones.

"These zones are ... points of contact between two different cultures, and involve certain dynamics, such as an imbalance of power between the two. From this constant and dramatic interplay, the culture itself becomes larger-than-life leading to the self-deception of the members of the culture who are invested in a set ideology as part of their self-image. If members of a contact zone, marginalized and dominant, imagine their communities as unified monocultures, then self-deception will almost certainly occur."—Gabrielle Micheletti, Deception, Delusion, and Division in American Politics: Fruits of the Contact Zone[53]

"It is not often that a campaign is so candid about its determination to slice-and-dice the electorate, to appeal to narrow sectarian interests and provide no overarching vision to draw the country together. But the Obama

---

[53].studentpulse.com/articles/168/deception-delusion-and-division-in-american-politics-fruits-of-the-contact

131

campaign is extraordinary—in its cynicism and arrogance."—Jennifer Rubin, the Washington Post, 2012[54]

Each issue discussed in later chapters is a mechanism used for gathering power to special-interest groups. Some black people hate white people because they think white people hate black people because black people tell them that white people hate black people.

In *Dreams from My Father*, Barack Obama observes young black children in the community he is organizing change from happy to haunted once they realize they are somehow less worthy than white people. He noted that these children had no exposure to anyone except other black people.

The lesson that white people hate black people came from other black people. These children never had the opportunity to enter school, the community, or the world at large without preconceived ideas. Hope wasn't taken from these children by white people or the government, but by neighbors and family.

"Anger's a requirement for the job and the only reason anybody decides to become an [community] organizer. Well-adjusted people find more relaxing work."–Barack Obama, Dreams from My Father

Women charge men with sexism because they have been led to believe men are guilty of sexism. Who tells these women they are victims of sexism? Other women. Women who are perfectly content and happy are often bullied into victimhood in order to build a bigger more powerful group of discontents.

The more women who believe they have been victimized the more powerful the group and the more control the leaders of the group have over newly victimized women. Many weren't victims until organizers told them they were. Women who refuse to be victims are considered traitors to the cause.

---

[54] washingtonpost.com/blogs/right-turn/post/politics-of-division

The latest buzzword is *misogyny.*[55] Most women can't spell it or define it, except to parrot what they've heard others say; that women are victimized by misogynists. I have been accused of being a misogynist because I refuse to believe that women are weak, powerless, or stupid. Those who accuse others of misogyny the loudest may be most guilty themselves.

> *"And why do you look at the speck in your brother's eye, but do not consider the plank in your own eye? Or how can you say to your brother, 'Let me remove the speck from your eye'; and look, a plank is in your own eye? Hypocrite! First remove the plank from your own eye, and then you will see clearly to remove the speck from your brother's eye."*— *Matthew 7:3-5*

Community and issues-organizing builds coalitions to acquire power and to identify someone who can be blamed for the ills of its members. The most frequent strategies involve blackmail, negative publicity, false accusations, and demands for financial reparations and/or apology for real or imagined insults.

No group protesting abortion limits, racism, sexism, homophobia, Islamophobia, or any other phobia is primarily concerned with feeding families, educating children, preserving family relationships, or building neighborhoods. The primary concern is gathering power and control to benefit the leadership of the protest organization.

Each group exists to improve its own circumstances at the expense of everyone outside the group. Every gain is made by taking something from someone else. Every remedy demanded simply creates another inequity. *There is no justice unless I get justice. No justice (for me or my opinion) No peace.*

Similar chants and sentiments have made headlines on a regular basis since the 1970s. More often than not, recent calls for "No justice, no peace" are racially motivated. Protest organizers keep

---

[55] Misogyny – dislike of, contempt of , or ingrained prejudice against women

dusting off the slogan because it's catchy, easy to march to, and tends to rile folks up, which is precisely what they want. Protestors generally want those protested against (or neutral bystanders) to feel at least a hint of threat. Slogans are often synonymous with, *"Gimmee what I want or I'll hurt you."*

On November 26, 2015, protesters successfully shut down Black Friday shopping on Chicago's Magnificent Mile. *"No justice. No shopping."* Protesters included the Nation of Islam marching under the banner of "Justice or Else", the Revolutionary Communist Party, and the Rev. Jesse Jackson's Rainbow PUSH coalition.

In the World

Making self the center of the world is the epitome of being self-conscious. What do people think about me? How do I feel? Am I happy? Am I depressed? Why don't people pay more attention to what I say?

What is the difference between narcissism and self-awareness? Narcissists have a grandiose sense of self-worth, exploit others for personal gain, feel a pathological sense of entitlement and consider themselves more valuable and unique than anyone else. Self-awareness recognizes character and personality, the role we play within a larger body, and how personal behavior benefits or damages others.

Most folks use such information to course-correct their behavior when it hurts someone they care about. Narcissists are totally self-absorbed, thinking only of themselves. They never truly feel sympathy or empathy for others. All humans are tempted by self-interest and self-indulgence. Narcissists are massive over-achievers of self-interest. Adam bought the lie sold by the serpent and we continue to blame our discontent on someone or something apart from self.

The world encourages our natural human desire for attention:

- Recognize me!
- Make it easy for me!
- Someone else is to blame for my discontent or failure.

Jesus has no use for people caught in webs of self-focus. James C. Maxwell[56] noted that "God uses people who fail because there aren't any other kinds around."

The foundational message of the Beatitudes is that we come to Christ with nothing of our own. *Blessed are the poor in spirit.* He provides Spirit, grace, mercy, and all that is needed to deliver us to heaven after fulfilling our mortal mission.

Jesus works through you, not with you. Chambers asks, "Which are the people who have influenced us most? Not the ones who thought they did, but those who had not the remotest notion that they were influencing us." Jesus never selects workers based on personal accomplishment but on their poverty of spirit and lack of ego. Jesus is the Master who makes the commonplace special.

> *"If absolute power corrupts absolutely, does absolute powerlessness make you pure?"—Harry Shearer*

> *"I must know Jesus Christ as Saviour before His teaching has any meaning for me other than that of an ideal that leads to despair. But when I am born again of the Spirit of God, I know that Jesus Christ did not come to teach only; He came to make me what He teaches I should be."—Oswald Chambers, My Utmost for His Highest*

The spirit of self-vindication is both revealed and destroyed by the work of the Holy Spirit. Christians operate in the world in two general ways:

1. They invest in the world while doing the least possible for God and His people, or
2. They invest in God and His people while doing the minimum for the world.

New Creations in Christ should be in the world but not of the world (John 15:19). How do you allocate your scarce resources of time,

---

[56] John C. Maxwell, contemporary speaker, author, and pastor.

cash, and energy? Do you invest in the world or in the body of Christ on earth?

When asked by the Pharisees if it was lawful to pay taxes to Caesar, Jesus knowing their hypocrisy said to them, "Why do you test Me? Bring Me a denarius that I may see it." So they brought it. The coin bore the image and inscription of Caesar. Jesus answered and said to them, "Render to Caesar the things that are Caesar's, and to God the things that are God's (Matthew 22:20-22).

What do you have that God didn't give you? No human ever truly creates anything. Jesus recognized the requirement that citizens contribute to legal governments. Anything beyond that comes from that which God gives us free choice to invest. What would the world say about spending most of your time, effort, and resources for the benefit of the brethren? Worldly people will call you fanatical or worse for doing what God asks you to do. He leaves the choice to you.

Who would you rather spend eternity with, Jesus Christ or the worldly?

First Love

ω

"Do you not know that to whom you present yourselves slaves to obey, you are that one's slaves whom you obey, whether of sin leading to death, or of obedience leading to righteousness?"—Romans 6:16

Those most desperately seeking to express their individuality are often the least original. Tattoos are so commonplace they're boring. Odd hairstyles or fashion choices are seldom truly odd. Body piercings seldom attract attention. The new fad is body-altering; actually changing, adding, or reworking permanent parts. In today's world, it takes a seismic fashion event to be noticed in a crowd screaming about its own uniqueness.

The only way to truly stand apart from the crowd today is by deviating from deviation. What used to be considered *normal* is now so rare it is remarkable. Social norms in western culture have completely shifted since the 1960's. By the time the latest fashion or fad has been adopted by people who yearn to be different, unique, their own person, or flaunt their own style, they are already just another face in the crowd.

Losing Your First Love

The pursuit of originality creates more slaves to fashion than free thinkers, though most aren't aware of it. *"My tattoo isn't anything like his. The bird on my arm is flying and is a completely different color."* When everyone is odd, no one is odd.

"I know your works, your labor, your patience, and that you cannot bear those who are evil. You have tested those who say they are apostles and are not, and have found them liars; and you have persevered and have patience, and have labored for My name's sake and have not become weary. Nevertheless I have this against you, that you have left your first love."—Revelation 2:2-4

Christians in the throes of first love for Jesus may not be able to quote massive quantities of scripture or discuss competing commentaries. Their entire being is full of gratitude and desire to know more about Jesus. They are eager and open, giving and receiving, and wholly engaged in learning to live as a New Creation in Christ. They are all in.

Does this prayer sound familiar? "Lord, I bring myself to You. Make me whiter than snow, free of sin, and holy in Your eyes." The focus of this prayer is self, not on God the Father, not Jesus the Son, not even the Holy Spirit. Jesus does not ask for anything more or anything less, than to completely abandon your right to yourself to Him.

In truth you have nothing that He didn't give you first. You cannot consecrate or commit what isn't yours to give. If I give you free access to my home, you cannot give me the gift of free access to my own home. You have no power to enter or to evict but what I cede to you.

You are a created being; God brought you in and He can take you out. The world would have you believe that the center of the universe is YOU, not HIM. This is the central theme of deceit. Satan seeks your destruction. The trap most successfully used throughout human history is distraction, pulling your focus away from the face of God to your own benefit. In the Garden, the deceitful serpent skillfully led Eve from obedience to God to seeking what was beneficial to her and Adam.

Right relationship is undisturbed by circumstance, location, or time. Jesus' disciples followed the Son of God when He was bodily present and when He was not. They were committed regardless of the situation or peril. Faith and the ability to maintain proper focus are gifts of the Holy Spirit. Every person has unique preferences when it comes to goodies, motivators, or stimulants. The same is true when comparing what totally distracts or tempts one person yet can't draw the attention of another for two seconds.

The things that provide motivation or meaning are not universal among people. What one considers punitive another thinks is great fun. Temptations are also unique to the situation at hand. A wonderful gift for one person may be the greatest of temptations to another. Things have no ultimate meaning or purpose in themselves. What seems an opportunity for great success or joy to one person may lead to someone else's failure.

"But beware lest somehow this liberty of yours become a stumbling block to those who are weak."—1 Corinthians 8:9

Satan knows the precise location of your weak spots. He knows the one thing almost guaranteed to distract you from listening to and waiting on Christ. Simple obedience is twisted into self-righteousness. Taking relationship with Christ for granted by misplaced familiarity, confidence, or presumption opens the door to error. Many preachers suggest that humans are more important to God's happiness than He is to ours.

First love fixates on:

- You alone are enough
- I desire to know thee more
- I desire to give; to serve; to pour out myself for Thee.

One of the greatest challenges is learning to look past a blessing in order to see God's face. Don't focus on the gift, seek the Giver. Some familiar prayers illustrate improper focus on the benefits of relationship with God.

Dear Lord,

- *I need you to* (the whiny Christian)...
- Make me complete.
- Fill me up.
- Provide for me.
- Make me loving.
- Make me ....
- Give me ....
- Help me ....
- Bring me ....

Those awash in first love long *to give, to spend,* and *to bless* the object of their affection. Nothing is more highly desired than to grow nearer; to close every gap between *my spirit/essence and Thine.*

Offer your affection, attention, and obedience to God as free gifts. Relationship with Christ is a miracle, not a transaction. We come, follow, go, or yield according to His will, His direction, and His vision. Correction is a gift of love, not punishment.

"As many as I love I rebuke and chasten."—Revelation 3:19

Rebuke and chastening have gotten a bad rap in recent decades. Parents won't correct their children because they fear rejection, and sometimes children escape consequences for bad behavior because it's just too much effort. Failure to correct children proves that a parent's first love has wilted.

If you know someone who places the interests and preferences of their children above the interests of Jesus Christ, the kids may be idols. There is no better way to demonstrate the depth of love for a child than leading him or her to Jesus. Christ is faithful. His love never changes. Can you say that about your own love for Him?

Have you exchanged engagement, giving, and being fully invested in Christ for just *trying* to be a good Christian? Do you negotiate transactions with the world to create common ground instead of having eyes only for God?

Where you find yourself fifteen minutes into eternity depends on your answer.

Tempted by Victimhood

Every human is born a self-centered narcissist. The first direct communication children usually offer is a hard-to-misinterpret physical gesture or verbal statement. Little-bitty self-absorbed hands grab a toy or cookie from sibling or playmate, clutch it tightly to their toddler-sized chest, proclaiming for all to hear, "MINE!"

Sharing, empathy, love, generosity, and selflessness are latent potentialities within the human heart, not characteristics expressed naturally. Something or someone on the outside has to coax them out and exercise them before they become habits. Deep in the nature of even the most admirable person lurk remnants of self-centeredness from the sandbox of childhood. We all harbor dark little temptations that lie in wait to strike the moment our guard drops.

Resolve to study God's Word, seek the soft voice of the Holy Spirit, and learn to behave as a loving Christ-follower. Do the right thing even if the idea isn't thrilling. Decades ago, psychologists discovered that behavior determines attitude and not the reverse. Adopt the behaviors of New Creations in Christ out of simple devotion to Him and you will be amazed how joy and peace begin to bless your daily life.

> *"But we all, with unveiled face, beholding as in a mirror the glory of the Lord, are being transformed into the same image from glory to glory, just as by the Spirit of the Lord."—2 Corinthians 3:18*

Where can we find such a mirror?

Most people are naturally drawn to their own reflections. Before mirrors were commonplace seeing what you looked like was a great curiosity. How would it feel not knowing what you looked like? Today that's hard to imagine because we've watched ourselves grow from infants to toddlers, teens to adults, and from middle-aged to old folks. Little children are fascinated by faces and usually recognize themselves in the mirror around 18 months of age.

Highly polished bits of copper and bronze were used for reflection as early as 4000 BC. Venice became a center of mirror production using the technique of coating glass with a tin-mercury amalgam in the 16th century. Glass mirrors from this period were outrageously expensive luxuries.

Until the 19th century only the wealthiest people were able to satisfy their curiosity about their appearance. The silvered-glass mirror invented by German chemist Justus von Liebig in 1835 paved the way for the eventual mass marketing of mirrors to the general public.

Reflections that matter most can't be seen in simple silvered-glass mirrors because they provide no context, reflecting only the surface. The glory of God is neither skin-deep, nor even describable. Little of eternal importance is discovered by looking at one's own reflection. The mirrors that best reflect the truth are the ones that reveal what lies beneath the surface. Little children, dogs, and horses are often more sensitive and receptive to the state of one's spirit than physical appearance. Kids and critters are reliably accurate barometers of character.

The only perfect picture of who you are is reflected from the face of God.

Tolerance vs Intolerance

ω

"Let me never fall into the vulgar mistake of dreaming that I am persecuted whenever I am contradicted."—Ralph Waldo Emerson, from his Journals

Accusations of intolerance in the 21st century are poorly disguised attempts to bully those who disagree. The definition of tolerance is not reserved to the majority, logical, faithful, or educated, but to the most powerful, passionate, or politically connected. The greatest irony in western cultures today is the outrageous intolerance exhibited by those who define tolerance.

"According to the new tolerance, to be intolerant toward another's beliefs is to be intolerant toward the person. And intolerance toward persons, incidentally, is the definition of bigotry. For practitioners of the new tolerance, intolerance is thought to be the supreme sin because it offends and disrespects persons. No one deserves to be offended or disrespected, and such an offense is considered an assault on their very dignity as a human being."—Ben R. Crenshaw[57]

Is it possible to respectfully disagree with someone's behavior or belief? Social justice experts say "No." In other words, you are guilty of intolerance unless you agree with everyone different than you and are therefore a bigot. But tolerance isn't a two-way street. Being called intolerant and bigoted isn't intolerant. The game and rules are stacked against anything traditional or Christian. Social justice experts might as well be honest and say, "Heads I win, tails you lose."

The word *discrimination* is losing its original definition. The primary definition used to be, "to note or observe a difference;

---

[57] "Shut up, bigot!" The Intolerance of Tolerance, thepublicdiscourse.com

distinguish accurately." It now means any word, thought, or act that prefers a traditional over a non-traditional choice. The present primary definition of *discriminate* (Dictionary.com) is, "to make a distinction in favor of or against a person or things on the basis of the group, class, or category to which the person or thing belongs rather an according to actual merit; show partiality."

> *"In real life the people who are most bigoted are the people who have no convictions at all. Bigotry may be roughly defined as the anger of men who have no opinions. It is the resistance offered to definite ideas by that vague bulk of people whose ideas are indefinite to excess. Bigotry may be called the appalling frenzy of the indifferent. This frenzy of the indifferent is in truth a terrible thing; it has made all monstrous and widely pervading persecutions. Bigotry in the main has always been the pervading omnipotence of those who do not care crushing out those who care in darkness and blood.*
>
> *Ideas are dangerous, but the man to whom they are least dangerous is the man of ideas. He is acquainted with ideas, and moves among them like a lion-tamer. Ideas are dangerous, but the man to whom they are most dangerous is the man of no ideas." – G.K. Chesterton, Heretics*

Social Justice Insanity

Microaggression is the latest pop-theory. Books, lectures, and university classes about it are becoming more prevalent. There is a website devoted to people sharing how others hurt their feelings—*microaggressions.com*.

Whether a smart aleck crack from junior high peers or a mother saying what mothers have said for centuries, people are hurt and humiliated by the same things that people have been saying to one another for decades or longer.

Parents used to teach children to suck it up and be nice to others even when the favor wasn't returned. Today children are taught that they should never have to suffer even an unintentional slight because "*You are responsible for how I feel.*"

You hurt people today. Other people hurt you today. If you can't remember when it happened or who else was involved, that's understandable. Microaggressions often occur at a subconscious level. It's like those mysterious black holes in space. They can't be seen and have no mass.

You wouldn't know they're there unless someone told you. In a nutshell, Microaggession describes how people are hurt and how they hurt others, often without anyone realizing it happened. Did you catch that? Not only are the guilty unaware but many victims have no idea they were victimized.

Microaggression is a form of "unintended discrimination." It is depicted by the use of known social norms of behavior and/or expression that, while without conscious choice of the user, has the same effect as conscious, intended discrimination. – Wikipedia

Any compliment to a woman, person of color, LGBT, or other marginalized person could be considered microaggressive. Say something nice at your peril, even if your sole intent is to support, reinforce, affirm, or compliment. To some you are guilty of a slight, indignity, put-down, or insult. Does it matter if you actually mean to be complimentary? No. It only proves you're unaware of your bad behavior. Does it matter if the person actually took it as a compliment? No, it only proves that they are unaware of how you victimized them.

Columbia instructor Dr. Derald Wing Sue's 2010 video[58] scripted several examples of folks interacting with others to illustrate what he considers microaggressive. One skit shows a business meeting where a woman's opinion is pretty much ignored.

---

[58] youtube.com/watch?v=BJL2P0JsAS4

The intent is to illustrate sexism. But why assume the cause is sexism? The woman in the meeting may have a history of offering insipid ideas. I've been in meetings with people like that of both genders. After a while it's difficult to pretend interest. The big question is, "Why is she/he still here?" Sometimes the best reaction is no reaction at all.

The University of Kansas recently banished gender specific pronouns like *his* or *her* because they are considered microaggressive. Singular pronouns have been replaced with plural pronouns. The UofK defended its choice to discard rules of language in favor of promoting gender neutral expression.

At UK you might read, Susie opened the door to their home where they lives alone. Before the policy changed the sentence would have read, Susie opened the door to her home where she lives alone.

The University of Tennessee also promotes the use of gender-neutral pronouns. Instead of microaggressive pronouns like he, she, his, or her, UT suggests students use ze, hir, zir, xe, xem and xyr—which remind me more of Algebra than English.

I suggest that Microaggression Theory is itself intolerant and insensitive. I'm not sure, but that might make me a bigot. In any case, discarding gender specific pronouns will make communication infinitely more difficult.

Riddle me this: Since microaggressive exchanges are usually unconscious, how do victims recognize they were victimized in the first place? How can the guilty be properly identified if victims are totally unaware that a crime was committed?

Microaggression is Manipulative

Dr. Sue, I am quite certain, believes he is well-meaning, kind, and moral. But the consequences of his unconscious and unintended messages are micro-aggressive in themselves. This is the very charge he makes about micro-aggressors. They are well-meaning, kind, and moral, but they victimize others in total innocence. I believe there's a scripture about that:

"Judge not, that you be not judged. For with what judgment you judge, you will be judged; and with the measure you use, it will be measured back to you. And why do you look at the speck in your brother's eye, but do not consider the plank in your own eye?"—Matthew 7:1-3

Critical Legal Studies

ω

"A nation is a society united by a delusion about its ancestry and by common hatred of its neighbours."—William Ralph Inge, The End of an Age: and other essays

Critical Legal Studies (CLS) is a movement in legal scholarship committed to shaping society to both consider and compensate for microaggressive inequities they believe are buried in existing institutions of law. CLS proponents work to upset traditional conceptions of law by disrupting existing legal practice and institutions. CLS formally appeared in 1977 but has roots dating back to 1960.

CLS includes a broad group of theorists at law schools on several continents. Spinoffs from CLS continue to increase and grow in popularity. Critical Race Theory (CRT) is probably the largest offshoot and has expanded beyond law schools to education, political science, and ethnic studies.

CRT "includes economics, history, context, group—and self-interest, and even feelings and the unconscious. Unlike some academic disciplines, critical race theory contains an activist dimension." (Critical Race Theory- An Introduction, Delgado and Stefancic, 2001, p 3)

Authors Delgado and Stefancic explain that CRT does not endorse liberalism because *"many liberals believe in color blindness and neutral principles of constitutional law."* (Ibid. p21) Equal application of law is an enemy when it doesn't make an exception for ME.

Critical Race Theory and its sister-theories have goals similar to Marxism and Communism. Instead of limiting social destruction activities to divisions defined by class or method of income, Critical Legal Studies breaks a single population into an endless number of social classes divided by race, gender, sexual preference and every other descriptor. The intent is to further fracture one united whole into vulnerable parts.

Every theory, religion, and –ism is doomed to failure because, except for one, each has a mortal flaw. One single thread stretches from the beginning of history until now and will continue as long as humans draw breath. The relationship between humanity and Jehovah God will endure because humans are real and so is the One who created them.

Human nature isn't a mystery to God. "And He said to them, 'You are those who justify yourselves before men, but God knows your hearts. For what is highly esteemed among men is an abomination in the sight of God'" (Luke 16:15).

God is not a respecter of persons. He doesn't care if you are male or female, black, white, or brown. Relationship with God explains every aspect of human experience. It provides the beginning, the middle, and sheds light on the end. Jesus Christ offers a solution for every concern of mankind. The first hiccup in the relationship between God and mankind was sin.

Battle lines were drawn the instant Adam and Eve put personal benefit above obedience to God. Human nature has warred against control by God and other humans ever since. Yet even from the very moment the serpent deceived Eve, God offered a solution permitting repair of the relationship.

The battle itself testifies to the error of human reason. Consider this comment by G.K. Chesterton about feminism: "It [feminism] is mixed up with a muddled idea that women are free when they serve their employers but slaves when they help their husbands." This same blindness and failure of logic proves that feminism (another –ism) is nothing more than selling a lie to one subset of humans.

A woman who feels more liberated punching time clocks than getting out of bed to share a pot of coffee with her husband proves little more than that she chose the wrong husband. But human nature always gravitates to doctrines that revolve around ME as the hub of the universe.

Why is it better to work than marry? Both require adherence to a set of norms and rules. Both subjugate some aspect of life to the relationship, whether employment or familial. Both restrict freedoms in some way. The difference is durability of commitment. Women who feel trapped in their job are no different from women who feel trapped in marriage.

The powers behind progressive feminism argue that it is easier to change employers than husbands. They don't mention the problem of who covers the bills between jobs. The purpose of the family God defines is security derived from the combination of efforts by the members. Unlike single women, women in traditional marriages don't lose their ability to enjoy shelter, groceries, and other security when illness or employment changes their routines.

Not surprisingly, there is a special area of critical legal study addressing the plight of women, Feminist Legal Studies (Fem Crit). Given the goal of CLS, it is easy to recognize Fem Crit as ultimately manipulative rather than supportive.

The primary tactic of the enemy is to divide, to separate, and to make vulnerable. Nothing is more vulnerable than one individual alone. Feminism preaches that women should become autonomic islands of insecurity. They argue that self-determination is empowering and more secure. Feminism, like every other –ism, plays to self-indulgence which is the heart and soul of human nature.

Say Goodbye to the Rule of Law

Justice is no longer blind and the rule of law is increasingly situational. Politics of personal identification replaced blind justice of previous eras. Dr. Martin Luther King, Jr. is hailed as a hero when convenient, but were he to express his principles and goals today they would be shouted down as intolerant, racist, sexist, and bigoted by many 21st century activists and educators.

Modern politicians, humanists, educators, and activists care little about the content of one's character and even less about equal treatment under the law or equal opportunity. Critical Legal Study proponents believe that equal application of the law is, by definition, discriminatory. Their goal is to tear down the foundations that promote or require any standard, not suggest an improved standard.

Critical Legal Studies suggest that how a person feels, or what the narrative of his social history suggests, is as meaningful as the actual facts of a case when presented as evidence in a court of law. In other words, in order to be just, justice must be totally subjective.

Death of Rules and Standards

Humanists and social activists consider all standards inherently intolerant. This creates a major problem when more than one person is in the room. Measurements are only meaningful when there is a fixed point against which progress or performance may be compared or computed. If you want to determine how far it is to work there must be a specific place you begin to measure the distance and a specific place where you stop.

Einstein's Special Theory of Relativity is simply written without footnote or reference: "Movement can only be detected and measured as relative movement; the change of position of one body in respect to another."

The line between right and wrong cannot be drawn without a set anchor point. Establishing fixed anchor points is unacceptable to humanists, making it impossible to define anything as absolutely right or absolutely wrong.

Today's academic legal theorists consider equal application of the rule of law a bad thing. That's why there is no consistency, no standard, and the gradual dissolution of the rule of law. CLS supports the doctrines of atheism/humanism. The only way to remove God from the public square is to establish a state religion of no religion. Absolute standards must be removed from public records and public discourse in order to make God's banishment permanent.

The choice to banish God today has eternal consequences.

Unconscious Sin

ω

"Those who dream by day are cognizant of many things which escape those who dream only by night. In their gray visions they obtain glimpses of eternity, and thrill, in waking, to find that they have been upon the verge of the great secret. In snatches, they learn something of the wisdom which is of good, and more of the mere knowledge which is of evil."—Edgar Allen Poe, Eleonora

Have you ever had a thought pop into your head that was lurid, violent, nasty, or blatantly sinful? Did you think, *Where did THAT thought come from*? The instant you became aware of the thought, you dismissed it, hoping to forget it happened. People have no concept of how deep sin nature lurks in the souls of men, and even less so in their own.

"For out of the heart proceed evil thoughts, murders, adulteries, fornications, thefts, false witness, blasphemies."—Matthew 15:19

Those bothersome thoughts we have from time to time come unbidden from places too deep to access or predict. Every parent has had a bad thought about a beloved child before sweeping it away as quickly as possible lest it require conscious consideration making it *real*. Horrific nightmares or improper dreams originate in places we can't visit while awake. The Holy Spirit is able to reveal and cleanse each area of hidden sin. Conscious conviction of sin makes it our responsibility to manage. Sins we aren't yet aware of are saved for future lessons.

"For what I am doing, I do not understand. For what I will to do, that I do not practice; but what I hate, that I do. For the good that I will to do, I do not do; but the evil I will not to do, that I practice. Now if I do what I will not to do, it is

*no longer I who do it, but sin that dwells in me."—Romans
7:15, 19*

The good news of forgiveness is that Christ forgives all sin, even
those you don't know exist. Paul's Romans 7 message is frequently
used to excuse conscious sin. I suggest it speaks rather to the
specific problem of subconscious sin; sin that flies under the
rational radar. How can you bridle a thought or behavior you don't
know exists until some wild mental, verbal or physical flash reveals
it to your surprise and (sometimes) horror?

Paul was not saying, "Hey, we all sin guys, even me! Don't sweat it,
just try to be good." Paul was saying, *I recognize as sin those things
I did without awareness or intent.* Another way to consider Paul's
confession involves the unintended consequences of otherwise
innocent actions.

A friend of mine repeatedly complimented a church acquaintance
on his beautiful head of hair. My friend was absolutely serious,
thinking how fortunate the man was compared to his own thinning
mane. One day, years into the exchange, the fellow came into
church without one hair on his head. Only then did my friend realize
he had been complimenting the man on his toupee. He was horrified
and feared his sincere compliment may have been taken as an
irritant or even been hurtful.

Did he say what he said? Yes. Did he understand the total
circumstance? No. Would knowing the truth have changed his
behavior? Absolutely. Yet, he had done what he would never do.

Everyone has unintentionally hurt someone else. Has something you
said caused pain to someone you cared for deeply? You didn't
intend to hurt them; nothing was further from your mind. You hurt
them. You did. But you would never have done it had you known in
advance. The difference between unintentional sin and
Microaggression is understood through relationship with Christ.
Some microaggressive behavior *is* intentional, but most
microaggressions pass beneath the awareness of both aggressor and
victim. In other words, they are often non-existent except in support
of some social justice theory or CLS case.

Paul tells us that sin lies deep within our souls. It is important to note that all error is NOT sin. Error is always unintentional. Some errors are simple mistakes without eternal consequence. Sin, however, can be either premeditated or completely unintentional. Nothing in the Bible suggests Paul was guilty of any premeditated sin. Think about that. Everyone sins. Paul didn't behave as he hoped, but as far as we know, he never sinned intentionally.

Is there forgiveness for intentional sin? Most people say there is. If so, why would it be and where in God's Word is that opinion confirmed?

The next time you sit before the Lord, tell Him why you think premeditated sin deserves forgiveness. Imagine yourself standing at the foot of the cross while Jesus labors to take one more breath. Look up. Trace the stream of blood running from the crown of thorns piercing His head down to tortured feet spiked to the tree. Sinning with full knowledge and intent chooses sin over salvation, denying the innocent blood pooling in the sand beside you.

> *"For if we sin willfully after we have received the knowledge of the truth, there no longer remains a sacrifice for sins."—Hebrews 10:26*

Remember that you and I have been deceived. Satan convinced Eve and Adam that God wasn't as much a stickler as they believed. "Surely God hath not said..." God indeed hath said. Where you find yourself fifteen minutes into eternity has a lot to do with whose message you believe: Satan's lies or God's Word.

The strength to reject temptation and to contend with your present circumstance is a gift of the Holy Spirit even when Satan continues to press the lie that "you deserve more!" Satan preaches the very popular gospel of self-indulgence. Not as popular, but eternally satisfying, is the self-denying gospel of Jesus Christ. Eve bought the lie that she could disobey God and escape the penalty He said would be rendered. If this Hebrews verse is true, how can one justify believing a "sacrifice for sin" still remains when the sin is willful?

The justification probably begins, *"Surely God hath not said"* --

From Pentecost to a Politically Correct Church

The God of the Bible either exists or He does not. Either the WORD made flesh, Jesus Christ, lived, died, and rose from the dead or He did not. Let us return to the two doors to eternity. One is the truth and the other a lie. One elevates Christ and the other idolizes self.

Views supported by God's Word are often dismissed as illogical or fanatical. Aristotle applied legendary skills of logic and debate to issues of his day. Some Christians dismiss parts of the Bible because they appear to lack logic or oppose scientific fact. Based upon the following points, I doubt Aristotle would buy into what is offered as the logical theory of macro Evolution. At the very least he would argue for the existence of a Creator.

In *Metaphysics*, Aristotle logically concluded that the seed of any plant or animal comes from other individuals who are prior and complete, meaning the first thing is not seed but something complete.

"We must say that before the seed there is a man; not the man produced from the seed, but another from whom the seed comes. There is a substance which is eternal and unmovable and separate from sensible things, without parts and indivisible (for it produces movement through infinite time and nothing finite can have infinite power). Such an eternal and unmovable substance must also be impassive and unalterable; for all the other changes are posterior [after]." [59]

This eternal actual substance must be a single *prime mover*, which, while the source of all process and change, is not itself subject to process or change. This substance does what the highest forms of life ought to do, namely to think.[60]

---

[59] scandalon.co.uk/philosophy/aristotle_prime_mover.htm

[60] logicmuseum.com/ontological/aristotleontological.htm

Is belief in one supreme God logical? Aristotle thought so, and no one stands above him on the pedestal of logic. If God is omnipotent and has the power and intent to bring human souls to heaven for eternity, then He can do it. If God were gentleman enough to allow a man to deny Him, to abuse Him, to lie about Him, to spend his entire life outside of His will, yet still welcome him to heaven, God would be a liar. False teachers suggest that God loves mankind so much that everyone will be saved and share eternity in a heavenly abode.

If God so loves that even human vermin get into heaven, why doesn't He simply transform every one of us into obedient little lapdogs for his court? Without free will (or free won't) relationship has no value. It isn't possible to love someone you can't distinguish from everyone else. God wants men to distinguish Him from everything and everyone else. Salvation isn't generic and isn't available to groups. Jesus died for men and women as individuals.

When Lazarus died *Jesus wept*. Jesus knew the difference between Peter and Thomas. Every disciple was special to Jesus in his own way. There is no value in a man confessing Christ as Lord unless he can freely choose to deny Him. Why doesn't God make little robots of us? Obedience without option is obedience without value.

God's Word is clear; one must be born again of His Spirit to enter the kingdom of heaven. New birth requires repentance and faith. If salvation required nothing of obedience, nothing of faith, and nothing of relationship, then what logic suggests anything else God said should be considered true? If God lied about anything, then neither door to eternity opens to heaven.

God does not desire Stepford children. He wants to be known as we are known and be loved for who He is. That means you have a choice, and your choice matters. Logic tells us that only those who know, love, and obey God will spend eternity with Him, because that's what He said.

> *Jesus answered, "Most assuredly, I say to you, unless one is born of water and the Spirit, he cannot enter the kingdom of God."—John 3:5*

Lynn Baber

"He who believes in Him is not condemned, but he who does not believe is condemned already, because he has not believed in the name of the only begotten Son of God."—John 3:18

The Unmentionables

ω

"... that we should no longer be children, tossed to and fro and carried about with every wind of doctrine, but the trickery of men, in the cunning craftiness of deceitful plotting."—Ephesians 4:14

Debates over climate change, abortion, gay rights, racism, religion, and evolution continue to create headlines. The engine of continuing argument is the absence of truth. Truth itself has become relative. If there are no objective definitions or limitations to gender, marriage, or sexual preference, why are people so eager to change labels? Either there ARE distinctions which inspire change or there are none which makes the whole concept of change ridiculously indulgent.

- Why do addicts want to change?
- Why do morbidly obese people want to change?
- Why does anyone want to change?

People seek change because they are dissatisfied with their present condition or circumstance. If there's nothing wrong with a person's present condition or circumstance, there should be no desire to change it. Satisfied people don't seek change. Regardless of the specifics, people seek change because they don't like how they feel about themselves; they don't like how they feel in relationship to others, or they desire some change in their surroundings.

Personal opinions now define gender, relationship parameters, race, and how to interpret the world around us. Is man-made climate change real? It depends on who you ask. Is mankind's oldest ancestor a rock? It depends on who you ask. Under what circumstances is killing a moral choice? It depends on who you ask.

Whatever happened to, "In the beginning God created the heavens and the earth"? To many, God is little more than an historical footnote or irritant. Personal Opinion is the new law of the land and happily partners with Humanist doctrines. Napoleon Hill's affirmation that "What a man can conceive and believe he can achieve" helped transfer the authority for defining truth from the Creator to the created.

Since 1859, upheavals in matters of faith, society, and medicine prove the truth of Hill's statement. Daily news reports testify to the normalization of things once considered impossible. The introduction of the computer laid the broad foundation for a new Tower of Babel that looms over everything from pet identification to intergalactic travel.

The next eight chapters tackle headline issues. Folks generally fall on one side or the other based on their associates and beliefs. We have all been deceived, yet there is reason to remain confident in the truth of God's Word. As you proceed, you may begin to wonder if what you've heard for years is actually true: true enough to serve as a basis for your eternity.

Abortion

(ω)

Women used to speak with wonder, gratitude, or resignation about "my baby." Fewer expectant mothers feel that way. "My baby" has become a fetus or *product of conception.*

> *"We teach them not to notice the different sense of the possessive pronoun. Even in the nursery a child can be taught to mean by "my Teddy-bear" not the old imagined recipient of affection to whom it stands in a special relation (for that is what the Enemy will teach them to mean if we are not careful) but "the bear I can pull to pieces if I like."*— C.S. Lewis, The Screwtape Letters

Until quite recently, pregnant women expected additions to the family. Grandparents and siblings began to dream of who would shortly arrive. Not what, but *who.* Pregnant women don't *expect* anything but a child. The emphasis on pregnancy today isn't expectation, but time frames. Many women happily share their due dates; the time when expectation becomes reality, a warm bundle of promise with mommy's nose and daddy's eyebrows.

As Chesterton observed, many women tragically think about "my baby" in terms of ownership and possession. Instead of a new person with a lifetime yet to experience, they think that if I own it I can *pull it to pieces if I like.*

Women who consider the death of their baby a legitimate and moral outcome of pregnancy don't think about due dates. They think about weeks in a sort of countdown. How long before I have to commit? How can I get an abortion once weeks become trimesters? How long can I keep my options open?

Abortion is frequently explained as a woman's right to control over her own body. The reason for most (not all) abortions is lack of control. Abortion is simply the remedy to absolve a woman of the consequence for blowing that control thing in the first place.

Lynn Baber

Call Abortion What It Is

Abortion kills babies; dismembering and crushing live humans for (1) convenience and (2) profit. God is not fooled and don't you be fooled. Critical Legal Studies suggest the weight of *the narrative* should trump simple facts in courts of law. One of the main players in Roe v Wade admitted as much. He was aware that the facts given to the court and the public were patently false. Proponents believed the "morality of our revolution" excused the lie. How can anything be right when it is based on falsehoods?

How the deception worked:

> *"In NARAL (the then-National Association for the Reform of Abortion Laws) we generally emphasize the drama of the individual case, not the mass statistics, but when we spoke of the latter it was always 5,000 to 10,000 deaths [from backstreet abortions] each year'. I confess that I knew the figures were totally false...But in the 'morality' of our revolution, it was a useful figure, widely accepted, so why go out of our way to correct it with honest statistics?"* Dr. Bernard Nathanson, one of the founders of NARAL and once the director of the busiest abortion clinic in the Western world. (Aborting America, Doubleday, 1979)[61]

What lies were sold as truth? How can the law of the land be based on lies?

> *We aroused enough sympathy to sell our program of permissive abortion by fabricating the number of illegal abortions done annually in the U.S. The actual figure was approaching 100,000 but the figure we gave to the media repeatedly was 1,000,000. Repeating the big lie often enough convinces the public. The number of women dying from illegal abortions was around 200-250 annually. The figure constantly fed to the media was 10,000. These false*

---

[61] grtl.org/docs/roevwade.pdf

figures took root in the consciousness of Americans convincing many that we needed to crack the abortion law. Another myth we fed to the public through the media was that legalizing abortion would only mean that the abortions taking place illegally would then be done legally. In fact, of course, abortion is now being used as a primary method of birth control in the U.S. and the annual number of abortions has increased by 1500% since legalization. As a scientist I know, not believe, know that human life begins at conception. Although I am not a formal religionist, I believe with all my heart that there is a divinity of existence which commands us to declare a final and irreversible halt to this infinitely sad and shameful crime against humanity.[62]

Planned Parenthood's website still endorses Dr. Nathanson's admitted lies. "In the two decades before abortion was legal in the United States, nearly one million women went "underground" each year for illegal operations. Thousands died for lack of medical care."[63]

Planned Parenthood gives no reference or source for this statement. According to the U.S. Centers for Disease Control, whose death statistics from legal abortions have been accepted and used by Planned Parenthood, in the year before *Roe v. Wade* (1972), there were 39 deaths from illegal abortions. In the year after *Roe v. Wade* (1974), there were 26 deaths from legal abortions. Does anyone else wonder what happened to the other 9,961 presumed deaths in 1972?

Proof of Deceit

How accurate are official federal records? Would you be surprised to learn that many are fabricated? Again, there is a great deal of latitude when attempting to pin down what is *is*. In the state of

---

[62] Nathanson, Bernard. "Confessions of an Ex-Abortionist" In The Hand of God: A Journey from Death to Life by the Abortion Doctor Who Changed His Mind (Washington, D.C.: Regenery Publishing, 2013

[63] .catholiceducation.org/en/controversy/abortion/confessions-of-an-ex-abortionist.html

Maryland during 1989, the Centers for Disease Control (CDC) reported ZERO abortion-related death, yet:

- Erica Kae Richardson (16 years-old) was admitted to an emergency room on March 1st with a punctured uterus from an abortion carried out earlier that day at a clinic in Laurel, Maryland. She died shortly after midnight on March 2nd.

- Paramedics arrived at an abortion clinic in Suitland, Maryland on July 12th to find Debra M. Gray (34 years-old) in cardiac arrest after being administered anesthesia without the presence of an anesthesiologist. She was taken to a hospital and died three days later.

- Paramedics arrived at an abortion clinic in Suitland, Maryland on September 10th to find Susanne Renee Logan (32 years-old) in cardiac arrest with an oxygen mask placed upside down on her face. It was found that she had been given anesthesia without the presence of an anesthesiologist, and when she reacted to it, was given another drug not indicated to mitigate the effects of the anesthesia. The paramedics resuscitated Ms. Logan; she stayed in a coma for four months and was generally paralyzed until her death in 1992.

- Gladys Estanislao, a 28-year-old college student, was found lifeless on a bathroom floor 17 days after undergoing an abortion procedure at a clinic in Bethesda, Maryland. Her autopsy revealed that the pregnancy was not in her womb but in her fallopian tube, which caused it to rupture and resulted in her death. This condition, called an ectopic pregnancy, is screened by a blood test or ultrasound, has a mortality rate of 1 in 2,000, and is typically diagnosed on the first visit to a gynecologist.

More Deceit

During the period 1981 and 1984 the CDC cites 30 legal abortion-related deaths in New York City." For the same time period, the CDC's Division of Reproductive Health reported a total of 42 deaths from legal abortions in the entire United States. If both numbers are accurate, it means that 71% of the legal abortion-related deaths in the United States occurred in one city where about 3% of the population lived.[64] I wonder if that curiosity was ever investigated.

Abortion in 1859

In 1859 the American Medical Association took pains to clarify its position on the horror of abortion. "The causes of this general demoralization are manifold. The first of these causes is a wide-spread popular ignorance of the true character of the crime--a belief, even among mothers themselves that the foetus is not alive till after the period of quickening.

> *[Another] reason of the frightful extent of this crime is found in the grave defects of our laws, both common and statute, as regards the independent and actual existence of the child before birth, as a living being. These errors, which are sufficient in most instances to prevent conviction, are based, and only based, upon mistaken and exploded medical dogmas. With strange inconsistency, the law fully acknowledges the foetus in utero and its inherent rights, for civil purposes; while personally and as criminally affected, it fails to recognize it, and to its life as yet denies all protection."*

During the mid-19th century spiritualism grew increasingly popular, giving in to Satan's deception. Spiritists of the period rationalized their propensity to dally with the supernatural (table-tipping, séances, and Ouija) as a logical and permissible part of Christianity. Good became evil and evil good. Married women of the *spiritist* revolution began to consider abortion a *Get Out of Jail Free* card to eliminate the complications of children born of sexual indulgence in affairs and spouse-swapping. How little has changed since.

---

[64] abortionessay.com/files/1859ama.html; justfacts.com/abortion.asp

165

[It is estimated] that during 1860, there may have been as many as 45,000 abortions performed on the roughly 600,000 spiritist women. When these married women first began seeking abortions from Dr. Charles D. Meigs in 1842, the Philadelphia doctor described them as "persons so ignorant of their own moral duties, or so uninstructed as to the character and duties of medical men, [that they came to him] with a bold-faced proposition to procure an abortion." His answer to such requests: "by common law [abortion] is felony, and by the law of God murder."

The National Abortion Federation (NAF) tells us that "by the 1870s, all states had criminalized abortion," and <u>it had almost nothing to do with religious pressure</u>.[33] According to the NAF, "physicians were the leading force in the campaign to criminalize abortion in the USA," arguing that abortion was "both immoral and dangerous."

AMA on Abortion in 1871

"[These are] men who cling to a noble profession only to dishonor it; men who seek not to save, but to destroy; men known not only to the profession, but to the public as abortionists. They seem impatient for the sacrifice... those innocent and helpless victims are not permitted ever to breathe that vital air which God in His providence has destined for their use in common with the rest of the human family. But, as is found in many other cases of murder, there is no extenuating circumstance here that can change or modify the character of his guilt. As in ordinary cases of murder, there is no anger to prompt him to the deed, no wrongs to be avenged, and no jealousies to be appeased. It matters not at what stage of development his victim may have arrived; it matters not how small or how apparently insignificant it may be; it is a murder, a foul, unprovoked murder. The abortionists are more destructive to human life than ten [foreign] armies." - Report on Criminal Abortion,

Transactions of the American Medical Association 22 (1871) 240-257.

It didn't take long for public sentiment to change. In 1904, Dr. Rudolph Holmes took his grievance against abortionists to the Chicago Medical Society which formed a Committee on Criminal Abortion. The committee went after all the newspapers in Chicago who sold veiled ads to abortion providers.

Ads disappeared from prominent display, yet in 1908 Dr. Holmes lamented:

> *"I have come to the conclusion that the public does not want, the profession does not want, the women in particular do not want, any aggressive campaign against the crime of abortion. Holmes concluded that while Illinois abortion law could not be improved on paper, a total lack of enforcement made such laws almost useless. He also noted the growing problem of national complicity. "It is not possible to get twelve men together without at least one of them being personally responsible for the downfall of a girl, or at least interested in getting her out of her difficulty."* [65]

Almost 140 years later, abortion remains, but the AMA's opposition has totally evaporated. Compare the AMA statements from 1859 and 1871 with its official position today:

> *The Principles of Medical Ethics of the AMA do not prohibit a physician from performing an abortion in accordance with good medical practice and under circumstances that do not violate the law.* [66]

Prior to the AMA's May 23, 2014 "Not Clearly Pro or Con" position above, the organization made a "Pro" statement in its Dec. 19, 2013 joint amicus brief from the AMA and the American

---

[65] abort73.com/abortion_facts/us_abortion_history/

[66] abort73.com/blog/the_american_medical_association_addresses_abortion/

College of Obstetricians and Gynecologists in support of abortion in the case of Planned Parenthood v. Abbott which stated in part: *"[We] oppose legislative interference with the practice of medicine and a woman's relationship with her doctor. Access to safe and legal abortion is an important aspect of women's health care. Abortion is one of the safest medical procedures performed in the United States."*[67]

Our society is so corrupt and irrational that Planned Parenthood kills babies of the same gestational age that NICUs (Neonatal Intensive Care Unit) work feverishly to save. New internet camera technology recently introduced to the NICU allows parents to watch their one, two- and three-pound babies fight to live. Who believes that a fetus of the same gestational age won't fight just as hard when the abortionist begins the ghoulish procedure that will kill it?

What justifies categorizing one 20-week-old fetus as a highly anticipated grandchild and another a valueless *product of conception*?

How could the death of one 20-week-old fetus be labeled a women's health matter and another the devastating loss of a son, daughter, grandson, granddaughter, or sibling? One is disposed of for tissue research; the other buried in a tiny white casket beneath a granite marker bearing his or her name.

> *"Before I formed you in the womb I knew you; before you were born I sanctified you."—Jeremiah 1:5*

There is either great value in the life of an unborn baby or there is not. Every unborn baby has value or none has value. To argue another position suggests that opinion drives value; namely MY opinion. If I think it's a baby it is. If I think it's a valueless mass of cells it is. "I" have become God.

> *"The Bible consistently uses the same word for a "born" or "unborn" baby. This is because the divine Author of the*

---

[67] abortion.procon.org/view.source.php?sourceID=012767

Bible did not recognize a material difference between the two. In Scripture, there is not some special event when a "human being" becomes a "person". Rather, he or she is a person from the beginning who goes through growth and development both inside and outside of the womb. In the New Testament the Greek word "brephos" is used to describe the unborn, newborns and youth. In Luke 1:44, the word is used to mean unborn baby: "For behold, when the sound of your greeting reached my ears, the baby leaped in my womb for joy." Then, in Luke 2:12, it means a newborn: "So they came in a hurry and found their way to Mary and Joseph, and the baby as He lay in the manger." And in Luke 18:15, "brephos" refers to a young child: "And they were bringing even their babies to Him so that He would touch them, but when the disciples saw it, they began rebuking them." – AbortionFacts.com[68]

Laura Young, a United Methodist minister who also serves as the executive director of the Ohio chapter, Religious Coalition for Reproductive Choice opined[69] that *"The religious right has really hijacked the conversation on this issue, and we need to let women know that there are people of faith who are in favor of safe and legal abortion."* There are indeed religious people favorable to abortion. Opinions of the faithful and religious are of no consequence. Ask God, who caused the spark of life to begin, for His opinion. Clergy has no power except to apply balm to itching ears.[70]

If you tell a lie often enough, publish it, and teach it, it becomes truer that actual fact. As we progress through other hot topics of our day, you'll notice how the template of deception repeats itself. Columbus didn't believe the earth was flat. No witches were burned

---

[68] abortionfacts.com/literature/the-christian-view-of-abortion

[69].christiannews.net/2015/10/18/apostate-clergy-bless-ohio-abortion-facility-thank-god-for-abortion-providers/

[70] Ezekiel 14:7, Mark 9:42, 2 Timothy 4:3

in Salem. Napoleon wasn't short. What will we learn about economics, climate change, and evolution? Read on.

Economics

ω

"For everyone to whom much is given, from him much will be required; and to whom much has been committed, of him they will ask the more."—Luke 12:48

There is a widely held assumption that Christ-followers consider Capitalism a proper application of gospel principles to a nation's economic system. Conservative traditionalists are generally assumed to be staunch capitalists while liberal progressives are considered some variety of Socialist or Communist. Truth, however, seldom jives with assumption.

A rich young ruler asked Jesus what he needed to do in order to inherit eternal life. Jesus said, *"Sell all that you have and distribute to the poor, and you will have treasure in heaven; and come, follow Me"* (Luke 18:22). The young man went away heartbroken. Some biblical scholars consider this a proof text for Socialism. Wealth is sinful. Only the poor enter heaven.

In a 2013 review of Killing Jesus published in The Daily Beast, Notre Dame Theology professor Candida Moss complained that "There's no mention of the free health care offered by Jesus and his followers or the insistence that the wealthy give away their possessions." Ms. Moss errantly believes the story of the rich young ruler proves that rich folk are barred from heaven.

Not all agree. Some liberal progressives suggest Jesus would endorse tax increases, unlimited social do-gooder programs, and equal income for all. Traditional conservatives counter with scriptures linking work to eating and reminding folks that the poor will always be with us. Such debates are pointless, because God owns everything. Men may be confused about that point, but I assure you the Creator of the Universe is not.

Since most folks are too busy earning a living and raising kids to study competing economic philosophies, allow me to offer a crash course in the four major economic systems. Once you know how to tell one from another we'll compare them to God's Word.

Capitalism

> *"Capitalism places every man in competition with his fellows for a share of the available wealth. A few people accumulate big piles, but most do not. The sense of community falls victim to this struggle."—Donald Barthelme, the Rise of Capitalism*

One might expect that Capitalism has been around as long as men have had goods to trade. The term first appeared in 1854 in William Makepeace Thackeray's novel, *The Newcomes*.[71] Thackeray used the term to mean "having ownership of capital".

Capital is money, accumulated wealth, or liquid assets available for investment in production, expansion, or development for the purpose of increasing the amount of capital an individual, organization, or corporation owns. Simply put, capital is a means of increasing capital. The amount of physical labor a man can perform in a day is not capital, nor is the power of one horse or one ox considered capital. Some might quibble, but capital is generally inanimate.

If capital is used to make more capital, then what is Capitalism?

My favorite definition found in Urbandictionary.com is short and simple: Capitalism is "an economic system based on private ownership of the means of production, in which personal bling can be acquired through investment of capital and employment of peeps."

Characteristics of Capitalism:

- Private ownership of capital and production of goods and services for profit (making more capital.)

---

[71] Oxford English Dictionary

- Production decisions are based on supply and demand; producing what someone is willing to pay for.
- Competition among producers for market share.
- Reliance on wage labor rather than shared ownership of capital.
- Legal and regulated commercial framework.
- Means to market and transport large volumes of goods.
- Capital owners seeking to accumulate more capital.
- Consumers hungry to consume increasing quantities of goods and services.

Capital and commercial trade have existed for millennia, but capitalism wasn't born until industrialization permitted private ownership of the major engines of production. Mass production blossomed when a class of people willing to sell their labor for a paycheck married new technology.

In pre-16th century England, legal and economic powers resided in the owner (Lord) of a manor. The household and estate were supported by the production of his land and those who worked it. Serfs worked for and were protected by the owner but also had the right to work certain plots of land for their own subsistence. In ways both large and small, people benefitted from working their own land with their own hands.

During the 16th century, ownership and control of land started to concentrate with fewer people owning larger estates. Instead of serf-owner relationships, capital was used to pay wages to employees with no direct interest in the ownership of their work. Workers no longer produced the necessities of life. Instead of working mostly for themselves they joined a growing consumer class.

Commercial trade was no longer exclusively business to business, but business to end user. Folks with the skills to produce goods for consumption owned small businesses of their own. Goods, services, food stuffs, and education were provided by individuals to individuals. Capital became money for wages. Wage earners brought home cash and used it to buy shelter, clothing, food, and education. As the Industrial Revolution progressed (1760-1840), industry replaced small business as the main player in capitalism, resulting in the decline of artisans and skilled entrepreneurs without sufficient capital to compete.

Capitalism is production for exchange, emphasizing high levels of wage labor and investing money (capital) to make a profit rather than pure production of goods to be sold. Capitalism separates owner and worker. Money became both the main method of exchange and the scale by which the relative value of people and products is measured.

Capitalism is the system where winners use what they have to get more of what they already have. The measure of success is money. Capitalism, like Monopoly, doesn't have a winner until all the money and property is in the hands of one person. There is no such concept as "enough."

Socialism

> "Socialism provides safety in numbers. And that's OK, if you don't mind trading your name—your identity and individualism—for a number."—Jarod Kintz, 99 Cents for Some Nonsense

In stark contrast to Capitalism and its predecessor, self-subsistence, Socialism is an economic and social system without private property. There is no private investment and no possibility of private profit. It sounds good in theory but has never worked and never will work. The reason Socialism will always fail is simple - human nature.

One of the greatest issues with Socialism is the lack of personal determination and control. Common ownership of everything is fine as long as everyone involved is willing to give up what they already have to those who don't have as much or don't have anything. Socialism requires 100% commitment to the total group no matter the personal cost. Socialism requires that the unwilling must relinquish all rights to ownership, by force if necessary.

Characteristics of Socialism:

- Ownership is either collective or governmental. There is no private property.
- Work is voluntary without any connection between output and reward because there is no concept of reward.
- Needs are met by taking what is needed from central stores or central distribution facilities.
- Widely considered an intermediate social and political step between Capitalism and Communism.
- Capital isn't necessary because there is no buying, selling, or need for money.
- The old slogan of "from each according to ability, to each according to needs" would apply.

Human nature doesn't understand work without reason. Hunter-gatherers hunted and gathered so they would neither starve nor freeze to death. Human nature invented the question, "What's in it for me?"

Robert Heilbroner (1919-2005) was a prominent American economist and lifelong student of economic philosophy. He authored the second highest-selling economic textbook of all time and was a socialist for most of his adult life. Heilbroner changed his mind when he saw the error of socialist philosophy and the actual failure of socialism in practice.

In 1989 as the Soviet Union was facing collapse, Heilbroner wrote the following in a New Yorker magazine article:

"Less than 75 years after it officially began, the contest between capitalism and socialism is over: capitalism has won...Capitalism organizes the material affairs of humankind more satisfactorily than socialism."

In 1992, Heilbroner wrote in the left-wing American quarterly magazine *Dissent*, that *"capitalism has been as unmistakable a success as socialism has been a failure"* acknowledging the superiority of free markets. Heilbroner observed that *"democratic liberties have not yet appeared, except fleetingly, in any nation that has declared itself to be fundamentally anticapitalist.*"[72]

Heilbroner also wrote that Socialism, defined as a centrally planned economy in which the government controls all means of production—was the tragic failure of the twentieth century. Born of a commitment to remedy the economic and moral defects of capitalism, it has far surpassed capitalism in both economic malfunction and moral cruelty. Yet the idea and the ideal of socialism linger on.

> *"During the 1960s the Soviet Union became the first industrial country in history to suffer a prolonged peacetime fall in average life expectancy, a symptom of its disastrous misallocation of resources. Military research facilities could get whatever they needed, but hospitals were low on the priority list. By the 1970s the figures clearly indicated a slowing of overall production. By the 1980s the Soviet Union officially acknowledged a near end to growth that was, in reality, an unofficial decline. In 1987 the first official law embodying perestroika—restructuring—was put into effect. President Mikhail Gorbachev announced his intention to revamp the economy from top to bottom by introducing the market, reestablishing private ownership, and opening the system to free economic interchange with the West. Seventy years of socialist rise had come to an end."[73]*

Socialism fails because it is foreign to human nature. No horse, dog, or human chooses to work and sweat without some reward. Children don't learn multiplication tables for giggles. People don't serve others unless there is something in it for them. New Creations in Christ willingly serve because the heart of Christ transforms human nature into something more. People take by instinct; they seldom serve by instinct.

---

[72] Richard Heilbroner - Wikipedia

[73] econlib.org/library/Enc/Socialism.html

Communism

"It [Communism] is not new. It is, in fact, man's second oldest faith. Its promise was whispered in the first days of the Creation under the Tree of the Knowledge of Good and Evil: "Ye shall be as gods." Other ages have had great visions. They have always been different versions of the same vision: the vision of God and man's relationship to God. The Communist vision is the vision of Man without God."—Whittaker Chambers, Witness

"Religion is the opium of the people."—Karl Marx, from his personal 1844 journal

If Socialism is an impossible dream, Communism is a nightmare. Some economic and political philosophers consider Communism a more advanced form of Socialism. Only people who deny the existence of evil could think of Communism as smarter Socialism.

Something, or someone, had to enter the equation to wrest the evils of Communism from the ideals of Socialism. That someone was Karl Marx. Marx believed that the value and rights of the individual were always less important than the collective; the group. People existed to serve the group so the group could serve the people. Only self-indulgent human nature can believe that such tortured logic is reasonable. Obviously, whoever defined and controlled the collective became both the throne and the power behind the throne.

Karl Marx (1818-1883) was a disgruntled Socialist who imagined something more. Communism was born in the evil places of Marx's all-too-human heart. Vladimir Lenin (1879-1924) nurtured young Communism and Joseph Stalin (1878-1953) brought it to maturity.

Marx was a privileged and discontented youth turned revolutionary socialist. Lenin was a privileged youth who renounced faith in God at age 16 when his father died. He discovered Marx's *Das Kapital* and became a dissident, translating *The Communist Manifesto* into Russian. Lenin and Stalin were two of the seven founding members of the Politburo founded to manage the 1917 Bolshevic Revolution. Stalin stepped into Lenin's leadership role after his death.

Joseph Stalin's (born Ioseb dze Jughashvili) home life was difficult and dysfunctional. He was a sickly and somewhat disfigured youngster with an abusive alcoholic father. Stalin was educated as a priest, but instead of increased devotion he became an atheist. He was a man with a grudge that festered until he became a monster.

Note on Karl Marx:

In 1859 Marx published *A Contribution to the Critique of Political Economy*, his first serious economic work. This work was intended merely as a preview of his three-volume *Das Kapital,* a critique of capitalism. Marx believed that the only "capital" able to continually produce profit was human capital (labor). Increases in profit must, by definition, exploit workers.

He believed machinery had limited ability to produce anything. Marx predicted the end of capitalism when workers had no more to give and overthrew capitalists, the owners of capital. Wouldn't Karl be surprised to learn the degree to which machines have replaced workers?

Marx believed workers were the backbone of capitalism. Once workers revolted, capitalism would be doomed. Marx was wrong. The power in modern capitalism doesn't belong to the worker class, but squarely in the hands of the consumer class.

Characteristics of Communism

- There is no private ownership. The means and materials of production are owned by the government or an autocratic governing body.
- Work and contribution are required, under duress if necessary.
- Communist revolutions succeed in primarily agrarian societies.
- Communism ushered in the Gulag system of forced labor camps and the Red Terror, a violent campaign against large-scale farmers with land, folks with capital, and the clergy.
- Communism killed millions of the people it professed to represent.

Power for the people is only possible when all power is taken from the people. Under Communism, agreement and consensus is either willingly given or taken by force. Leaders don't care which. Lenin knew he would have to steal the land from tens of millions of peasants who would not willing give it up. Communism endorses government theft, even if it requires the death of resistant property owners.

Lenin tried to seize power by controlling food distribution. Casualties in the millions forced his retreat, but resistance was futile. Stalin was successful in grasping power through his "terror famine," *sending millions of the more affluent peasants (kulaks) to Siberian slave labor camps and starving the rest into submission. The exiled kulaks had been the most advanced farmers, and after becoming state employees, the remaining peasants had little incentive to produce. But the government's quotas drastically increased. The shortage came out of the peasants' bellies. The communists' willingness to wage total war on their own people sets them apart.* – Bryan Caplan[74]

Estimates suggest as many as 100 million people were murdered by Communist regimes in the 20th century. Communist leaders include Joseph Stalin (Russia), Kim Il Sung (North Korea), *Chairman* Mao Zedong (China), Ho Chi Minh (Viet Nam), and Pol Pot (Cambodia.)

Communism suggests that people exist to serve the group, so the group can serve the people. This is the same rationale used by many groups featured in headline news today. The government exists to care for the people. The most affluent people (those with capital) are increasingly expected to feed the government so the government can affirm and feed the people.

Government is also expected to provide cell phones, entertainment, education, transportation, housing, acceptable food, equal outcomes, and safe spaces. Who provides the government with means to give stuff away to the people? The people.

---

[74] econlib.org/library/Enc/Communism.html

Abortion is considered a sacrament of Communism. The Communist Soviet Union offered legal abortions free of charge. Only a fraction of pregnancies were carried to term. The majority ended in abortion with most Soviet women having repeated abortions. Whittaker Chambers' book *Witness* (1952), explains his conversion from Communism to Christianity.

Once pregnant, Chambers and his wife discovered how much they actually wanted children, receiving permission to carry the first to term. Through the miracle of life, on their working farm and in the faces of their children, they discovered what could not exist if Communism was true. They discovered family, love, nature, hope, beauty, and God.

> *[The 20th century] "Is the first century since life began when a decisive part of the most articulate section of mankind has not merely ceased to believe in God, but has deliberately rejected God. At every point, religion and politics interlace ... as the conflict between the two great camps of men – those who reject and those who worship God – becomes irrepressible. The most menacing form of that rejection is Communism."—Whittaker Chambers, Witness*

Whittaker Chambers became a national figure in 1948 when he testified against Alger Hiss (1904-1996.) Hiss was a high-ranking Communist Party operative and high-ranking US State Department official who attended the Yalta Conference[75] (1945) as an adviser to Franklin Roosevelt and later served as temporary secretary-general of the United Nations. Richard Nixon, a little-known Congressman from California, bucked the system to investigate Hiss. Nixon was elected Vice-President of the United States in 1952 and President in 1968.

---

[75] Franklin D. Roosevelt, Winston Churchill, and Joseph Stalin made important decisions at Yalta about the future progress of the war and the postwar world.

"Throughout the most trying phase of the Case, Nixon and his family, and sometimes his parents, were at our farm, encouraging me and comforting my family. My children have caught him lovingly in a nickname. To them, he is always "Nixie," the kind and the good, about whom they will tolerate no nonsense."—Witness

The United States has a long and colorful history of Communism. The opium of religion is being replaced with the opium of Communism. Communists infiltrated the highest levels of government, academia, and the media in the mid-20th century. Communists, both active and "sleeping", were rampant in Washington D.C. and in all likelihood still are today. Let's begin in the White house.

Frank Marshall Davis (1905-1987)

Frank Marshall Davis has been described as a card-carrying member of Communist Party USA (CPUSA). He edited and wrote for Party-line publications such as the Chicago Star and the Honolulu Record.

The federal government certainly took notice. In December 1956, the Democrats who ran the Senate Judiciary Committee summoned Davis to Washington to testify on his activities. He pleaded the Fifth Amendment. No matter, the next year, the Democratic Senate, in a report revealingly titled, "Scope of Soviet Activity in the United States," publicly listed Davis as "an identified member of the Communist Party."

Davis insisted that anti-Communism was un-Christian and nothing more than veiled racism and fascism. In Chicago in April 1948, Vernon Jarrett and Davis put their minds together for the Packing-House Committee and their pens to joint service defending Chicago's oppressed proletariat. "The duty of this Committee," declared their statement "is to give publicity to…the plight of the workers."

Today, their political heirs put their minds to joint service at 1600 Pennsylvania Avenue. In 1983, Jarrett's son, Dr. William Robert

Jarrett, married a young woman named Valerie Bowman. Valerie Bowman became Valerie Jarrett, who today is Barack Obama's top adviser.

Robert Taylor was the first African American head of the Chicago Housing Authority. He also appears in the major 1944 congressional report "Investigation of Un-American Propaganda Activities in the United States." Taylor was the maternal grandfather of Valerie Jarrett.

Barack Obama acknowledged Davis' influence in his book *Dreams from my Father*. Frank is a recurring part of Obama's life and mind by Obama's own extended recounting. From Hawaii—the site of visits and late evenings together—to Los Angeles to Chicago to Germany to Africa; from adolescence to college to community organizing, Davis was always one of the few (and first) names mentioned by Obama at each mile-marker on his historic path from Hawaii to Washington DC. When Davis is not physically there, Obama literally imagines him—pictures him there, visualizes him.[76]

Communism is brutal. Communism is punitive. Communism is evil. Communists are smart. They blend in and have great patience. Communists don't carry protest signs and wear funky t-shirts. Communism exists to change the world. Communism exists to deny God's existence. Communism is an invention of Not God. The genesis of Communism was born in the Garden of Eden.

The mechanics of Communism that worked in the early 20th century won't work in the 21st, but there is still a desire for some economic system other than what exists. Dispossessed and disenchanted members of society continue to yearn for something that makes them feel relevant, special, and equal to every other member of society.

Children and young adults now expect the state (whether a collective or federal government) to care for their needs without demanding much in return. The link between obedience and security is being built from the bottom up; from preschool to law

[76] spectator.org/articles/34799/dreams-frank-marshall-davis

school. People look to governments for food, shelter, education, work, security, and entertainment. Everything is provided in return for your obedience.

Religion is no longer the opium of the people as Marx concluded. The plan today is to legalize opium itself. Anything that appears to define or set limits smacks of God and is considered foolish, discriminatory, intolerant, or just plain evil.

Of the 20th century Whittaker Chambers (Witness) concludes, "If it [Communism] fails, this will be the century of the great social wars. If it succeeds, this will be the century of the great wars of faith." There are two doors to eternity. One opens through relationship with God. The other opens by simple human nature that longs to believe that "Ye shall be as Gods."

Distributism

G.K. Chesterton, the Apostle of Common Sense, introduced me to the economic model of Distributism. I studied economics in college and lived out the truths and applications as both employee and employer. Distributism was never mentioned. Chesterton believed that while God has limitless capabilities, man has limited abilities in terms of creation. As such, man therefore is entitled to own property and to treat it as he sees fit.

> *"Property is merely the art of the democracy. It means that every man should have something that he can shape in his own image, as he is shaped in the image of heaven. But because he is not God, his self-expression must deal with limits; properly with limits that are strict and even small."* *Chesterton summed up his distributist views in the phrase "Three acres and a cow".* [77]

Distributism appeared on the economic scene on the heels of Socialism and Communism. Socialism is an impossible ideal and Communism plays on human nature to the detriment of humans.

---

[77] Wikipedia - Distributism

Distributism attempts to recognize and reward what is best about human nature rather than exploiting the darker side of human nature toward ultimately dark purposes. Simply put, Capitalists, Socialists, and Communists love the darkness, while Distributists attempt to cast a broad light on as many as will look on it. Distributists understand that no one can serve two masters.

Characteristics of Distributism:

- The possibility of property ownership is an inalienable right conferred by a Creator.
- The capacity and means of production should be widely distributed with little, if any, centralized state control.
- The emphasis is to produce for oneself, not work for wages.
- Promotes local controls and independent communities.
- Effort expended is directly proportionate to rewards generated.

Distributism has often been described in opposition to both Socialism and Capitalism, which Distributists see as equally flawed and exploitive. In contrast, "distributism seeks to subordinate economic activity to human life as a whole, to our spiritual life, our intellectual life, our family life."[78]

Capitalists and Distributists both recognize the existence of others who produce the same thing they do. Capitalists call such entities competitors. Distributists tend to see them as brothers. Everyone understands that both Coca-Cola and PepsiCo seek to attract market share from the other. Millions, if not billions, of dollars are spent for no other purpose than to tempt Pepsi drinkers to Coke or Coke drinkers to Pepsi. This is a huge simplification of capitalist competition, but you get the idea.

Farmers traditionally regarded one another as friends or colleagues, not competitors. Barn raisings, harvests, and combines worked one field after another without competitive concerns. Farm families helped one another when tragedy befell a neighbor.

[78] Thomas Storck quote - Wikipedia

"The church ahead will either concentrate on a business view or seek to answer the question, 'What does God want us to do now?'"—John Tielepape, Director of Missions for Parker Baptist Association 79

Most churches today consider other churches as competition. Each seeks to draw as many bodies and pocketbooks to its congregation as possible. Congregations try to expand market share by offering something the church down the street doesn't. Most modern churches are ideological Capitalists, seeking growth purely for growth's sake.

Around the start of the 20th century, Catholics [writers] G. K. Chesterton[80] and Hilaire Belloc[81] drew together the disparate experiences of the various cooperatives and friendly societies in Northern England, Ireland, and Northern Europe into a coherent political ideology which specifically advocated widespread private ownership of housing and control of industry through owner-operated small businesses and worker-controlled cooperatives. In the United States in the 1930s, Distributism was treated in numerous essays by Chesterton, Belloc and others in "The American Review."

Although a majority of distributism's later supporters were not Catholics and many were in fact former radical socialists who had become disillusioned with socialism, distributist thought was adopted by those concerned with promoting localized and independent communities, challenging the establishment position, but from a perspective of renovation, not revolution; seeing themselves as trying to restore the traditional liberties of England and

---

[79] Quote used with permission noted during an interview by author Lynn Baber

[80] G.K. Chesterton (1874-1936) British novelist, journalist, Catholic and Christian apologist.

[81] Hilaire Belloc (1870-1953) French/British writer, historian, political activist and staunch Catholic.

Lynn Baber

her people which had been taken away from them, amongst other things, since the Industrial Revolution.

Much of Dorothy L. Sayers's writings on social and economic matters have affinity with distributism. She may have been influenced by them, or have come to similar conclusions on her own; as an Anglican (Protestant), the reasoning she gave are rooted in the theologies of Creation and Incarnation, and thus are slightly different from the Catholic Chesterton and Belloc. —Wikipedia

Distributism encourages people to support themselves without outside investors or reliance on non-ownership employees. Entrepreneurs or families who built businesses from the ground up might be considered Distributists. Larger businesses are possible when talents, property, and equipment is combined by families, partners, or communities with shared ownership.

Capitalism isn't the natural or proper economic and political system one should expect based on God's Word. It uses capital to accumulate more capital based on the work of wage-laborers with no ownership in the enterprise. Profits (additional capital) accrue only to the owner(s) of the capital. Someone with a big bank account can establish a big business with nothing more than cash and an idea. No expertise or personal (non-capital) assets are necessary. The goal is to use money to make more money, then use it to make even more money.

Wealth accumulation is not necessarily synonymous with capital accumulation. Abraham, for instance, was a very rich man with what amounts to a family collective. Abraham didn't seek venture capitalists; he ordered his flocks and households to produce enough for all. As the collective grew, so did the size of the flocks and the relative responsibilities of those in the collective.

Moneychangers were an early example of Capitalism. Money alone was used to make more money which in turn was used to make even more money. The system in place wasn't true Capitalism, but there have long been smaller segments of different economic and social systems within larger ones.

Jesus told His disciples not to store up earthly treasures but treasure in heaven. *"For where your treasure is, there your heart will be also."*[82] Jesus and the apostles taught against the error of capital accumulation on many occasions.

> *"Now godliness with contentment is great gain. For we brought nothing into this world, and it is certain we can carry nothing out. And having food and clothing, with these we shall be content. But those who desire to be rich fall into temptation and a snare, and into many foolish and harmful lusts which drown men in destruction and perdition. For the love of money is a root of all kinds of evil, for which some have strayed from the faith in their greediness, and pierced themselves through with many sorrows."—1 Timothy 6:6-10*

> *Jesus said, "Take heed and beware of covetousness, for one's life does not consist in the abundance of the things he possesses."—Luke 12:15*

Capitalists do not serve God in the pursuit of capital accumulation. Workers with no options other than being wage-laborers regularly face temptation. No one can serve two masters (Matthew 6:24.) When family and employer needs compete, wage laborers are forced to choose which takes precedence.

Socialism is built on common ownership. Nothing is owned and labor is optional. Socialism always fails because human nature takes all it can and gives only what it must.

Distributism seems to fit the parameters of societies more closely aligned to God's order. Husbands are more committed to wives who have borne them children. People are more committed to being good stewards over land, livestock, and other personal assets they rely on to support themselves and their families.

The only illustration necessary to prove the point is the difference between a rented house and one owned by the occupants. People

---

[82] Matthew 6:19-24

use and often abuse that which they rent. Care of the object is the problem of the owner. Paying the price to hire the use of an object is the only responsibility most folks feel. Many renters resent the capitalists who own the homes and feel justified in treating them without care. Capitalist relationships are based on money. I pay you to work. You pay someone else to help you work for me. Hired employees are seldom treasured by the employer. If a wage earner gets used up, someone else will step in. Wage earners can be "owned" by the wage payer.

The flip side is also true. If a capitalist buys a machine he doesn't know how to operate, he hires an experienced operator. Unless there are hordes of such operators around every corner, the capitalist may be "owned" by the wage earner.

Distributism endorses the idea of everyone having skin in the game. Marriage is a commitment that binds a man and wife together. Ownership of one's property and means of service or production binds society and family together in ways that Capitalism does not.

Evaluate your economic ideology by God's Word, which is quite specific:

- Treat others as you would be treated (Matthew 7:12)
- Work hard to support yourself (1 Timothy 5:8, 2 Thessalonians 3:10)
- Surplus goods are to be shared with others (Ephesians 4:28)
- Give cheerfully and as led by the spirit (2 Corinthians 9:7)
- Give in secret (Matthew 6:3-4)

The goal for followers of Christ is, *To seek first the kingdom of God.* (Matthew 6:33) How will you choose your door to eternity?

"Give, and it will be given to you: good measure, pressed down, shaken together, and running over will be put into your bosom. For with the same measure that you use, it will be measured back to you."—Luke 6:38

Decline of Currency

ω

"She planted that terror of debt so deeply in her children that even now, in a changed economic pattern where indebtedness is a part of living, I become restless when a bill is two days overdue. A thing bought on time was a thing you did not own and for which you were in debt."—John Steinbeck, East of Eden

Capitalism separates the labor of wage earners from ownership. Over time, the linkage between man, property, and production weakened, resulting in mobile workers; parents and grown children who haven't lived in the same state since graduation with loyalty that only lasts until a better offer arrives. Mobile workers move from state to state, community to community, and house to house. The ties that bind become fewer and more tenuous.

Marriages often end when one wage earner gets a new job in another location. Little today has lasting value because people have been conditioned to think in terms of take-home pay. When families lived above the shop or on their own producing land, relationships were deep, lasting, and society was blessed. Extended family lived and worked together.

How did we get to the point where it is nearly impossible to communicate value, cause and effect, accountability or responsibility? What led to the disparity between the ways one group lives compared to others? Why do the rich get richer and the poor poorer? Why can't anyone figure out how to straighten things out?

Relationships between labor, buying power, and cash are nearly severed. The result is economic, social, and political chaos. Socialism promises you everything you need without requiring anything in exchange. Little wonder socialism is trying to claw its way out of the grave in the 21st century.

189

Consider the relationship between money and labor. The connection is obvious to generations born before 1965 but may be nebulous or nonexistent to younger folk. Family units were largely self-sustaining until more complex societies developed.

Hunting or gathering met the needs of the individual or group. There was no 7-11 on the corner selling meat, spears, hides, or berries. If you wanted something you had to go out and get it. Division of labor within families or clans was made to benefit the whole. This arrangement still exists in parts of the non-industrialized world.

Trade, barter, and the exchange of goods and services began when one human community began to interact with others. Perhaps a traveler traded dried fish for your wool. You may have exchanged tools with some nomad in order for you both to expand the options in your toolboxes.

Transactions or exchanges were easily managed when the owner of the assets involved knew the value of each item and dealt accordingly. As time passed, the exchange of assets grew a bit more complex.

The concept of value matured, and money became the norm. Trade wasn't simply a horse for a cart, but the exchange of goods or labor for currency with no value other than value. Early exceptions included salt or precious metals that had utility apart from establishing baseline value among different peoples and nations.

The link between currency and labor was firm. Throughout the majority of human history men and women worked as many hours as necessary to obtain the minimal necessities of life. If their labor was more valuable, they had the option to accumulate more stuff or work less. The connection was fairly direct and well understood by everyone.

Wage workers received credit at retailers (often the company store) or cash for labor until the introduction of the paycheck. The regular use of checks began in the 18th century. Workers traded their effort and expertise for a paycheck. The number on the paycheck represented spendable money once it was deposited in a bank or exchanged for the real stuff. The link between currency and labor remained strong.

No one had money to spend unless it was in his pocket or he could borrow a bit from a friend or family member. If you only had three dollar bills with a week left before payday, you knew you had to make the three bucks last. Budgeting wasn't optional in the good old days; it was a necessity.

Checking Accounts

Along with many other major transitions, consumer direct demand or checking accounts became popular in the late 19th century. The first fully printed banknotes, precursors of the modern printed check, were issued by the Bank of England in 1853.

In 1862, California allowed women, whether married or not, to open their own individual checking accounts for the first time. The use of personal checking accounts increased on a national level as the 19th century gave way to the 20th. The number of checking accounts in the USA doubled between 1939 and 1952. The first ATM (automated teller machine) was installed in suburban Columbus, OH in 1959. Congress approved the (1978) Electronic Funds Transfer Act in 1979, and by 2014 nearly 90% of all households used checking accounts.[83]

The days of receiving payment in hard cash at the end of each day or week ended with the advent of the paycheck. Payday morphed from cash in hand to receiving a negotiable instrument that could be either cashed or deposited.

Electronic Funds Transfer

Within twenty years of Congress approving Electronic Funds Transfer (EFT), paychecks started moving from pay envelopes to direct deposit. Cash and checks evolved into entries on a monthly bank statement. Employers provided pay stubs; employees entered the amount in a check register and wrote checks against it.

---

[83] banks.com/articles/history-checking-account#sthash.Sy8tnFGY.dpuf

The connection between currency and labor began to blur. Pulling cash from pocket or purse and counting out bills and coins to pay the grocer or service station attendant made spending more painful than writing a check. *Empty pockets* no longer meant pockets without cash, but check registers reflecting tiny or negative balances. The pain of writing *one hundred* on a check isn't nearly as great as pulling 100 dollars in cash from your pocket. Writing a check for $10.00 or $100.00 is the same procedure except for the infinitesimal amount of ink necessary to add one extra zero and four extra letters (*ten* vs *hundred*). The check itself is exactly the same.

Dawn of Charge Cards

Fast forward a few years. Charge cards first entered the scene in the 1940s and 50s requiring payment in full each month. The Bank of American offered the first modern credit card in 1966. The link between labor and currency value was vaporizing.

How many hours of work are required to buy a Big Mac, fries, and a large Coke? How much was the bill the last time you treated the grandchildren to lunch? How many hours did you have to work to buy your athletic shoes? Few people know the answer to those questions because they paid the bill with a credit card. It doesn't matter if they only have three dollars in their checking account with a week left before the next paycheck is transmitted for deposit. If they overspend, the difference is automatically covered by new debt.

Remember years ago when food stamps were made of real paper distributed in books? Buying $12.00 of food with stamps meant you had to tear out enough stamps to equal $12.00. Empty stamp books bought nothing. People learned to budget their stamps to save enough for basics like bread and milk.

Launched in 1999, the American Express Centurion Card is the most exclusive credit card in the world. The full details of how one becomes a cardholder aren't public but include being an American Express Platinum cardholder for over one year and charging at least $250,000 during that time. The Black Card is by invitation only, comes with an initial fee of $5,000 and annual dues of $2,500.

Electronic Benefits Transfer

Electronic Benefits Transfer (EBT) is a system allowing recipients to authorize transfer of government benefits from a Federal account to a retailer account to pay for purchases. EBT is used in all 50 States, the District of Columbia, Puerto Rico, the Virgin Islands, and Guam. EBT has been implemented in all States since June of 2004.[84]

What do EBT cards, credit cards, gift cards, and the Black American Express Centurion card have in common? What could food stamps, welfare, and the exclusive Centurion Card possibly have in common? All are plastic cards of the same size with access to electronic funds transfer or transaction capability. Only the card design differs, as well as the source of funding. The first delivers government benefits to individuals while the latter is a limitless charge card.

SNAP EBT cards look like any other gift or credit card. Welfare plastic looks the same as personal plastic. Plastic cards representing extraordinary wealth look just like plastic cards that represent no wealth at all. The link between labor and value is nearly gone. Using a plastic EBT card requires no labor output at all. Little children cannot process the difference between the little piece of plastic that buys one person a boatload of great stuff and the piece of plastic Mom says limits their family to the basics.

Little wonder protests over unequal outcomes and social disgruntlement are getting louder. The direct link between labor and purchasing power is gone. Folks are peeved.

Children No Longer Understand Value

Recently I met a lady who wrote math curriculum for kids entering elementary school. I peppered her with questions because I couldn't figure out why someone had to work so hard when there are plenty of textbooks available. The answer she gave was totally unexpected.

---

[84] fns.usda.gov

Few children starting school today understand the concept of value. When I was a kid everyone knew how many pennies made a nickel; how many nickels a dime; how two dimes and a nickel made a quarter; and how much change was needed to get a dollar bill. Not many children or adults know how to make change today. Transactions are made with plastic and everyone's plastic pretty much looks the same.

The relationship between labor and purchasing power is either skewed or extinct. Why should folks get a job and WORK when they can get their own piece of plastic from the government for free? Why would children raised in welfare homes look for gainful employment? In many areas, working is the exception and not the rule. Not working is a completely rational choice in the 21st century.

In centuries past able-bodied people worked to feed themselves and their family. Today, housing, food, cell phones, education, and other goods and services are not labor dependent, they are plastic dependent.

Socialist Plastic

Plastic cards are socialist in nature; everyone gets one and nothing is required in exchange for purchasing power. For many people the linkage between the choices we make today and eternity is just as blurry as the link between labor and the ability to obtain goods and services. Trying to convince someone who has no need that work is a blessing is an uphill battle. Logic asks "Why?"

People enjoying the bloom of early stages of Socialism are thrilled to get without having to give. Human nature loves to receive! Trying to convince satisfied and comfortable people that they need a Savior is also an uphill battle. Human reason rightly asks "Why?"

Human nature opens one door to eternity. Which door do you plan to open?

Education

ω

"Intellectual curiosity will not take us one inch inside moral problems, but immediately we obey [God] in the tiniest matter, instantly we see."—Oswald Chambers, My Utmost for His Highest

"Christians in modernity thought their task was to make the Gospel intelligible to the world rather than to help the world understand why it could not be intelligible without the Gospel."—Stanley Hauerwas, Sanctify them in the Truth: Holiness Exemplified

Etymologists may study butterflies for a lifetime, but no amount of committed study will ever transform an academic into a butterfly. Biblical scholarship is not faith. A man may study Jesus Christ for a lifetime yet never truly meet Him. However, one cannot be a student of the Bible if one cannot read the words and understand what the words mean.

Public education in the United States originated as a means to teach children how to read and understand their Bible. In 1647 the General Court of the Massachusetts Bay Colony ordered every town with 50 families to establish an elementary school and every town of 100 families to provide a Latin school. The goal of this first New World school system was to teach Puritan children to read the Bible for themselves.

Secularists insist that the wall of separation between church and state extends to the schoolhouse. Re-history (changing history to suit those with the power to do so) suggests that God, prayer, Biblical instruction, and the Ten Commandments were introduced into public schools by accident or evil design.

Secularists believe that schools returned to their true intent in the 20th century; teaching children to see the world intellectually and not from the distorted view of religion. Yet, there is no doubt that

Christianity was the major player in founding institutions of higher learning in the United States.

> *"Education in Religion was central to our Founders: Benjamin Rush signer of the Declaration of Independence wrote, "...the only foundation for a useful education in a republic is to be laid in religion. Without this, there can be no virtue, and without virtue there can be no liberty, and liberty is the object and life of all republican governments." The type of education that shaped our Founders character and ideas was thoroughly Christian. It imparted Christian character and produced honest, industrious, compassionate, respectful, and law-abiding men. It imparted a Biblical world-view and produced people who were principled thinkers."—April Shenendoah85*

Harvard

Harvard College is now an ivy-covered bastion of liberal academia. Established in 1636, Harvard required students to obey eight "Rules and Precepts."[86] Rule 2 was quite specific:

"Let every Student be plainly instructed, and earnestly pressed to consider well, the maine end of his life and studies is, to know God and Jesus Christ which is eternal! life, John 17:3 and therefore to lay Christ in the bottome, as the only foundation of all sound knowledge and Learning. And seeing the Lord only giveth wisedome, Let every one seriously set himself by prayer in secret to seeke it of him Prov. 2, 3."

William and Mary

Chartered by English King William III and Queen Mary II in 1693, the foundation for the College of William and Mary was laid in 1695, offering a grammar school, divinity school, school of

---

[85] tysknews.com/Depts/Educate/history_part3.htm

[86] bible-history.com/quotes/harvard_university_1.html

philosophy, and a school for the education and conversion of native Indian boys to Christianity.

Yale

Yale University traces its roots to the 1640s. In 1701 the charter was granted for a school "wherein Youth may be instructed in the Arts and Sciences (and) through the blessing of Almighty God may be fitted for Publick employment both in Church and Civil State." (yale.edu)

For more on the founding of Ivy League schools, refer back to *History of the Christian Church.* 1859 was a pivotal year in academic advancement in the United States of America.

Post-secondary Schools founded or opened in 1859:

- The University of Michigan Law School
- The Cooper Union for the Advancement of Science and Art - New York
- Valparaiso Male and Female College–Indiana
- Medical College of Alabama
- Northwestern (Lind) University School of Medicine–Chicago
- St. John Academy (Catholic)–Indianapolis
- Stanford (University of the Pacific) School of Medicine–California
- Auburn University (East Alabama Male College)
- South Carolina School for the Deaf and Blind
- Michigan School for the Blind
- Berea College (racially integrated)–OH
- Manhattan College–NY
- Maryland Agricultural College
- Rutgers College–New Jersey
- Southern Baptist Theological Seminary–Kentucky
- Medical College Virginia, 1859/60
- Lenox College–Iowa

- Adrian College (Christian, antislavery and women's rights)–Michigan
- Humboldt Medical College–St. Louis, MO
- University of Illinois College of Pharmacy
- Wheaton College (founded by abolitionists)–Illinois
- Amherst College Department of Hygiene and Physical Education (first Department of Physical Education in an American college)–Massachusetts
- Whitman College (founded as a seminary)–Washington state
- Trinity College (upon affiliation with Methodist Church)–North Carolina
- University of Toronto–Canada
- Luther College (Norwegian Lutheran)–Saint Louis, MO
- Pontifical North American College (to train Catholic clergy)–New York

Educators in the 21st century believe education is the panacea for every ill the same way government believes government is the cure for every societal imbalance. The more established any human institution becomes, the less effective its actions. Failed education adds more of the same, yet somehow expects a different result. Einstein defined insanity in precisely those terms.

Education demands more education when enough students fail or enough parents complain. Government adds more government when enough systems fail or enough citizens complain.

3 Truths Educators don't know or don't believe:

1. You get more of what you reward and less of what you punish.
2. Punishment never made a kid smarter, stronger, or healthier.
3. Education provides ability, not motivation.

Children who identify with peers who skip school, harass teachers, and ignore authority figures will also begin to skip school, harass teachers, and ignore authority figures. Simply throwing more tax dollars at the problem won't fix it. Adding more money (fuel) to an educational system already going down in flames makes it burn hotter, not smarter.

Children devote time, attention, and study to what they think is valuable or relevant. For most that means music, fashion, and improving proficiency with social media and video games. Study habits, good character, and productivity must first exist within a person before he or she begins to value them.

> *"While they promise them liberty, they themselves are slaves of corruption; for by whom a person is overcome, by him also he is brought into bondage."—2 Peter 2:19*

Education Does Not Create Habits

Consistent practice and repetition create habits. Unless children show up and consistently practice correct behaviors positive habits will not develop. Kids must be required to attend school. Parents must be accountable for their attendance. Once kids show up, educators must apply effective motivation to entice participation. Children without discipline, respect for authority, or willingness to go along must be required to tear down old habits and build new ones.

Quantifying Education Success

You can't define or measure anything without objective standards. Educators police themselves. The government evaluates itself. Both claim objective measures like unemployment statistics, poverty rates, graduation rates and student test scores. Each is number defined, adjustable, and judged subjectively. Subjectivity is not a firm foundation for objective measurement.

What could possibly go wrong in a closed system where only those in the system determine success?

Government statisticians routinely manipulate data, formulas, and restate performance results. So do educators. Oft times they are one and the same. A single keystroke alters one's body score from obese to normal, one's economic status from middle-class to poverty, and one's faith from religious freedom to hate speech.

Kids used to learn to read, calculate, write, and communicate coherently as well as basic life skills like relationship, agriculture, and history. Kids today don't know where hamburger comes from or how to grow a carrot. They rely on batteries to read, calculate, write, and communicate. Basic skills of relationship, agriculture, and history no longer appear in most public-school curricula.

Educational and governmental institutions teach children that personal failure is the result of victimization. I don't disagree. Children are victims—of education and government institutions with bloated budgets working tirelessly to separate the innocent from faith and family.

> "In a word, we may reasonably hope for the virtual abolition of education when 'I'm as good as you' has fully had its way. All incentives to learn and all penalties for not learning will vanish. The few who might want to learn will be prevented; who are they to overtop their fellows? And anyway the teachers--or should I say, nurses?--will be far too busy reassuring the dunces and patting them on the back to waste any time on real teaching. We shall no longer have to plan and toil to spread imperturbable conceit and incurable ignorance among men. The little vermin themselves will do it for us." —C.S. Lewis, The Screwtape Letters (1941)

Evaluating Teacher Proficiency

It is imperative that teachers distinguish the student who is unable to learn from one who is unwilling to learn. Three-year olds understands the difference between "I can't" and "I won't," yet the distinction appears to elude most educators.

Punishing inability is abuse. Using a heavy stick to rap the tender knuckles of a first grader will not improve his testing performance. Failure to motivate unwillingness guarantees failure. Not only does the unwilling student fail to learn what the educational systems promised, but he is rewarded for his unwillingness to learn. What does that teach the unwilling kid? It proves the educational system is either punitive or ignorant and reinforces his decision to ignore or resist future teaching efforts.

It also suggests that the Word of God is not true when it states that standards exist and there are consequences for unwillingness. Do you get more grace the more you sin? Paul says no. James says no. God says no.

Kids today easily recite the hottest lyrics. They remember minute details from the Kardashian Twitter feed. They know the celebrities their friends know, what styles are popular and where to get a tattoo. Kids know how to organize social activities, even if many are flash mob or protest events. Advertising executives would love to achieve the same level of success kids do when promoting events.

Kids are wily and smart. Educators should take a page out of the teen and preteen playbooks. They might learn something useful. Many teens today have skills to manipulate, promote, obfuscate, and confuse that Cold War era KGB brass might admire. Students of every age out-maneuver educators at every turn.

> *"Train up a child in the way he should go, and when he is old he will not depart from it."—Proverbs 22:6*

You get more of what you reward. Institutions of higher learning and government are no exception. Since they insist on doing more of the same, why should we believe they aren't getting precisely the results they want?

> *"As educators we should always be able to debate our profession. The problem we have, as does anything that involves politics, is that we cannot seem to move forward together. There are state and national leaders so consumed with being right that they cannot, and will not, budge."—Peter DeWitt, Education Week, January 2014*

Isn't it curious how students of yesteryear learned far more advanced material than students today? Technology in the 17th, 18th, and 19th centuries was pretty much limited to being present for lectures and studying printed or written words. They had candles and writing materials. Why were educators and students far more successful in centuries past than they are now?

Questions from an 1895 exam for eighth graders:

1. Name the Parts of Speech and define those that have no modifications.
2. What are the Principal Parts of a verb? Give Principal Parts of do, lie, lay and run.
3. What is the cost of a square farm at $15 per acre, the distance around which is 640 rods?
4. Give the epochs into which U.S. History is divided.
5. Describe three of the most prominent battles of the Rebellion.
6. What is meant by the following: Alphabet, phonetic orthography, etymology, syllabication?
7. Give two rules for spelling words with final 'e'. Name two exceptions under each rule.
8. Name all the republics of Europe and give capital of each.
9. What is climate? Upon what does climate depend?

Six questions from an 1870s teacher's college test:

1. Define and give the etymology of verb, pronoun, conjunction and adverb. Give example of a defective, an auxillary, an impersonal and a redundant verb. How many kinds of pronouns are there? Give examples of each.
2. Define metonymy, catachresis, and hyberbole; and state the difference between a metaphor and a simile.
3. Write a word containing a diphthong, one containing a digraph, and one containing a trigraph.
4. What effect has multiplying both terms of a fraction by the same number, and why; and why in dividing one fraction by another do you invert the divisor and multiply the terms together?
5. Why do we reckon 180 degrees of longitude and only 90 of latitude?

6. Through what waters would a ship pass in going from Duluth to Odessa?

American colleges and universities were largely founded to teach God's Word and promote Christian values and truths. Standards were established and upheld. Today the very idea of standards is intolerant and upholding anything is judgmental. Why? Because God's Word is not permitted in school.

Children don't have time to study. They have too many social engagements, athletic commitments, social media or entertainment obligations. Children who aren't completely scheduled usually have the opposite situation; no one is home. No one monitors what they do. No one asks about school. No one cares.

"But whoever causes one of these little ones who believe in Me to stumble, it would be better for him if a millstone were hung around his neck, and he were thrown into the sea."— Mark 9:42

Who is responsible for teaching children? Their parents; unless you live in a western culture that insists it takes a village to raise a child. That means child-rearing by committee which is, in essence, socialistic childcare. That means no one is in charge and no one has to take the blame for failure. Such folks won't recognize or desire a heavenly Father who notices all and keeps perfect records.

Families used to teach new generations important stuff like:

- How to grow food
- How to care for children
- Not to get drunk, steal, or lie
- Not to play with matches
- Not to poke bears or tease dogs

But then, perhaps these lessons are simply no longer practical. When families lived above the shop and operated farms and small production shops children needed to be useful. Today children aspire to larger wages. Others will simply apply for plastic cards offering purchasing power and access to services.

Few children of the most recent generations were educated by their families. Government regulators and regulations raise most kids today.

Governmental funding drives most of the information students receive from:

- Schools
- Programs
- Entitlements
- Public service messages
- Advertising
- Enforcement of regulations

Perhaps mathematics, language, and science aren't really that important. What appears to be of greatest significance is how students feel, how tolerant they are of diversity, and how quickly they swallow anything spewed by those in authority.

Indeed, what's the point of teaching facts and standards when many educators consider facts and standards inherently divisive? Institutions of higher education issue impossibly restrictive laws in the name of freedom and liberty when in fact they shackle the intellect, sense, and behaviors of all who submit to their servitude. Gender specific pronouns are gradually being phased out along with gender specific bathrooms.

> *"A Nebraska school district has instructed its teachers to stop referring to students by "gendered expressions" such as "boys and girls," and use "gender inclusive" ones such as "purple penguins" instead. Furthermore, it instructs teachers to interfere and interrupt if they ever hear a student talking about gender in terms of "boys and girls" so the student can learn that this is wrong.*

> *"We don't get involved with gender preferences. We're educating all kids . . . and we can't be judgmental,"*

[Superintendent Steve Joel] said."–Katherine Timpf, NationalReview.com,[87] October 2014

What have children learned once they identify as purple penguins and not boys and girls? Public education teaches children to be gender neutral, that dinosaurs evolved and roamed the earth millions and millions of years ago, that having two mommies or two daddies is normal, and that global warming is starving the polar bears. Sadly, science has yet to prove anything based on morals or faith.

What are children really learning? That God does not exist. That He did not create the earth. That the Bible is a judgmental fairy tale. Education has fallen into the deluded mire of human nature. What are your children learning? How will they know which door to eternity is the right one?

---

[87].nationalreview.com/article/389862/school-told-call-kids-purple-penguins-because-boys-and-girls-not-inclusive

Evolution

ω

"[G.K.] Chesterton argued that it would have been more productive to discover 'what is actually known about the variation of species and what can only plausibly be guessed and what is quite random guesswork', but 'the Darwinians advanced it with so sweeping and hasty an intolerance that it is no longer a question of one scientific theory being advanced against another scientific theory. ... It is treated as an answer; and a final and infallible answer.'"[88]

The Big Bang Theory is accepted by most in the scientific community. It is also thought probable by most Bible believers. Agreement is limited, however, to the notion that a Big Bang occurred at some point in history. After that, ways part dramatically. Curiously, the Big Bang is a more logical explanation for the physical beginnings of the universe for Creationists than Evolutionists.

The Big Bang Theory suggests that all matter came into being in an instant when a really dense point exploded. BOOM! (Tick-tock.) The universe was born, grew, and matured in the twinkling of an eye. Did space and time exist prior to the big bang?

Astrophysicists Steven Hawking, George Ellis, and Roger Penrose all say no. Their calculations lead them to believe that time and space had a definite beginning and that beginning corresponds directly with the big bang. In other words, the big bang was the beginning of everything.

"Natura non facit saltum" is Latin for "Nature does not make a jump." Aristotle accepted this as fact. No newer or more plausible theory has yet been suggested. Curiously, the Big Bang Theory flies in direct opposition to *"natura non facit saltum."* There is no bigger

---

[88]creation.com/gk-chesterton-darwinism-is-an-attack-upon-thought-itself

jump possible than fielding an entire universe in the blink of an eye. From nothing to everything in *tick tock.*

> *The principle of "Nature non facit saltum" expresses the idea that natural things and properties change gradually, rather than suddenly. In the biological context, the principle was used by Charles Darwin and others to defend the evolutionary postulate that all species develop from earlier species through gradual and minute changes rather than through the sudden emergence of new forms.* - Wikipedia

If natural things and properties change gradually, how did the universe appear in a moment? Does that mean the universe is outside of nature and the principles accepted by most scientists?

If species evolve through gradual and minute changes, why did most creatures appear in a very short period of time (the Cambrian period) with no evidence of precursors? Fossil evidence directly contradicts the theory it purportedly proves. Early animal phyla representing all subsequent body types appeared at roughly the same time. Nothing led up to the explosion and it was never repeated. Whatever types of critters didn't exist prior to the Cambrian period were there at the end.

> *"The rapid diversification of lifeforms in the Cambrian, known as the Cambrian explosion, produced the first representatives of all modern animal phyla."—Wikipedia*

Darwin's theory on the origin of life rests on the principle that nature does not jump. Either nature made a huge leap in the Cambrian Period in opposition to Darwin's theory or his theory is wrong.

If nature does not jump, evolutionary theory is pretty much toast. You can't successfully argue against religion based on faith when Evolution is a religion based on the same thing; faith that there is a yet undiscovered fossil graveyard holding all the missing links between amoeba and ape, monocell and monkey, bacteria and brontosaurus. Little complications like the absence of a supporting fossil record aren't sufficient to dampen the faith of true believers in Evolution.

Does nature jump? God's Word addresses the question in Job 11:12. "For an empty-headed man will be wise, when a wild donkey's colt is born a man."

The universe apparently didn't evolve but came into being when a cosmic switch was flipped. Think of a huge football stadium standing empty in the pitch dark. When the master switch is thrown massive banks of lights create instant brilliance until the entire stadium is ready for action. The Big Bang stands apart from the norms of nature (*natura non facit saltum*) but is a perfect explanation of how the first light switch may have been thrown by the Master Illuminator. "*Let there be light.*" (Genesis 1:3) That was one powerful switch!

Speaking of the Big Bang, is the universe (1) expanding, (2) contracting, or (3) is it reassuringly stable and steady? The answer depends on which astrophysicist you ask. I guess that means we really don't know. Settled science apparently exempts the formation of the universe from other accepted scientific principles in the same way evolution is exempted from other basic scientific principles.

There was a Big Bang; it happened when God spoke. Creatures did appear on the earth at the same time because that's how God said He created them.

Human Envy Denies Creation

No human ever truly creates anything. We re-purpose, re-arrange, or combine what already exists. A seed planted, watered, and properly tended creates a plant. The gardener didn't create the plant, the water, or the seed.

Artists "create" something new by using pre-existing materials in new ways. Babies aren't created by men and women. Pre-existing biological materials combine to form new lives. No human has ever truly created anything. Many will disagree, because many deny God.

Science as God

As God sat about Heaven one day a scientist said, "Lord, we don't need you anymore. Science has finally figured out a way to create life out of nothing. In other words, we can now do what you did in the beginning."

"Oh, is that so? Tell me..." replied God.

"Well," said the scientist, "we can take dirt and form it into the likeness of You and breathe life into it, thus creating man."

"Well, that's interesting. Show me."

So the scientist bent down to the earth and started to mold the soil.

"Oh no, no, no..." interrupts God, "Get your own dirt.

Because men cannot create anything, we find it impossible to understand or accept that Someone else could. The idea of a Creator God is a real annoyance to many. Atheists who realize that men create nothing original find it difficult to explain where it all came from because, if there is no God, then what?

How foolish men are. They can't create a thing yet *worship the works of their own hands* (Jeremiah 1:16).

The Little Problem with Scientific Dating Systems

Every elementary school textbook has a chapter beginning, "Millions of years ago" suggesting that someone was there to record and date events. Of course, there wasn't anyone around millions of years ago. Have you wondered how scientists determine the age of old bones, hides, and wood?

The question about the age of the earth is a source of continuing kerfuffle. Is it an old earth or a young earth? How old is it really?

Some folks believe it is actually possible to KNOW how old something is. Others disagree.

The most widely discussed method for dating materials is radiocarbon dating using the isotope Carbon 14. Permit me to share a brief explanation from Wikipedia. I'm sure it's more than you ever wanted to know but it does explain why radiocarbon dating is hardly accurate or reliable. To be fair, radiocarbon dating isn't reliable enough to bet the farm, but it is reliable enough to satisfy scientists who are comfortable with really good guesses.

As you read the following description of radiocarbon dating, take particular notice of the *number of variables* mentioned in time, amounts, and the wide fluctuations documented since this tool entered the scientific toolbox. The use of underlining in this chapter is my own emphasis, except for the lines used within a mathematical formula.

The idea behind radiocarbon dating is straightforward, but years of work were required to develop the technique to the point where accurate dates could be obtained. Research has been ongoing since the 1960s to determine what the proportion of C14 in the atmosphere has been over the past fifty thousand years. The resulting data, in the form of a calibration curve, is now used to convert a given measurement of radiocarbon in a sample into an estimate of the sample's calendar age. Other corrections must be made to account for the proportion of C14 in different types of organisms (fractionation), and the varying levels of C14 throughout the biosphere (reservoir effects). Additional complications come from the burning of fossil fuels such as coal and oil, and from the above-ground nuclear tests done in the 1950s and 1960s. Fossil fuels contain no C14 and as a result there was a noticeable drop in the proportion of C14 in the atmosphere beginning in the late 19th century. Conversely, nuclear testing increased the amount of C14 in the atmosphere, to a maximum (reached in 1963) of almost twice what it had been before the testing began.—Wikipedia

Simply stated, the process of using radioactive dating systems to age anything is to measure what presently exists and plug it into a formula (extrapolate) to estimate age. Extrapolation uses known facts to form opinions or make estimates about something else using mathematical formulas that assume other facts. Before going further, please note; mathematical formulas often make huge assumptions that miraculously become constant and reliable.

For example, nuclear decay reactions are said to be independent of temperature and the chemical or physical environment. That assumption is sometimes applied to physics as a fact. But this "fact" of constancy appears to be at odds with reality once you take out all the "buts" identified in the preceding description.

Michael Benton, Action Bioscience[89], describes methods for "absolute" dating in the follow way.

> *The best-known <u>absolute dating</u> technique is carbon-14 dating, which archaeologists prefer to use. However, the half-life of carbon-14 is only 5730 years, so the method cannot be used for materials older than about 70,000 years.*

> *Radiometric dating involves the use of isotope series, such as rubidium/strontium, thorium/lead, potassium/argon, argon/argon, or uranium/lead, all of which have very long half-lives, ranging from 0.7 to 48.6 billion years. Subtle differences in the relative proportions of the two isotopes can give good dates for rocks of any age.*

How do you measure the half-life of an isotope? Even the shortest time frame, 5730 years, precludes anyone from doing a measurement to determine when the half-life was reached and verify that the change occurred in a precisely consistent/linear manner. And no one argues that bean counters have been monitoring isotope behavior for 48,000,000,000 years. Estimates

---

[89] actionbioscience.org/evolution/benton.html

are made based on formulas. Does this sound like I'm rejecting radiometric dating as absolute? I am.

> *"The rejection of dating by religious fundamentalists is easier for them to make, but harder for them to demonstrate. The fossils occur in regular sequences time after time; radioactive decay happens, and repeated cross testing of radiometric dates confirms their validity."—Michael Benton*

I don't discount absolute dating simply because I believe God's Word. I'm skeptical that it is of any use whatsoever because of basic math and science principles. The problem arises from how assumptions and formulas are used, not whether or not fossils and radioactive decay exist.

Fossils do occur in regular sequences—except when they don't. Fossils of animal and plant life supposedly separated by millions of years are found in the same geological strata of the same fossil bed. That means they arrived at roughly the same time. Second, radioactive decay does happen, but cross-testing of a single item may agree or vary by significant margins.

The rate of radioactive decay is the key to dating systems. Measurements are taken of how much of an isotope remains in a fossil. Using a mathematical formula, the age is determined by plugging that value into a formula with a <u>variety of other variables</u>.

First one must <u>assume</u> how much was there to begin with. Then one must <u>assume</u> the rate of decay, and then one must <u>assume</u> the rate of decay was constant, and once all the <u>assumptions</u> are calculated an "absolute" age is determined.

I won't bore you completely, but I want to share some concerns with dating systems. Darwin's evolution is based on "millions of years." Unless things are datable as millions of years old it's pretty hard to support the theory of evolution—even for atheists and agnostics.

It's been decades since I've taken a math or physics class. I don't pretend to know much about this stuff except to critically examine the presentation of constants and variables. It's reasonable to think that constants shouldn't vary, and variables are, by definition, inconsistent. To the irritation and chagrin of a number of teachers and professors I asked what seemed obvious questions.

When the instructor's answer finally ended with a declarative "it is assumed", the Q&A ended. I was left to wonder why "it is assumed" was considered an acceptable scientific response. This was my introduction to "settled science."

If your eyes begin to glaze over just move on. For information junkies and trivia geeks I'll share a bit more about the pitfalls of dating systems. Measuring decay and the half-life of an isotope is key.

How to Measure the Half-life of an Isotope[90]

The number (#) of radioactive decays per second equals (=) Lambda (λ) times (x) the number (#) of radioactive atoms.

Lambda (λ) is a constant of proportionality, the inverse of the mean lifetime. *In other words, Lambda is a constant based on a computation.* The constant is, in essence, an assumption.

The half-life is = 0.693 (natural log of 2) divided by Lambda (λ).

I must admit, I have no earthly idea why the natural logarithm of "2" is meaningful. If I thought it was important to this discussion I would have studied further so I could explain it. I doubt many readers are disappointed that I'm leaving this particular rabbit trail unexplored.

How do we know how many atoms we have at the beginning?

Mass of Substance x 6.022 x 10^{23}

Atomic Number

Radioactive dating systems are spectacular laboratory achievements. They stack variables and computations of variables and assumption on top of one another then divide by more

---

[90].youtube.com/watch?v=I2abTNq4AZs Dr. Harold Yorke, Senior Research Scientist,

computed variables and computed constants. The result is somehow considered an "absolute" dating system. They may offer profound benefits in the practice of nuclear medicine but are hardly rock-solid when it comes to dating something as millions of years old.

> *"Absolute dating complements relative dating by providing a specific (not necessarily precise) chronological age for a given specimen, such as '50 million years before present.'"—Glen Kuban [91]*

The parenthetical "not necessarily precise" is part of the original Kuban quote, not an editorial comment on my part. In other words, absolute dating is not really absolute and the terms specific and precise don't necessarily mean the same thing.

I visited Nature.com for a specific (and accurate) illustration of what is accepted as *settled science*.

> *"Based on the primate fossil record, scientists <u>know</u> that living primates evolved from fossil primates and that this evolutionary history took tens of millions of years."*

How do scientists <u>know</u>? The whole problem of the missing link(s) means the fossil record fails to show how any particular primate evolved into another. How do scientists <u>know</u> that such supposed evolution took tens of millions of years?

> *"Fossils can be useful tools for understanding the relative ages of rocks. Each fossil species reflects a unique period of time in Earth's history. Index fossils are used to determine the age of the strata in which it is found and to help correlate between rock units. The principle of faunal succession allows scientists to use the fossils to understand the relative age of rocks and fossils".—Nature.com*

---

[91] paleo.cc/kpaleo/fossdate.htm

Relative dating compares fossils and rocks. Fossils are used to date rocks and rocks are used to date fossils. Circular reasoning is always fascinating, using A to prove B which then proves A. Of course, absolute dating systems are also used to determine the age of fossils, using absolutely specific, non-precise, variable and assumption based methods of radioactive decay.[92]

Scientists agree that even <u>absolute</u> radiometric dating systems leave a large coverage gap in which fossil age is difficult to estimate. The gap is generally considered between 40,000 and 200,000 years ago. Bible believers discount such estimates, but even evolutionists admit the limitations of radiocarbon and potassium-argon systems.

> *"Human evolution demands precise dating of the relevant fossils. Evolutionists now admit that the dates for the human fossils in the significant Middle Stone Age period and elsewhere are uncertain. It means that there is no such thing as a legitimate evolutionary fossil sequence leading to modern humans. It also means that evolutionists cannot make accurate statements regarding the origin of modern humans based on fossils discovered thus far. Their continuing to do so reveals that their statements are based on a belief system, not on the practice of a rigorous science."—Marvin L. Lubenow, M.S., Th.M., The Dating Gap*

Error by Extrapolation

Simple algebraic formulas based on extrapolation often yield inaccurate results, yet evolutionists use extrapolation to determine <u>absolute</u> dates. Climate change adherents (more about that later) also use extrapolation to track global heating and cooling data and predict future temperatures and outcomes. Such formulas measure changes in temperatures over a period of time then estimate what

---

[92].nature.com/scitable/knowledge/library/dating-rocks-and-fossils-using-geologic-methods-107924044

the temperature will be in the future (or what it was in the past) based on the known measurement history.

How Extrapolation Works

For example: If Susie earned one dollar per day for the past five years ($1 x 5 x 365 = $1825) how much will Susie earn in the next ten years? The extrapolated answer would be $3650, or twice as much. That is a specific answer, but not necessarily a precise predictor of what Susie will <u>probably </u>earn over the next ten years.

Everyone knows about Leap Year. Depending on when Leap Year fell within the five-year baseline period the amount Susie earned would be a dollar or two more. There must also be a small adjustment to allow for Leap Years during the next ten years.

But what if Susie worked less than full time for part of the past five years and she hopes to work full time for the next ten? How would that change the estimate of her earnings? What if Susie has a new job and will earn substantially more per day over the next ten years? What if Susie opens her own business?

What if Susie's records for the past five years are incomplete and there is a factual record of her gross earnings for only 83 days out of the total of 1825? That would be okay for scientists; they would write an equation allowing for small potential discrepancies or assume that the 83 days are representative of the other 1742. What if Susie earned unreported tips? How might that affect the estimate of future earnings?

A quick overview of the quoted note on radiocarbon dating reveals nearly a dozen variables. That means the level of C^{14} is not consistent. If we restate the C^{14} issue into Susie terms, not only do we not know what Susie earned, how long she worked, if she plans to keep working in the future, or if Susie ever truly existed.

Here's a simpler illustration. Let's say the temperature three days ago was 74 and two days ago was 75. Yesterday it was 76. Today it is 77. We can project the temperature 3 months from now by extrapolation. If the temperature rises one degree per day – and it has with perfect consistency – we can estimate the temperature in

90 days to be 90 degrees warmer than today, or 167 degrees. Whew!

In a controlled laboratory setting it's easy to measure changes and make educated guesses about future results, all things remaining constant. That's the trouble. Radioactive dating systems study events in controlled settings then guess what effect random and drastic changes over the past however-many thousands of years may have caused.

Old Earth vs New Earth

There are numerous theories about the age of the earth and the role of humans relative to the rest of nature. If you believe God created man and Genesis is true, do you think God created Adam as a newborn baby? If so, who would have cared for him? There wasn't anyone else. Was Eve created from Adam's little-bitty baby rib thus leaving two helpless infants for the critters to raise and care for?

Most creationists believe Adam was created as a mature man and Eve a mature woman. When Adam was truly one second old he probably looked like he'd been around for a long time. If Adam walked into a fully outfitted crew of anthropologists and physicists, they would swear he had been born, grew, survived puberty, and was somewhere between 25 and 50 years old. They would never believe this full-grown human was but one second old, yet this is precisely how scientists say the Big Bang happened.

What if God didn't create a baby planet? Perhaps He created trees, seas, creatures, and man as fully developed beings and systems. Scientists see something that walks, talks, and acts like an old planet so conclude that it is. Who could blame them? Perhaps a 500-million-year-old planet appeared in an instant; just like the universe. Bang! A mature planet.

God's Big Bang was spectacular. Creating one little mature planet is nothing when compared to setting an entire universe in place in the twinkling of an eye.

Population Growth

Depending on the source, evolutionists believe humans first appeared between 100,000 and 6,000,000 years ago. Obviously the date that dawn first broke over humanity is not "settled science." The most popular guesstimate suggests men and women have roamed about for 200,000 years.

Curiously, this is precisely the time frame outside most "absolute" dating systems.

According to current projections, the global population will reach eight billion by 2024, and will likely reach nine billion by 2037. Projected figures vary depending on underlying statistical assumptions and the variables used in projection calculations, especially the fertility variable. Long-range predictions to the year 2150 range from a population decline to 3.2 billion in the "low scenario", to a "high scenario" of 24.8 billion.[93]

Population projections a mere 135 years into the future vary from 3.2 to 24.8 billion. In other words, everyone is either guessing or throwing a dart at a board with numbers on it. The likelihood that population estimates from 35,000 BC are accurate is infinitesimal.

Making more-or-less educated guesses is not the same type of science as observing, documenting, and conducting experiments using the Scientific Method.

Bill Nye, the Science Guy, has a lot to say about climate change and evolution. When it comes to population, Mr. Nye said, "The evidence now is that at one time there were about a hundred humans, a tribe or a large group of tribes, but we squeezed through the evolutionary sieve and here we all are."[94]

One of the operative words in most published accounts of what researchers discover about the evolution or humans is "thought." The following examples of how precise and concrete the evidence

[93] en.wikipedia.org/wiki/World_population
[94] .salon.com/2015/11/06/bill_nye_demolishes_climate_deniers_im_not_a_scienti st_therefore_im_not_going_to_use_my_brain/

for human evolution is were excerpted from a single scholarly article:[95]

Quotations include spelling and grammatical errors. I really wanted to correct them but resisted the urge

- "It is <u>thought</u> that changes in the climate …"
- "The founder populations cannot have been very big."
- "… are <u>thought</u> to have first evolved"
- "It is <u>thought</u> that by 150,000 years ago …"
- "… discovered in Israel and are <u>thought</u> to be around 100,000 years old"
- "It has long been <u>assumed</u> that human success in spreading around the world was due to their adaptability and hunting skills. The latest research, however, <u>suggests</u> [otherwise]"
- "… quarter of a million years but are <u>thought</u> to "
- "… is <u>thought</u> to have been recolonised by modern humans after the last ice age "
- "There seems to have been a huge amount of <u>luck</u> involved "
- "… <u>believe</u> they have strong evidence "
- "We did not find a single individual [through DNA analysis] that could be *considered* the decendants of homo erectus"

What scientists used to "thought" isn't what they think today:

The idea that all non-African humans are descended from a single group of individuals contradicts previous theories that the different modern races evolved separately from a human ancestor known as Homo erectus, but in different parts of the world.

What about other sources?

"Homo is the genus of great apes that emerged around 2.4m[illion] years ago and includes modern humans. …The remains at Dmanisi are thought to be early forms of Homo

---

[95].telegraph.co.uk/news/science/science-news/5299351/African-tribe-populated-rest-of-the-world.html

erectus, the first of our relatives to have body proportions like a modern human. ... Experts believe the skull is one of the most important fossil finds to date, but it has proved as controversial as it is stunning. Analysis of the skull and other remains at Dmanisi suggests that scientists have been too ready to name separate species of human ancestors in Africa. Many of those species may now have to be wiped from the textbooks."[96]

What was thought to be scientific proof of evolution, down to the naming of species, may now "have to be wiped from the textbooks." It appears the entire line of human evolution may have to be scrapped as well. DNA evidence appears to have eliminated the lineage of homo erectus from human ancestry, at least for all non-African humans.

If the great apes evolved into *homo erectus*, then humans are not evolved from great apes. Oops, so much for settled science. I wonder when this bit of news will get a mention in the mainstream media.

Bastions of respected science may not be any more trustworthy than certain media outlets. Thousands of giant human skeletons were rumored to have once been housed at the Smithsonian Institute. Yet none remain and no one seems to know anything. But an August 2015 story finally proved that the Smithsonian intentionally trashed every bit of evidence that giants not only lived in the world, but in areas now within the borders of the USA. Evidence at odds with the priests of Evolution has been known to simply disappear.[97]

How Long Does it Take for Something to Petrify?

Depending on the conditions and who you ask, petrifying wood takes either *millions of years* or *just a couple of days*. If you add natural materials and heat—Shazam!—perfectly petrified wood

---

[96].Theguardian.com/science/2013/oct/17/skull-homo-erectus-human-evolution

[97].theeventchronicle.com/study/smithsonian-admits-to-destruction-of-thousands-of-giant-human-skeletons-in-early-1900s

over the weekend.[98] During petrification of wood, the walls of every cell are replaced by a dissolved rock solution, such as a silicate or limestone. This has to happen before the cells decay.[99]

When pressed, scientists agree that petrification doesn't really take all that long. Cells must hold their original shape and properties in order to petrify in recognizable form. Once there is decay or rot there can't be petrification. How do they come up with millions of years then? Because petrified trees have been discovered around fossils presumed to be millions of years of old.

Mother Shipton's Petrifying Well[100] (waterfall), Knaresborough, England, has been petrifying objects from animals[44] to teddy bears for hundreds of years. It is considered the oldest tourist attraction in England. Teddy Bears (sold in the gift shop) petrify in about three months.

The only thing we can reasonably assume from something petrified is that it didn't decay or rot immediately. Petrified trees didn't lie around slowly petrifying for millions of years. Trees in the Petrified National Forest in Arizona are 100 feet deep. How did that many trees pile up in a short enough period of time to petrify without rotting or decaying?

There is widespread agreement that they were deposited there by some water source, eliminating the theory that the dry heat of prehistoric Arizona preserved the trees. Any thoughts on what water source might have been powerful enough to move an entire forest? I'll give you a hint; Noah.

Dating Petrified Fossils

Fossils are often petrified remains of life forms. We've already learned that petrification can take as little as a few days but cannot take place over centuries or millennia because original tissues don't last that long.

---

[98]todayifoundout.com/index.php/2012/05/how-things-become-petrified/

[99] johnpratt.com/items/docs/lds/meridian/2005/petrified.html

[100] mothershipton.co.uk/the-park/petrifying-well/

Once you start talking about petrified fossils, the doctrine of basic fossil dating begins to fall apart.

> *"Petrifaction or petrification is the process by which organic material is converted into a fossil. Petrification takes place through a combination of two similar processes: permineralization and replacement. These processes create replicas of the original specimen that are similar down to the microscopic level, and require a minimum of about 10,000 years to take place."*—Wikipedia, Petrifaction

Scientists agree that fossils of organic material cannot take more time to create than the original tissues or substances are able to survive decay or rot. And yet, sources declare without caveat that petrification takes at least 10,000 years; unless they're of the two-day wonder variety demonstrated by Dr. Yongsoon Shin, Department of Energy, at the Pacific Northwest National Laboratory.

If you've read more about dating systems and evolution in the previous few pages than you ever wanted to know, it's easy to understand why so many people believe evolution is settled science. Who wants to burrow in rabbit holes of imprecise science?

Here's the bottom line: Evolution is only settled science because people must either confess evolutionary doctrine or face social ostracism.

If you believe humans evolved from rocks or other animals, you don't believe God's Word. If you believe any form of life died before the Garden of Eden was fully populated by flora, fauna, and man you don't believe God's Word.

Genesis clearly states that death did not exist on earth until God sacrificed animals for hides to clothe sinful Adam and Eve, newly chastened by their nakedness. Human sin invariably causes the innocent to suffer. It was true for the first sin and is still heart-breakingly true today.

If you're a serious student of geology and how things came to be as they are, most of earth's history is easily explained by Noah's flood.

The evidence for a global flood about 4000 years ago is equal to, or better, than all evolutionist *thought*.

No matter how long the argument continues, evolution cannot answer foundational questions both timeless and timely:

- Is where you came from related to where you'll eventually go?
- What do you believe? You must believe something or you would be less than a rock.
- What is true? For anything to be true it must also be true in the extremes. If something is only true in limited circumstances then it is merely a generality, relative, or comparative.
- How were right and wrong first distinguished? Have some things always been right and some wrong? If not, how did the distinguishing line change?
- Humanism worships mankind. But "mankind" is a heterozygous group. Humans do not agree. How do you categorize or theorize right, wrong, truth, and behavior? I'm a human, do you worship me?
- How can my sin be your sacrament and your sacrament my sin? A mere difference of opinion? How do we know we aren't both wrong?
- Why are there different sexes? Have there always been? How do you know and how is that material to sex/gender issues today?
- Why is it right to murder a cow but not a person?
- What's wrong with torture? If you just don't like to see something suffer then that's your problem isn't it? Or is there a bigger reason?
- Why enforce some laws but not others? All laws are opinions and benefit someone over someone else.
- Why should #BlackLivesMatter more than #AllLivesMatter?
- Are people more important than animals?
- Are animals more important than plants?
- Is the environment more important than people?

- How do you know that dogs aren't the highest species? Because you don't understand them? Because you can destroy them? Hitler destroyed millions of people; did that mean he truly was superior? Then why did the USA wage war against him?
- Why are people charitable?
- How do you know your children are really yours? How do fathers know they are really the dads? Was there a DNA test? Did you conduct every aspect of the DNA test yourself? Did you build the equipment, invent and conduct the test? Unless you invented, built, collected samples and used lab machinery and every item used in the test, your belief is based on faith.
- Which door to eternity is true and which the lie?

To date, God's Word is the only source of answers to every question and issue facing mankind.

Last Call for Darwin Fans

If you skimmed or dismissed everything in this chapter and insist that humans evolved from non-humans, I'm going to make one last call for consideration:

If humans evolved from some lesser animal yet you base your eternity on faith that Jesus died for the sins of all, how many human "ancestors" do you expect to meet in heaven? *Homo erectus*? Gorillas? Lemurs?

If you don't believe Jesus died on the cross for a lemur, where exactly do you draw the line between the last human-type animal not eligible for salvation and the next one who is? How far back in the long, slow, bumpy evolutionary process did the blood of Christ become ineffective or moot?

No matter what date you prefer, Jesus died millennia after recorded human history began. How far back does the cross reach? What is its limit? If it goes back to the Garden of Eden to include Adam and Eve, how much further back? What animal produced Adam? Was his mother saved? What about his sire?

The moment you dismiss the fact of God's Word you open a can of worms that is as impossible to put back as the evils from Pandora's Box. If humans evolved, then so did salvation. That means Jesus may not have died for all and there may be some folks and some sins that will not be covered. If you're willing to go that far, then there's a pretty good chance you'll be spending eternity with some very interesting folks. The bad news is, Jesus won't be there with you.

Global Warming—Climate Change

ω

"While the earth remains, seedtime and harvest, cold and heat, winter and summer, and day and night shall not cease."—Genesis 8:22

Christian apologists have been around for centuries. These are people blessed with spiritual gifts and specific education who debate, discuss, and entertain both questions and accusations from non-believers. Christians love to talk shop about Jesus, God's Word, creation, and enthusiastically wander off into the weeds when folks challenge or object to Christian tenets.

Atheists and naysayers aren't shunned as mental midgets or monsters but respected as people created by the very God they deny. God told Elijah to get over himself when he wailed that he was the last prophet (1 Kings 19:14-15). He was not. God has people ready to carry His message when and how He desires. Someone is always willing and able to take on critics and opponents, but isn't a task assigned to all.

Climate change has much in common with religion. Those who believe are steadfast and increasingly intolerant of speech or opinion that suggests climate change doctrine is untrue. "Deniers" are considered scientific or social outcasts by the priests of global warming. In the 21st century Christian apologists are the poster children of true tolerance. Not so the acolytes to climate change (global warming).

Bill Nye (The Science Guy) seems a nice enough fellow, but writes, Part of the solution to this problem or this set of problems associated with climate change is getting the deniers out of our discourse. You know, we can't have these people—they're absolutely toxic.[101] It's certainly a different take on science; calling

---

[101]salon.com/2015/11/06/bill_nye_demolishes_climate_deniers_im_not_a_scientist_therefore_im_not_going_to_use_my_brain/

227

for the end of further investigations just because you like the conclusions reached thus far.

Do most climate scientists agree that global warming is a massive problem?

In 2009 a college student surveyed 3,146 people worldwide for her master's thesis. Known as the Zimmerman-Dornan study, it concluded that "97% of climate scientists agree" that global temperatures have risen and humans are a significant contributing factor. Note that the survey suggests that human activity is a contributing factor but does not measure what respondents think about rising temperatures. Are they a concern? If so, a great concern or no concern at all? The study is silent.

The mythical but much reported 97% consensus refers to responses from a tiny group of 79 out of the total 3,146. If you compare consensus replies to the whole, instead of 97% it is less than 3%.

The actual result isn't an overwhelming consensus, but a smaller number that the 5% statistical error gimme, and thus evidence of nothing at all. Is this study really solid enough to inspire a scientific religion that excommunicates all who refuse to worship?

In 2010, college student Love Anderegg examined the views of 200 of what he considered the most prolific writers on climate change (among thousands.) He concluded that 97-98% of his small sample agree that human generated greenhouse gasses are responsible for most global warming. There is, however, no indication if the respondents consider the changes significant or of particular concern. Is this research a sound basis for excluding scientific *apostates* from discussions on climate change?

In 2013 an Australian blogger and a few of his buddies did a little research project of their own. They compared the abstracts of papers from a ten-year period and concluded that 97% either said or kinda said that humans are responsible for some warming. Is the warming significant?

Are humans responsible for the vast majority of whatever warming there might be? Both the blogger and buddies are silent. When the blogger's source material was reviewed by a team led by a university professor, former director of the University of Delaware's Center for Climatic Research, the results were slightly different. Instead of 97%, the team of academics found that only one percent (1%) of actual opinions agreed that humans caused most of the warming. Four of the people whose work was reviewed specifically objected to misrepresentations made by the blogger and his buddies.

Surveys published in 2010 by German scientists Bray and von Storch discovered that most climate scientists disagree on the reliability of climate data and computer modeling. The Petition Project based in LaJolla, California has 31,000 (9,000 PhD's) signatories who believe "there is no convincing scientific evidence that human release of . . . carbon dioxide, methane, or other greenhouse gases is causing or will, in the foreseeable future, cause catastrophic heating of the Earth's atmosphere and disruption of the Earth's climate."[102]

The Petition Project isn't alone in the field of climate change apologetics. A Reuters/New York Times article states that Scientists conclude: "We found that, while climate change does exist, it is cyclical, and the anthropogenic role is very limited," he said. "It became clear that the climate is a complicated system and that, so far, the evidence presented for the need to 'fight' global warming was rather unfounded."

"Data show no slowdown in recent global warming" declared NOAA's October 2015 press release. The suggestion is that global warming continues at an alarming and catastrophic rate. The statement is, however, entirely true; the total absence of global warming in the past 20 years remains unchanged. There is still no global warming. Context is key![103]

---

[102] The Myth of Climate Change – 97%, Bast-Spencer article, Wall Street Journal online, May 26, 2014. wsj.com/articles/

[103] .breitbart.com/big-government/2015/10/29/noaa-attempts-hide-pause-global-warming-disgraceful-cover-since-climategate/

"Climate change," says noted (Democrat) theoretical physicist Freeman Dyson, "is not a scientific mystery but a human mystery. How does it happen that a whole generation of scientific experts is blind to obvious facts?" Dyson admits that "Obama got it wrong."[104]

How have we wandered so far afield of the truth? In 1859 John Tyndall discovered that some gases block infrared radiation. He suggested that changes in the concentration of these gases could bring about climate change. 1859 was a pivotal year, moving human investigation from the observable to the mythical—even regarding climate change.

---

[104].newsmax.com/Newsfront/Freeman-Dyson-Obama-democrats-wrong-climate-change/2015/10/14/id/696280/

Racism and Slavery

ω

"Masters, treat your slaves justly and fairly, knowing that you also have a Master in heaven."—Colossians 4:1

There is one institution infinitely older than the Roman church; slavery. Domination and slavery are human norms. Mankind was given dominion (stewardship) over the animals in the Garden. God's design permitted no death and no suffering until Eve swallowed Satan's lie, "Surely you will not die..." (Genesis 3:4). Death came by sin.

Mankind's fall from grace is the product of deception. Sin produced death, dominance, deceit, suffering, and slavery. Race is not the cause of slavery. Slavery within races is historically commonplace. Domination, self-indulgence, and a sense of entitlement produce slavery.

Humans first made slaves of animals believing them to be inferior to humans. All who enslave others must create at least an illusion of superiority. To do otherwise admits a willingness to do evil or excuse narcissistic behaviors. Few (if any) of us are willing to think of ourselves as evil, so we create some palatable excuse for the horrible things we do.

Once the concept of slavery was introduced it rapidly progressed:

- One tribe of humans made slaves of another tribe believing it inferior to their own.
- One religion made slaves of another believing it to be inferior.
- One economic class made slaves of another believing it inferior to their own.
- One social class made slaves of another believing it inferior to their own.
- One nation made slaves of another believing it to be inferior.

Victors in war frequently made slaves of the vanquished. Superiority is often decided by who has the power of life and death over another. People in many places continue to sell their children into slavery for food and safety.

African Slave Trade

Slavery was a traditional part of African society—various states and kingdoms in Africa operated one or more of the following: chattel slavery, debt bondage, forced labor, and serfdom. Between 1450 and the end of the nineteenth century, slaves were obtained from along the west coast of Africa with the full and active co-operation of African kings and merchants.[105]

Portugal was one of the first nations to take advantage of this new source of labor. Racial divides and stereotypes didn't cause slavery but are the result of slavery. Contrary to general thought, more Africans entered the Arab slave trade than the transatlantic slave trade which included the United States. That slave trade was outlawed in both Britain and the USA in 1807.

The Arab slave trade began in the 8th or 9th centuries with the transportation of Bantu Africans into the Middle East. European and American historians assert that between the 8th and 19th century, 10 to 18 million people were bought by Arab slave traders and taken from Africa across the Red Sea, Indian Ocean, and Sahara desert.

Arabs also enslaved Europeans. Between 1 million and 1.25 million Europeans were captured between the 16th and 19th centuries by Barbary pirates, who were vassals of the Ottoman (Turkish) Empire, and sold as slaves. The Ottoman

---

[105] africanhistory.about.com/od/slavery/tp/TransAtlantic001.htm

wars in Europe brought large numbers of European Christian slaves into the Muslim world.[106]

In the beginning there was some level of mutual respect between the Blacks and the more lighter skinned Arabs. However, as Islam and the demand for enslaved Blacks grew, so did racism toward Africans. As casual association with Black skin and slave began to be established, racist attitudes towards Blacks began to manifest in Arabic language and literature. The word for slave – Abid – became a colloquialism for African.[107]

The United Nations estimates that roughly 27 to 30 million individuals are currently caught in the slave trade industry. Mauritania (Islamic Republic in North Africa) was the last nation to officially abolish slavery, doing so in 2007; yet 4.3% of the population still remains enslaved. Despite being illegal in every nation, slavery is still prevalent today.[108]

Slavery has existed for most of human history. Slavery is not necessarily punitive. It created employment, fellowship, and provision for millions of people. Some slaves were considered property while others eventually assumed familial relationship. Family pets can be slaves or gods. People are slaves to electronics, controlled by the beep, vibration, or silence of the smart device of their choice.

Hagar, Ishmael's mother, is the first named bondwoman, but Joseph is the first slave mentioned by name in the Bible. Egypt already had a mature slave culture when Joseph was sold into slavery by his envious brothers (Genesis 37:28). A curious note about slavery is found in Jesus' genealogy. The brother who suggested Joseph be

---

[106] Wikipedia – Arab Slave Trade

[107] atlantablackstar.com/2014/06/02/10-facts-about-the-arab-enslavement-of-black-people-not-taught-in-schools/2/

[108] Wikipedia – Contemporary Slavery

sold to the Ishmaelites was Judah, the only brother in the lineage of Jesus.

> *"So Judah said to his brothers, "What profit is there if we kill our brother and conceal his blood? Come and let us sell him to the Ishmaelites, and let not our hand be upon him, for he is our brother and our flesh."*—Genesis 37:26-27

Slavery is found throughout the Bible from Genesis to Revelation because slavery is a norm of human nature.

Ten percent of England's population in 1086 was slaves. Slavery existed in the New World just as it had in the Old.

> *"Slavery among Native Americans in the United States includes slavery by Native Americans as well as slavery of Native Americans. Tribal territories and the slave trade ranged over present-day borders. Some Native American tribes held war captives as slaves prior to and during European colonization, some Native Americans were captured and sold by others into slavery to Europeans, and a small number of tribes, in the late eighteenth and nineteenth centuries, adopted the practice of holding slaves as chattel property and held increasing numbers of African-American slaves. What further aided the Indian [Native American] slave trade throughout New England and the South was different tribes didn't recognize themselves as the same race dividing the tribes among each other. The Chickasaw and Westos for example sold captives of other tribes indiscriminately in effort to augment their political and economic power."[109]*

Slavery has been a human institution almost as long as there have been humans. Race isn't the genesis of it, nor is religion. It is elevating one's own power and economy above that of a weaker individual or group. The east African slave trade (into the Mideast)

---

[109] Wikipedia – Slavery among Native Americans in the United States

was far greater than the west (into Europe and the USA.) Indigenous peoples of every continent engaged in slavery as slave or slave master, and sometimes both.

Anti-slavery Issues

In 1859 the United States of America stood on the verge of civil war. One Southern congressman after another rose in Congress to declare that promoting a "Black Republican" (anti-slavery) president would justify secession. Republican congressmen answered that secession would be met with coercion. The divisive issue was slavery. Congress convened in December 1859, shortly after John Brown's unsuccessful October raid on Harper's Ferry, a raid designed to free slaves by force of arms. Democrats announced that Brown's raid was the natural consequence of Republican antislavery agitation.

In 1859 and 1860 the conflict between slavery and antislavery inspired debate over free speech in Congress. The goal was to repress antislavery speech and press in much of the South, including the prosecution of an antislavery minister in North Carolina for circulating Hinton Helper's book, *The Impeding Crisis of the South*, which concluded that slavery hindered the South's economic development when compared to that in the North (according to the 1850 census.)

In 1859 criminal procedure guarantees were especially pertinent because some Democrats implied that the Republican Party was not a normal political party, but instead was a criminal conspiracy because of its position against slavery. Democrats wanted anti-slavery Republicans jailed or punished for the crime of standing against slavery. [110]

---

[110].scholarship.kentlaw.iit.edu/cgi/viewcontent.cgi?article=2904&context =cklawreview

LGBT

ω

"Therefore God also gave them up to uncleanness, in the lusts of their hearts, to dishonor their bodies among themselves, who exchanged the truth of God for the lie, and worshiped and served the creature rather than the Creator, who is blessed forever. Amen. For this reason God gave them up to vile passions. For even their women exchanged the natural use for what is against nature. Likewise also the men, leaving the natural use of the woman, burned in their lust for one another, men with men committing what is shameful, and receiving in themselves the penalty of their error which was due."—Romans 1:24-27

God's message has not changed. The text of the Bible has never changed in any material way. Translations based on newly discovered but more ancient scrolls or scroll fragments yield additional nuance, but none has ever changed the message. Recent adaptations of God's Word have been produced; one of the most recent being the *Queen James Bible*.

The Queen James Bible is based on The King James Bible, edited to prevent homophobic misinterpretation. Homosexuality was first mentioned in the Bible in 1946, in the Revised Standard Version. There is no mention of or reference to homosexuality in any Bible prior to this—only interpretations have been made (Amazon.com description).

The implication is that if God was that concerned about homosexuality He would have mentioned it. He did! This nit-picking concerns the actual word "homosexuality." Hebrew and Greek words used in the original texts weren't translated in English to homosexual until the early 20th century because the word itself did not exist in the English language until 1892 when it appeared in a translation of *"Psychopathia Sexualis"*, a German reference work on sexual perversions.

Lynn Baber

*"We have to acknowledge that you don't translate a word
from Hebrew and Greek into the English if there is no
English equivalent. So, using the term "homosexual" in the
English Bible could not have occurred until after the word
had entered the English vocabulary."—Matt Slick*[111]

Folks who desperately wish to alter God's Word continue to try and
continue to fail. The authors/editors of *The Queen James Bible*
didn't change God's message, though they will have to answer for
the attempt one day.

The latest iteration of sexual deviance in western societies testifies
to the growing chasm between God's view of spiritual and sexual
deviancy and that of the present culture. The divide may already be
a breach of separation beyond repair, with the shaky bridge
connecting God and worldly man nothing but smoldering embers.

It has been suggested, argued, and legislated that limiting genders to
only male and female is too confining. No definition that forces a
person into the box of male or the box of female is permissible in a
tolerant progressive society. At least that's the deception being
played upon the gullible.

*Gender is something everyone thinks they understand, but
most people really don't. Here, it's broken into three
categories: identity, expression, and sex. It's less "this or
that" and more "this and that."*[112]

Since God created Eve there have been two genders or sexes: male
and female. Gender identity (in the world of gender-speak today)
deals with all the possibilities on a line that admits *man* (male) on
one end and *woman* (female) on the other. Proponents suggest there
is an endless possibility of gender-identities on any and all points
between man and woman.

---

[111] Christian Apologetics and Research Ministry - carm.org/word-homosexual-english-bible-1946

[112] .itspronouncedmetrosexual.com/2011/11/breaking-through-the-binary-gender-explained-using-continuums/#sthash.xlrzojsu.dpuf

Gender expression is where an individual falls on the continuum between masculine and feminine. Gender identity is what you think you are, and gender expression is how you show the world what you think. Sex (biology) is nothing more than a chromosome test result; XX, XY, or another result that occurs on very rare occasions.

The other component generally lumped into gender issues is sexual orientation; whether someone is carnally attracted to males, females, or *all of the above*. Who turns you on has nothing to do with chromosomes or social gender identification. Interjecting love or elements of attraction into debates about the science of sexual/gender assignment is nonsensical.

What drives the demand for genderless humanity? Self-indulgence feeds the delusion that any choice between A and B is too limiting if someone doesn't feel *really comfortable* with one choice or the other. The foundation of self-indulgence is the desire to opt for something other than God or Not God. It's a desire based upon a pretty lie that continues to work. The most vulnerable are those with the greatest education, intellect, ego, curiosity, or fear.

People believe same-sex unions based on love and passion not only make sense but are equal to marriage. God didn't say a man and a woman were united in marriage in order to fulfill their passion, but to create children who would be reared in fear of Him. Arranged marriages were not between two men or two women. They were arranged to create strong relationships; whether familial, economic, social, or powerful.

Few marriages in the Bible began from shared passion between a man and a woman. Marriage isn't about scratching a sexual itch or sharing the same bed. Covenant marriage is about commitment and creation. Same-sex couples CANNOT create new generations. Same-sex marriage proponents argue in favor of gay marriage by pointing out the failure of heterosexual marriage. They have a point. The problems causing marriage failure today have nothing to do with the gender of the couple, but the total lack of commitment and reverence for God. Denying God in favor of self-indulgence is a human sin, not one reserved to any gender or ideology.

Betrayed by Insecurity

Only fundamentally insecure people force others to publicly agree with them. Recant or face retribution! You may not agree with me on any number of issues. Does that mean I should require you to agree and make such agreement public? Certainly not. The growing number of public apologies (or demands for apology) illustrates people's insecurity. They need others to agree. When necessary they are willing to use force to get "agreement."

No follower of Christ thinks unbelievers should be forced to confess Christ as Lord. To do so would cast holy pearls before swine. False professions of faith do not honor our Savior. Denying God's plan in support of same-sex marriage doesn't strengthen God's plan; it completely mischaracterizes it.

The stridency of those who endorse climate change, evolution, and the removal of all barriers to expressions and rights of every gender and sexual preference prove how fragile those beliefs are. People who dare to believe in God's Word and historical human norms are beginning to suffer rabid intolerance and abuse. And it will get worse.

Pastors, scholars, and other sinners who teach that God's Word can change to suit someone's personal preference will not end up in the eternity of their choice. There has been one social and legal goal for the past 150+ years, to tear down all absolutes, standards, definitions, and rules for the purpose of denying God.

White people insist they identify as black (i.e. Rachael Dolezal.) Men insist they identify as women (i.e. Bruce Jenner.) Women insist they identify as men (i.e. Chastity Bono.) I challenge any of them to define what man/woman or black/white actually means. In the present social and political climate, it's hard to defend claims that a body or skin color doesn't match the inner spirit.

To define, describe, and quantify what male and female means requires setting divisive standards. Such attempts (when made by traditional parties) are considered exclusionary and intolerant. Since race/sex/gender doesn't really mean anything, why the big push to change?

Why the hullabaloo about Bruce/Caitlyn Jenner? Is Jenner a man or woman? Arguments exist because there is no definition other than "Jenner identifies more as a woman." How would Jenner know? There's no longer any acceptable discrete definition. What is the difference between a man and a woman? All we know is that Jenner wasn't happy with Jenner.

It is a ridiculous example of circular reasoning. God is not fooled nor is He amused.

What Jesus Said About Homosexuality

LGBT proponents who comment on God's Word argue that homosexuality is fine because Jesus never said "Thou shalt not commit homosexual sex." Some argue that explicit condemnations of homosexuality in the Bible don't apply to consensual sex, but only to same-sex acts of rape.

Jesus as God specifically outlawed gay sex. He specifically outlawed fornication and adultery. Marriage outside of a covenant union as prescribed by God is fornication and still a sin. God does not rationalize. We may be deluded, but He is not. Jesus doesn't care how we parse God's Word; *It changeth not.*

Some folks insist Jesus said nothing about homosexual activity because there is no red type comment in the New Testament. All who hold that position deny the Trinity because God is Jesus is the Holy Spirit. Anything God (Jehovah) said Jesus said. To suggest Jesus was silent on the subject excludes homosexual activity from the broad category of sexual immorality. Does anyone really believe sex between individuals of the same sex gets a free pass but sex between a man and a woman is subject to stricter limitations? Fornication is a sin, regardless of the respective genders of the participants.

So what did Jesus say about homosexuality? Actually, a whole lot less than many imagine which may be hard to believe given the fierce rhetoric Christians employ regarding homosexuality. Only seven passages in the Bible refer directly to homosexual behavior and none of them are specifically associated with Jesus. Compare that to the more than 250 verses on the proper use of wealth or more than 300 on the responsibility to care for the poor and to seek justice. One should quickly appreciate that homosexuality was not a major biblical theme.

Maybe little was said because it was an open and shut matter. Perhaps biblical references are limited because the topic didn't require extensive parsing or explanation. God created. God defines. God set the standards. God alone will judge. No human can meet the standard and any failure is total failure.

Homosexuality: The Great Debate

Homosexuality was not considered normal until the 21st century. It was considered deviant for the entire length of previous human history.

As far as we know, homosexuality does not occur in animals, even though there are behaviors that people interpret as homosexual. Two males hanging together may be life-long buddies, not lovers. Bachelor groups are common in the animal world. Unless an observer can interview the birds or animals engaging in "homosexual" behavior to determine the state of their hearts and the true meaning of what they see, they're making it up.

If a male penetrating another male is evidence of homosexuality, what do you call a man who penetrates a vacuum cleaner hose or any other handy item? (I wouldn't know about such things except I used to work in an emergency room). What about bestiality? The Bible denounces it right along with homosexuality.

God's position on homosexual behavior has never changed. However, there are many opinions about the subject in Christian circles. When it comes to eternity, it doesn't matter what a pastor, scholar, theologian, counselor, author, or scientist believes unless what he or she believes is true.

There are only two possibilities. Either homosexual marriage is fine with God or it is not. There is no third option.

While researching this topic I discovered a fascinating pair of articles written by two Christians. Both are gay and once shared the common belief that homosexual behavior is sinful. One of the two remains celibate and faithful to God's requirement to abstain from sexual immorality.

The other has *evolved* and now lives as a practicing gay Christian endorsing same-sex marriage. Both lengthy articles may be found on the Gay Christian Network website. Executive Director Justin Lee, a practicing gay Christian leader shares his evolved opinion[113] in the "Great Debate" with Ron (no last name published).

Justin writes:

> It's certainly true that God designed our bodies with heterosexuality in mind; that's how new human beings come into the world. I don't think anyone can deny that heterosexual sex is the way our bodies were built to function. But does that mean that using our bodies in any other way is sinful? There are no same-sex marriages in the Bible. But that's what we'd expect anyway. Same-sex marriages weren't a part of the cultures in which the Bible was written, so obviously we wouldn't expect to see stories of men and women with same-sex partners. Many things aren't mentioned in the Bible, either because they weren't part of the culture at that time (e.g. computer porn) or because they weren't especially important issues to the Biblical authors (e.g. masturbation).

And yet the Bible clearly mentions homosexual behavior which was part of the culture at the time. Justin suggests that opponents can't explain why God would condemn monogamous homosexuality to his personal satisfaction; therefore it has no explanation and no foundation requiring obedience.

But, God did explain Himself. There are 52 references to His creating male and female in the Old Testament and four in the New Testament. God designed the human body to join and procreate. Justin doesn't argue the point. However, to suggest that deviating

[113] gaychristian.net/justins_view.php

from the intended design and use is not necessarily of concern is fanciful. God's design and His Word is clear about what bodies are supposed to do.

> *"For this reason God gave them up to vile passions. For even their women exchanged the natural use for what is against nature."*—Romans 1:26

God expects us to consider and come before Him with our questions. God designed the male and female bodies to function together naturally. No male/female coupling is permissible unless the relationship is approved by God. Couples who are not married to each other or are related in forbidden ways sin when they "do what comes naturally."

The caveat about marriage answers all the questions that could be asked. A father cannot marry his daughter. A son cannot marry his mother. Rape is never involved in covenant marriage. Little children cannot marry. Nothing in scripture suggests men can marry men or women marry women. Without covenant marriage all sex is fornication.

> *"And He [Jesus] answered and said to them, "Have you not read that He who made them at the beginning 'made them male and female.'"*—Matthew 19:4

Justin:

> *No matter how wordy, complex, or sophisticated they get, every Christian Traditionalist argument I can think of ultimately relies on this basic principle: God has a rule against same-sex relationships, and even if we don't fully understand or can't explain the rationale behind it, in the end we're just expected to obey, like Abraham being willing to sacrifice Isaac. Basically, the evidence for a rule against same-sex relationships consists of a few Bible passages where homosexual behaviors are condemned.*

Do you expect God to justify what He does before you will submit to His judgment? Arguments in favor of same-sex marriage forget that God created everything and doesn't need to answer petty demands from the created.

One definitive Bible verse should be sufficient. Mr. Lee admits that God condemns such behavior. Why keep arguing? Jesus stood condemned before Herod and Pilate. Men spat at Him and mocked Him. Jesus permitted men to lay out their charges, express their opinion, and crucify Him on a cross. He was judged a man and raised a Savior. On one occasion Jesus stood before the throne of a man. No excuse, no opinion, no whining, and no hissy fit will sway Him. He died to cleanse us of sin, not excuse it. God established the rule and will never stand in judgment before men again.

Justin:

> *If you're fortunate enough to know a Christ-centered gay couple, you'll notice something remarkably different. These relationships are actually bearing good fruit. The fruit of the Spirit are in abundance in such relationships — love, joy, peace, patience, and all the rest. You can argue all you want about the meaning of this passage or that passage; the fact remains that I know monogamous, Christ-centered gay couples whose relationships are living proof of God's blessing on them. Bad trees don't bear good fruit.*

Note the obstinacy of this argument: *What God's Word may or may not say is immaterial because "the fact remains that I know."* Self-indulgence never bears good fruit but those who have been deceived will argue the delectability of even the most rancid fruit. Ask Eve.

Ron (no last name published), a member of the Gay Christian Network, believes gay Christians are called to lifelong celibacy.

Ron wrote[114]:

---

[114] gaychristian.net/rons_view.php

Humility is important in the Christian life, and I have tried to write with the humility of one who will be judged by Christ. I have had to learn (and it is one of life's most difficult lessons) to be humble enough not to make myself judge of God's revelation ... and refuse to obey until it has satisfied all my objections.

It seems to me quite significant that when Jesus speaks of marriage, He begins by reminding the Pharisees that God made us male and female and says that a man shall be joined to his wife.

The linguistic problem seems to me to be exactly analogous to this: suppose I have an Old Testament text which says, "it is unlawful to lay bricks," and I have a New Testament text that says "bricklayers are lawbreakers." It would seem inconceivable to me to say that "Greek scholars don't know exactly what bricklayer means." Yet Mel White claims (with an apparently straight face) that "Greek scholars don't know exactly what arsenokoitai[115] (men having sex with men) means."

For myself, I finally came back to the view that the Bible forbids gay relationships, in part because though I could see the reasons to doubt the traditional position, I couldn't see any solid evidence to support the idea that God blesses gay marriages. And the more I sought to find in the Scriptures principles which could be used to support gay marriage, the more I realized that the basic principles in the Scripture for guiding sexual expression would rule out gay relationships.

This brought alive for me the Gospel's logic: "We know that the law is spiritual; but I am carnal, sold under sin. I do not understand my own actions. For I do not do what I want, but

---

[115] gotquestions.org/arsenokoitai.html - literal translation, "men having sex with men." Reverend Mel White is a linguistic scholar who promotes homosexuality as an approved choice for Christians.

I do the very thing I hate. Now if I do what I do not want, I agree that the law is good" (Romans 7:14-16).

Can Homosexuals Be Christian?

Much of the literature and debate about homosexuality and Christianity deals with the question, "Can homosexuals be Christian?" May I suggest that this is entirely the wrong question? It's analogous to asking a man, "When did you quit beating your wife?"

The question is a two-parter:

1. Can sinners be Christian?

2. Can people who deliberately sin with the full intention of continuing in sin be Christian?

The answer to the first is that all Christians are sinners. The answer to the second could be rephrased as, *Can someone who choses idolatry over Christ be Christian*? Lust and self-indulgence is idolatry. To consciously choose sin over Christ is pretty shaky ground.

"No temptation has overtaken you except such as is common to man; but God is faithful, who will not allow you to be tempted beyond what you are able, but with the temptation will also make the way of escape, that you may be able to bear it" (1 Corinthians 10:13).

Unless regenerated by rebirth in the Holy Spirit, human nature chooses to sin in full view of Christ. Sin is natural. Sin is human. Jesus understands the temptation and distractions common to all men and women. There are two doors to eternity. Human nature chooses one. Is that your choice?

"Matthew Vines' book *God and the Gay Christian* for example states that 'Christians who affirm the full authority of Scripture can also affirm committed, monogamous same-sex relationships.' "

Christians can affirm the moon is made of green cheese. Most Christians would disagree and God doesn't care what you affirm. Separate your affirmations from His at your peril.

Compassion

"The answer is that no Christian is called upon to make that choice. The text of the Bible on one hand, and full equality for gay and lesbian people on the other, is a false dichotomy. God would not ask or expect Christians to ever choose between their compassion and their faith."—Patheos.com [116]

Like many other non-biblical preferences, it causes great pain to Christian LGBT practitioners when scriptural doctrine isn't adjusted to embrace them. For this reason, some argue, God would agree that personal feelings trump Christ's death on Calvary. This logic argues that compassion excuses sin. If compassion is the standard of establishing what approved behavior is and what it is not, who arbitrates differences of opinion about compassion?

Do you feel compassion for an animal going to slaughter? If so, is it sinful to kill it? Who is in the wrong, the one feeling compassion or the one set on murder? The Bible requires us to be good stewards and compassionate toward animals yet permits their use as a food source in Genesis 9.

Animal rights activists insist that using animals for food is wrong. Would they also argue that *"God would not ask or expect Christians to ever choose between their compassion and their faith"?*

Would you feel compassion for a teenager who killed an entire family while driving under the influence? If so, should there be no crime, no charges, no judgment, and no penalty? I suspect you might have a problem with that if the victims were members of your own family.

Compassion towards gay and lesbian people does not require us to choose between empathy and God's Word. The false dichotomy suggesting that compassion eliminates accountability isn't found in

---

[116].patheos.com/blogs/johnshore/2012/04/the-best-case-for-the-bible-not-condemning-homosexuality/

the text of the Bible. Compassion encourages prayer, support, friendship, and commiseration during difficult times. In the courts of men compassion doesn't affect whether someone is or is not guilty, but how he or she is to be treated.

Sadly, convicted rationalization has become synonymous with both *logic* and *tolerance*. Judges may feel compassion for a convicted criminal, but it should not affect orders assessing penalty. In the case of the teenage driver, should the sentence be mitigated because of a lack of youthful control? What if this is the third offense? Compassion never excuses habitual sin though many false teachers insist it should.

Compassion is the product of human nature. Synonyms include kindness, benevolence, empathy, sympathy, and humanity. There are significant differences among these human *feelings*. Sympathy with someone who is angry means we share their anger; empathy means we understand the anger but don't become angry ourselves.

Sympathy joins in camaraderie. Empathy understands and attempts to understand or change the situation. Compassion may be shown sympathetically or empathetically. We can feel right along with the plight of another or we can understand why they might feel as they do.

Sympathy for a person trapped in a deep dark hole with no escape is demonstrated by jumping into the pit with them. Empathy understands how the person got there but doesn't include hopping in. Practical compassion motivates us to try and rescue the one trapped and all who may have jumped in out of sympathy.

Throughout the Bible we see ourselves in the feelings and behaviors of sinners. We understand why they made the choices they did. It took three years for Jesus' disciples to learn the difference between human nature and Jesus. Jesus understood human nature and laid down His life that we might overcome it.

One might empathize with a person who finds God's will difficult. Every person who enters heaven found the path difficult somewhere along the way. Sympathy says we share the difficulty, share the feeling, and walk the path together. Sympathy says I will hurt along with you. Empathy says I understand why you hurt. Depending on the circumstance, compassion may lead us to walk the path with someone we care about or try our best to lead them off the path of destruction.

Compassion is the testimony of human nature based on feelings. Feelings can be temptations to deceit. Human nature rebels against God when it refuses to admit that anything could be greater than ME.

God fully understands human nature. Satan understands it well enough to deceive. One of the two doors to eternity is opened by human nature. The one to eternity with Jesus Christ is opened by the nature of God in the form of the Holy Spirit. The Holy Spirit convicts us to get off the broad way leading to destruction and walk the narrow path leading to the very gate of heaven.

Can followers of Christ have compassion for folks who are drawn by feelings (human nature) toward same-sex or gender-neutral choices? Certainly! True compassion seeks to steer them from the path that leads to destruction to the narrow path of Matthew 7. Can we imagine how they feel? Certainly! What breaks the heart of those who care about people lost in deceit is not a difference of opinion, but love.

Addicts are perfectly happy when they're high. Why not make the object of the addiction legal and provide the means to be high all the time? Why try to change them? The trigger that led them to addiction is human nature. There are two main reasons people become addicted, searching for pleasure or seeking relief from pain. Each person has his or her own road and cannot choose for another. Compassion dictates whether we share the path to destruction or attempt to lead someone who has gone astray to a better one.

Which door is true and which the lie? One opens by human nature the other by the nature of God. Human feelings change from moment to moment, but God never changes. Do not be deceived. God asks every man to choose between feelings and Him.

Gender Changes in Children

Denying the existence of absolutes has turned the simple life of children upside down. An ever-increasing number of children discover on the first day of elementary school that there is no such thing as gender. The terms *boys* and *girls* are too limiting and intolerant. How will you react when innocent 6-year old Amy tells you there are boys in the school bathroom?

The Lincoln, Nebraska school district "instructs teachers to interfere and interrupt if they ever hear a student talking about gender in terms of boys and girls so the student can learn that this is wrong."[117] District training materials suggest teachers call all children purple penguins or line up based on their preferred choice of pet; dog or cat. Teachers are encouraged to avoid any plan that will configure or "create a gendered space."

When do kids know if they are a boy, girl, or neither? Parents hear their 18-month old little girl declare, "I am a boy!" and she becomes a he. If a little girl doesn't like frilly barrettes or a little boy prefers playing house to playing war, maybe there's a gender issue. When children naturally choose behaviors and attire outside of what is considered normal for little boys or little girls, is it a gender mistake or ridiculous constraints on what is considered normal behavior for boys and girls?

As a child I loved animals, dirt, playing sports with the boys, and remember risking punishment with three memorable snit fits. I refused to wear a dress with bows on the sleeves, nixed the very fashionable pair of saddle shoes my mother liked, and was less than thrilled (behaved badly) when I was forced to get a permanent wave at age eight.

I am positive I said, "I want to be a boy" more than once because boys *did funner things* than most of the girls. The girls I played with liked the same things I did. Dolls made us grimace, horse models made us happy, and we usually went home very dirty.

---

[117] Katherine Timpf, National Review Online, October 8, 2014

More than a half century later I haven't changed much. I don't wear dresses, you won't find me sporting a bow, and I live in a barn and get dirty on a regular basis. And I still really like grown up boys, especially my best friend to whom I've been married for well over three decades.

If I were a California kid today there's a good chance some well-intentioned teacher or school counselor would suggest I be transitioned from tomboy to real-boy. Guess what? I grew out of wanting to be a boy around the same time I realized boys weren't just buddies, but kind of interesting in other ways.

Western society is as irrational as it is well-intentioned. How does the dress code for little boys differ from the one for little girls? What hair style is exclusively male or exclusively female? Who raises an eyebrow if a boy wears a necklace or bracelet? Are manicures gender exclusive? Fashion was far more gender neutral in early human history. Adam and Eve wore unisex outfits, and in the time of Christ everyone wore long robes.

Attire differentiated as a result of occupation, climate, and social status more than gender. Many early American paintings of children challenge viewers to determine if the subject child is male or female. Little boys and girls both wore dresses and sported similar hair styles.

Men wore high heeled shoes before women. Persian diplomats visiting Europe in 1599 left local aristocrats with a taste for high heeled footwear. Louis IV of France was an avid shoe collector who inspired other snappy dressers with cash and clout to adopt heels. Women started wearing heels to prove they were equal to men. Have things really changed that much?

Fashion has always been a breeding ground for ostentation, experimentation, and exhibitionism. The desire to be noticed, even for being odd, is not unique to one gender. It's just another example of human nature lusting for greater self-indulgence and self-expression.

An Oakland, California little boy began a new life as a little girl at age 3 ½.[118] Oregon law prevents 15-year olds from getting tattoos, drinking, driving, and even using tanning beds. But, as of January 2015, Oregon 15-year olds can get sex change procedures without parental notification and the state will even pick up the tab. Included under the umbrella of procedures are cross-sex hormone therapy, puberty-suppressing drugs, and gender-reassignment surgery.

Anyone subjecting a child to a mutilating medical procedure without parental agreement is guilty of kidnapping and assault, unless it's for sex change therapy/surgery or abortion. How is it possible that a 15-year-old cannot consent to a sexual relationship with a teacher but can decide to change sexes?

Why are sex changes necessary for 15-year-olds? Because, it is argued, they might face bullying by others. If a 15-year-old can't deal with being bullied by a peer, he or she is not mature enough to even entertain such a drastic choice, much less make it.

The worldly seek to separate children from family, from nature, and from God. Telling a kid to do whatever he feels in order to "find himself" results in that kid finding himself alone. In the wild, predators separate the young, the lame, and the old in order to take them down. Human predators follow precisely the same scheme. You can fool a child, you can fool an adult, and maybe you can fool a nation, but you can't fool God.

Children who believe they're in the wrong bodies may be suicidal, or so advocates would have you believe. Children are suicidal because they are totally focused on themselves and find the picture less than delightful for any number of reasons. Fifteen-year-olds are often emotionally stunted by dependence on social media and a far too permissive society. Kids need to learn how they fit into the norms before making the decision to dynamite the norms to smithereens.

---

[118].dailycaller.com/2015/07/04/california-family-discusses-4-year-old-transgender-child/

People today can pretty much act and look as odd as they please. Changing soft-tissue configuration and hormone levels with chemicals won't change a blasted thing. Gender does not change. There is nothing more categorically sexist than telling a kid that he (she) was born the wrong gender.

What Happened to Great Thinkers?

ω

"Where is the wise? Where is the scribe? Where is the disputer of this age? Has not God made foolish the wisdom of this world?"—1 Corinthians 1:20

Great thinkers think about big things and big places. There are no Great Thinkers in this post-Christian era because modern thinkers think in tiny places about tiny things. Thinking is limited by personal ideology, social acceptability, and personal experience.

The attention span of western people in 2000 was 12 seconds. In 2013 it plummeted to 8 seconds, one second less than a goldfish.[119] Today's Christians are content to think for a moment; any thought taking more than a moment to process is dismissed.

Post-Christian thinkers believe the little glass snow globe in which they live is all there is. Until 1859 most people weren't conflicted about how big God is. They knew they originated elsewhere, that there is a Being (or beings) far more powerful than they, and that one day they would be released from the smallness of the visible world.

In order to tap into the power and vision of God's Spirit that opens up something greater we must first think smaller; limiting distractions that separate us from our surroundings. We must get alone with God without crutches or labels. The only way to find right relationship with God is to come empty-handed. The idolatry of self-importance must be rejected. Only the Holy Spirit can guide your vision, perspective, awareness, and spirit into what is more, and then into much more.

Blessed are the meek, mournful, poor in spirit, merciful, pure, and peacemakers. Only by accepting limitation can God do with us what is necessary to usher us into the realm of what is greater. Limiting

---

[119] time.com/3858309/attention-spans-goldfish/

God slams the door on greatness and condemns us to the constraints of our own smallness.

Greatness often comes from accepting smallness. Great thinking sometimes originates in prison.

- The Apostle Paul
- The Apostle John on Patmos
- John Bunyan – Pilgrims's Progress
- Martin Luther
- Martin Luther King, Jr. from Birmingham
- Dietrich Bonhoeffer
- Victor Frankl
- Corrie Ten Boom

Saul of Tarsus was blinded on the road to Damascus. Before Jesus revealed Himself, he first reduced Saul's world to what he could touch and smell; he neither ate nor drank. Jesus limited him visually and spatially until he was prepared to receive Jesus' direction.

"In that hour Jesus rejoiced in the Spirit and said, *"I thank You, Father, Lord of heaven and earth, that You have hidden these things from the wise and prudent and revealed them to babes. Even so, Father, for so it seemed good in Your sight."*—Luke 10:21

God often uses small things to do great things. He doesn't imagine great things then send out the small to accomplish His goals by their own puny power. You should be familiar with the stories of little David's victory over the giant Goliath and how Jericho's mighty walls fell with little more than a siege of footsteps with a trumpet finale.

The Lord left Gideon with a remnant of 300 men from a beginning army of 32,000. The number was purposefully small *lest Israel claim glory for itself against Me, saying, 'My own hand has saved me.'*

> *"So Gideon and the hundred men who were with him came to the outpost of the camp at the beginning of the middle watch, just as they had posted the watch; and they blew the*

trumpets and broke the pitchers that were in their hands. And every man stood in his place all around the camp; and the whole army ran and cried out and fled."—Judges 7:19, 21

"And when the servant of the man of God arose early and went out, there was an army, surrounding the city with horses and chariots. And his servant said to him, "Alas, my master! What shall we do?" So he answered, "Do not fear, for those who are with us are more than those who are with them." And Elisha prayed, and said, "LORD, I pray, open his eyes that he may see." Then the LORD opened the eyes of the young man, and he saw. And behold, the mountain was full of horses and chariots of fire all around Elisha."—2 Kings 6:15-17

The greatest thinkers are those who take the loftiest and seemingly most difficult questions of life and restate them simply.

"If you can't explain it simply you don't know it well enough."—attributed to Albert Einstein

"I didn't have time to write a short letter, so I wrote a long one instead."—attributed to both Mark Twain and Blaise Pascal

"Out of intense complexities intense simplicities emerge."—Winston Churchill

"Assuredly, I say to you, whoever does not receive the kingdom of God as a little child will by no means enter it."—Mark 10:15

Complexity is a distraction of the world. Great thinkers of earlier times weren't distracted by cell phones, email, texts, the stock market, and 24/7 coverage of events across the globe. Great thinkers only thought great things because they weren't focused on ME to the exclusion of all else.

Great thinkers realized that having too much breaks people just as much as having nothing at all. The reason people are broken is because they don't place value where it belongs; in the person of Jesus Christ. A soul that has nothing collapses upon itself. A soul weighed down by too much collapses under the weight.

Great thinkers knew how easy speaking boldly is when you have everything. They also knew that speaking boldly comes easily to those with nothing left to lose.

Security based on the protection provided by wealth is unreliable. There is always someone with more. Security based on the promises of the King of Kings allowed the apostles to boldly proclaim the gospel to all who would listen because no one had more power. They went peacefully to martyrdom because the only thing of true value could never be lost—eternity with Jesus Christ.

Choose today whom you will serve.

In the Midst of Judgment

ω

"If you were of the world, the world would love its own. Yet because you are not of the world, but I chose you out of the world, therefore the world hates you."—John 15:19

To be secure *in* the world without being *of* the world requires a primary identity and vision that places Jesus Christ first; first above everything and everybody else, including ME. Nothing in life should register in your conscious mind without first passing through the lens of Christ.

Sin is a problem. Since Genesis 3 sin has always been THE problem. When the issue of control is distilled to its absolute essence, the competition for control is between ME and THEE.

One of the doors leading to eternity is the result of control by ME. The other door leads to eternity controlled by THEE – by the God of the Bible. One of the doors is chosen by human nature and the other by the nature of God.

Few sane people believe they have the power to direct, change, produce, or restrain eternity. Unless deluded by God's hand, few admit the desire to enter the door leading to eternity that's "All about me—forever!"

The door of truth can only be opened with the proper key—Jesus Christ. The taproot of deception is so deep that truth is called a lie and a lie truth by many who believe they believe.

Only One Thing

There is only one thing of consequence to God. Theologians, philosophers, romantics, warriors, politicians, activists, and others filled with passion for any one of 100 million reasons spin their wheels in vain unless the source of their passion is the Lord Jesus Christ. The only thing that matters to God is who you are in relationship to Him. Is His truth your truth? Is His word the final word? Do you believe what He said about Himself, about the world, and about eternity? Regardless of which door to eternity you chose, one day every truth about God will be proven.

"The Lord knows the thoughts of man, that they are futile. Blessed is the man whom You instruct, O Lord"—Psalm 94:11-12

"Although they knew God, they did not glorify Him as God, nor were thankful, but became futile in their thoughts, and their foolish hearts were darkened."—Romans 1:21

Does God Make Mistakes?

This is a foundational question. Your answer is the framework for every belief you hold and decision you make. If God makes mistakes, then your eternity is insecure and you better look for a cosmic insurance policy or cross your fingers and hope the Nihilists are correct. If God makes mistakes there is no heaven, Jesus cannot save you, and you're on your own.

If God does not make mistakes, then His Word stands and you will be judged accordingly. To charge God with making mistakes, from natural disasters to being born in the wrong or imperfect body denies any profession of faith in His deity. Human opinions about God's creation carry as much weight as a toddler's opinion of Einstein's Theory of Relativity. The little tyke would rather have Jello anyway.

Too many professed Christ followers get suckered into debates about the topics that divide the body of Christ. Don't fall prey to the wily serpent of Eden. He hasn't changed his slither or his pitch. The tactic that convinced Eve to eat forbidden fruit is the very same one that sells the lie that abortion and gay relationships are okay with God.

The pertinent question remains, "Does God make mistakes?"

Once you fall for the inanity of macro evolution (humans descended from a rock) it's easy to believe that (1) life has no ultimate meaning or rules, or (2) God evolved right along with His creation.

The issue isn't evolution; the issue is GOD. Does the God of the Bible exist or doesn't He? There isn't a third option to that simple question. It's one or the other. Has God evolved?

God's Word speaks for itself:

> "You are My witnesses," declares the LORD, "And My servant whom I have chosen, so that you may know and believe Me and understand that I am He. Before Me there was no God formed, and there will be none after Me."— Isaiah 43:10

The following message was shared on social media by "Jennifer", a proponent of same-sex marriage:

"I am a child of God and deserve to be treated as an equal in the world that he created. God doesn't judge us, he forgives our sins, and he loves us for our own individual lives on this earth. Everyone is welcome to their beliefs; it makes you who you are and your own person."

The issue of marriage equality isn't the topic of concern. It's the wrong topic and wrong discussion. The main issue is false teaching.

Where does God's Word say that:

- Children of God deserve to be treated as equals in the world?
- God doesn't judge, but forgives sins?
- God loves people for the individual way they choose to live?

Many of the most illustrious men who ever professed Christ as Lord were martyred for their faith. Jesus shared a different message than the one in "Jennifer's" social media post.

Blessed are the poor in spirit, those who mourn, the meek, those who hunger and thirst for righteousness, the merciful, the pure in heart, the peacemakers, and those who are persecuted for righteousness' sake, for theirs is the kingdom of heaven.

Blessed are you when they revile and persecute you and say all kinds of evil against you falsely for My sake. Rejoice and be exceedingly glad, for great is your reward in heaven, for so they persecuted the prophets who were before you.

Christians do not demand equality on earth because they know they are strangers here with a home waiting in heaven. For some, the world was not worthy of them.

> *"Others were tortured, not accepting deliverance, that they might obtain a better resurrection. Still others had trial of mockings and scourgings, yes, and of chains and imprisonment. They were stoned, they were sawn in two, were tempted, were slain with the sword. They wandered about in sheepskins and goatskins, being destitute, afflicted, tormented—of whom the world was not worthy."—Hebrews 11:35-38*

Fruit-producing Christians exhibit characters of service, humility, adherence and respect for God's Word, consistency, faithfulness, and are more other-directed than self-indulgent. Followers of Christ seek to be just but not to expect justice from others. Petty demands for equality, tolerance, exception, respect for individuality, and all other me-ishness are anathema to the Holy Spirit.

God does love His children. He sent Jesus Christ to die in our place. All who believe on Him and are born anew with the Holy Spirit are saved from eternal condemnation. Salvation is not a *Get Out of Jail Free* card though some obviously think so. Such thoughts lead to eternal separation from Christ, not eternal life.

> *"For the Father judges no one, but has committed all judgment to the Son."—John 5:22*

Don't be suckered into social or scientific debate about gender, sexuality, or who may legally marry whom. Don't get suckered into social or scientific debate about when life begins. God IS and has not changed. He speaks through His Word and His Spirit. Don't be tempted to debate what is not debatable.

Some people begin reading the Bible at Genesis 1, "In the beginning, God", while others start with Proverbs and discover that the fear of God is the beginning of wisdom. Still others need a more gradual introduction to God's word and read that for "God so loved the world that He gave His only begotten Son, Jesus Christ, to die."

Every verse in the Bible is inextricably linked to every other. No matter where you begin, the message is still the same, "I AM". There is one source of truth and one foundation on which eternity stands.

The final testament arrived in 1859. Dickens' A Tale of Two Cities begins; It was the best of times. It was the worst of times.

It ends; It is a far, far better thing that I do, than I have ever done; it is a far, far better rest I go to than I have ever known.

> "If then you were raised with Christ, seek those things which are above, where Christ is, sitting at the right hand of God. Set your mind on things above, not on things on the earth."—Colossians 3:1-2

The End Leads to the Beginning

> "The coming of the lawless one is according to the working of Satan, with all power, signs, and lying wonders, and with all unrighteous deception among those who perish, because they did not receive the love of the truth, that they might be saved. And for this reason God will send them strong delusion, that they should believe the lie, that they all may be condemned who did not believe the truth but had pleasure in unrighteousness."—2 Thessalonians 2:9-12

It doesn't matter what you believe at your last breath unless what you believe is true. The lies of the world have no power in eternity. There is only one source of Truth. It not only matters *why* you believe *what* you believe, it matters if what you believe is *real*.

Almost everything wrong in western cultures today was either introduced or altered course in 1859. It was the beginning of humanism, settled science, modern medicine, progressive sociology, and a theology based on human nature rather than God's Holy Spirit.

Where you find yourself in eternity depends on what you believe and what you do about it. You must declare your choice because there is no more time on the clock. Mortals cannot measure the span between 23:59 and 24:15. The passage from life to eternity is known only by God.

> *"It was the best of times; it was the worst of times."*— *Charles Dickens, 1859*

No unity remains in the United States of America except to agree that we disagree with one another. Such disagreement is neither genial nor agreeable but based on fear. Human nature seeks to exclude, banish, contain, or exterminate those who aren't *like we are*. Because "they" are different, we can't predict what "they" will do.

There is nothing everyone in the USA would agree on. There is nothing every Christian would agree on. Nothing unites and the result is infighting. The USA is no more immune to human nature than were the Israelites. Human law changes based upon which "we" is in charge.

The only law unchanged from the beginning is that established by God. God has been banished from our land because human nature fears, rejects, and seeks to eliminate that which it does not understand or is not *like we are*.

Determine to do what is far, far better than anything you have ever done before. An eternal choice waits. Choose wisely because Eternity is but a heartbeat away.

> *"Choose today whom you will serve. As for me and my house, we will serve the LORD."*—*Joshua 24:15*

About the Author

ω

Lynn Baber is an author, coach, and speaker with a passion to inspire and help others find the source of their own power, authority, and confidence. She combines God's truth with daily life, using creative illustrations and a bit of humor.

Lynn has worked with ministries, equine therapy barns, leaders, authors, boards, and as a teaching cheerleader for business owners, non-profits, and other horse trainers.

Topics guaranteed to spark spirited conversation include commitment, respect and obedience, relationships, using questions to achieve goals, and finding peace and joy in a complex world. Challenges and obstacles become solvable using simple gospel principles and choosing between two timeless options (there are always two.)

A World and National Champion horse trainer and breeder, Lynn is also a best-selling author, proving, as she says, that God has a sense of humor.

Horses are never wrong. Feelings are always real. God's word is always true, and the road to fulfillment winds through the valley of resolving differences without conflict.

Connect with Lynn at www.LynnBaber.com

Lynn Baber's Books

ω

Gospel Horse Series

Amazing Grays, Amazing Grace – Book 1

He Came Looking for Me – Book 2

Discipleship with Horses – Book 3

Breath of Horse Crazy – Book 4

Christian Living

Rapture and Revelation

Fifteen Minutes into Eternity

Ebooks

The Art of Getting to YES

www.ingramcontent.com/pod-product-compliance
Lightning Source LLC
Chambersburg PA
CBHW051714020426
42333CB00014B/983